Outsider Rules

Roger Fleming

Elderberry Press

OAKLAND

Copyright © 2020 by Roger Fleming
All rights reserved.
Distributed to the trade by
Elderberry Press
1393 Old Homestead Drive
Oakland, Oregon, USA 97462
editor@elderberrypress.com
Our books are available from your favorite bookseller in print and ebook.
Publisher's Catalog-in-Publication Data
Outsider Rules / Roger Fleming
ISBN: 978-1-934956-77-9 [soft cover]
ISBN: 978-1-934956-76-2 [hard cover]
1. Congress—fiction.
2. Politics—fiction.
3. Washington D.C.—fiction.
4. Political Parties—fiction.
5. Montana—fiction.
6. Drug Cartels—fiction.
7. Native American—fiction.
8. Crow Reservation—fiction.
I. Title

*For my first friend, Claudia Valentine, who taught me
the basics of life and how to truly appreciate the simpler things*

This is a work of fiction and the usual rules apply. Although, like much fiction, it is sometimes inspired by real events, none of the characters are real. Most events depicted in the book never happened. The narrative does draw on a few legislative efforts debated or voted on in the Montana State Legislature or the U.S. Congress. Where the story touches close to actual events, I have provided endnotes in an attempt to briefly explain the related events. In all other instances, the events are imaginary. Neither this fictional story nor the notes are intended to address every aspect of the sometimes controversial subjects covered in this novel or in any manner account for all the different political perspectives on them.

Outsider Rules

I returned and saw under the sun, that the race is not to the swift, nor the battle to the strong, neither yet bread to the wise, nor yet riches to men of understanding, nor yet favor to men of skill; but time and chance happeneth to them all.

— Ecclesiastes, 9:11 (ASV)

Bozeman, Montana

Summer 2006 The Campaign Trail

Nick Taft awoke on a cool cement floor. His knuckles were scraped and scabbed. Untouched metal cots were attached to bare walls. His client, dried blood on his face, lay next to him seemingly unconscious.

Faded letters beyond the iron bars read, Gallatin County. How stupid had they been? His favorite client did like to drink. No, his friend was a drunk. Kale McDermott had been his close friend for years, but divulged information that night that severely changed their relationship. A violent fight broke out between them and they were arrested ten miles down the road from Teasers bar. Their public display was a threatening development. The local headline would certainly read: "Senator Waters Implicated in Lobbyists' Arrest."

He nudged Kale with his boot. His client struggled to sit up.

"You're a piece of work, you know that? Have you lost your senses?" Nick said.

"Oh please, Nicky. Give me a break."

"You don't need a break. You need alcohol rehab."

"What?" Kale asked, indignantly.

"You're an alcoholic."

"If I was an alcoholic, I'd want a drink right now. And *I do not* want a drink. In fact, I'll bet you a $100, no make that $200, that I'm not an alcoholic. Seriously, $250 right now."

"You're on." Though he excelled at drinking, gambling was Kale's number one vice.

There were days when Nick wished he had taken a pass on the money and stayed within the guarded halls of Congress. Lobbying had its pluses, being paid to drink, hand out checks, play golf and ski at nice resorts. However, telling the same story over and over regardless of its veracity came with a price. He was a good lawyer in Congress and advocated well on the issues, but found few opportunities to use those skills in his current job.

Sometimes Nick thought he should have stayed to help his party where he could have fought for what was best for his country rather than what was profitable for a few corporations. However, second-guessing all those decisions since 1997 would neither help him nor the one politician he desperately needed to see re-elected that fall. Nick was constantly distracted, however, by the campaign's insatiable hunger for money, and woefully unaware of how pivotal one campaign would be in altering his life fundamentally and forever.

Washington, DC

A less experienced Nick Taft sat optimistically on the edge of a leather chair in the middle of a long mahogany conference table. Then he witnessed a psychological pummeling, the likes of which he was unaccustomed. He remained out of the target zone only because he was the newest and youngest member of the corporate government relations team and had been given no assignments to screw up.

Those people don't seem incompetent, he thought. *How could they all have performed so poorly?* But they each hung their heads as if guilty. Hally Peters, the senior vice president of congressional affairs for the American Communications Coalition (ACC) was a dark haired, slightly buck-toothed, lanky woman in her late fifties whose chalky complexion turned red when she was mad. Nick thought at first she was just sunburned.

The recently-formed ACC was not the coolest of the DC organizations made up of telecom companies, but was Nick's only offer to leave Congress and salvage a private sector career. With only twenty member companies, it wasn't nearly as prestigious as the larger formal associations, but he was excited to be there. He had started out with a law firm in his home town years before, but the boredom of litigation overcame his wish to continue his family's legacy. His father was proud of his nascent legal career, but disappointed when he took a job in Congress. He could still hear his father's words when calling him at his congressional office, "Okay, put the newspaper down and get your feet off the desk." Nick would redeem himself even if his father had long since passed on.

The stilted meeting ended and all sheepishly retreated to their separate offices. Nick didn't know his new colleagues well but wanted the lowdown on what had just occurred. That inquiry would have to wait. It was the beginning of his second week as manager of congressional affairs for the ACC and he was to have lunch with a former Hill colleague at a restaurant overlooking the Capitol.

Running late, Nick jumped in his car and floored it to the Hill. It was 17 degrees and starting to snow. He parked illegally on a street between the Senate office buildings and Union Station where the lined spaces were reserved for cars with special government stickers. He learned to abandon his car there when late as there was practically nowhere else to park. He was only ten minutes behind schedule when he sat down for lunch.

"So, how's it feel being in the big-time lobbying world?" asked his previous colleague, a counsel in the U.S. House. His friend was leaving at the end of the year to return to the private practice of law in his hometown. He'd had enough of DC.

"It is different," Nick admitted. "I certainly don't miss your Monday morning staff meetings."

"Oh, don't remind me. They get earlier every week. You enjoying it over there?"

"Well, our team meetings aren't so early but they are lively. I saw one of my colleagues get his ass handed to him at a meeting today."

"For the record, you were never on time to a single meeting, Nick. How would you possibly know how early they were? What did your colleague get dressed down for?"

"Oh, something he was apparently supposed to get done last week."

"Who's the boss over there?"

"Hally Peters."

"Never heard of her. Does she lobby the Hill?"

"Occasionally. She's not really around much. And when she is, she's in her office on the phone with the door closed."

"What's she doing behind her door?"

"I don't know. Someone suggested campaign-related work, like fundraising."

"For what campaign?"

"Don't know."

"Well, keep an eye out for warning signs. A lot of sketchy crap goes down in this town under the guise of congressional affairs. Don't need your new career ended before it even gets started."

They both looked out a vintage paned glass window over the Senate toward a frigid Capitol Dome. There was a new inch of clean snow on the ground. Three Marine helicopters crossed the skyline toward the White House. "Where'd she come from?"

"She was a telecom lawyer at the Massachusetts Department of Public Utilities, then very involved with the Republican Party there. She was some muckety-muck on the last presidential campaign.

The one that lost."[1]

"That's it?"

"Yeah. She's asked me twice when the Chairman of the Telecommunications Subcommittee is up for reelection." A waiter took their orders. "I've explained to her twice that House Members are up every two years and Senators are up every six." Nick shook his head.

"That sounds like quite a challenge, my friend. But, that's why they hire brilliant strategists like you, right? Are you covering my committee?"

"As a matter of fact, yes," Nick laughed, "and I have a list of specific questions for you."

"And yet you're aware, I know absolutely nothing about telecom law," his friend said, smiling.

"Just don't tell anybody or I won't be able to buy you lunch."

As he cautiously walked a snow covered sidewalk back to his car, Nick noticed a large pink card with black print showing through the white ice on his windshield. It read:

THIS VEHICLE DOES NOT DISPLAY A VALID PARKING PERMIT AND IS THEREFORE PARKED ILLEGALLY ON U.S. SENATE GROUNDS

A notice of infraction had been issued by the Office of the U.S. Senate Sergeant At Arms. It was just a warning though, no fine was imposed. He stuffed it in his glove box along with several others.

When back at his desk trying to be productive, Nick's office door swung open. Standing there was Thaddeus (Tad) Larson, the guy who hopelessly campaigned for Hally Peters' job but was instead offered a legal advisory role in the coalition due to the political divide within. Hally was a conservative, and Republicans had stunned the Washington political class two years prior by taking control of Congress for the first time in forty years. The head of the coalition, Mike McDuffie, a somewhat apolitical, long-time industry Independent, was compelled to fill the congressional affairs post with a Republican, but didn't want to turn away a good Democratic lawyer like Tad despite that he had to hire Hally.

Tad wanted to talk, but not there. "Can I buy you a cup of coffee down the street?"

They walked quietly down the hallway past an array of fiber telecom equipment displayed along the lobby walls toward the gurney-sized elevators. Tad was years older than Nick and though born in Europe, he was raised in Bermuda. He looked a combination of Jamaican and Bahamian with olive skin, blue-gray eyes and thick hair. Politely described as ambitious, he was single and also a recovering litigator. Silence lingered during their elevator ride. They walked out the front door of the old converted medical building into a transitional neighborhood and past the corner liquor store. Next to the sidewalk, a jackhammer pounded at the asphalt preparing to lay out more optic cable for potential new telecom providers.

Once seated by a window at a local deli, Tad looked around to see who could hear them. Those at the closest table were speaking a foreign language, but Tad spoke quietly regardless.

"Nick, I know everyone thinks Republicans own the world now. But we still have the White House. I'm telling you straight, if you think for one second that most of this coalition's political action committee (PAC) money is going to Republicans in the House or Senate, you're mistaken.[2] This industry's money will help impact who controls this country, and it's going to affect Republicans and Democrats equally."

Their conversation was overwhelmed by sirens as a government motorcade passed by. Tad continued, "Look, I guess Hally's as conservative as they come, but I'll fight you guys tooth and nail to ensure we give equal amounts to Democrats. You don't fuck with my priorities, and I won't fuck with yours, *comprendes*?" Nick nodded.

Coincidentally, the next morning began with a meeting at the ACC to determine how to spend its PAC money for the next fiscal quarter. The coalition's larger members were some of the biggest telephone companies in the country. They were part of what remained after a federal judge dismembered the largest corporation in the world, AT&T, pursuant to an antitrust decision, and broke it into one long-distance company and several big telecom companies. These Big Telcos and the American Communications Coalition had about a million PAC dollars among them to spend on upcoming campaigns for Congress.

Banter among the lobbyists around the conference table turned to the latest Hill gossip including the grim news of a staffer to a freshman congressman recently found dead. Once all were seated, they began a review of Members of Congress to determine for whom they would host a fundraiser. After negotiating down a long list, Nick asked for money for Senator Clarence Waters since he had been assigned to cover Montana. Initially bemoaning that it was

1997 and Waters wasn't up for reelection for three years, the group budgeted $20,000 for him anyway. Democrats ended up targeted for half the money. Tad Larson was smiling.

A red-faced Hally all but shoved Nick into her office after the meeting. "What, are you running the fucking show now?"

"What?"

"Hitting that group up for money for Waters? That's not a priority of this coalition. I've got enough Republican senators running for reelection who need money *this* election cycle. Waters isn't up again until 2000."

Unbeknownst to most, Hally's path to her lofty position at the ACC went directly through some conservative DC insiders involved with the powerful, *Greater America Foundation*. One of the reasons her lack of DC experience was downplayed was her commitment to heavily fund conservative candidates running in 1998.

"Hally, he's chairman of the Senate Communications Subcommittee, one of the most important legislative bodies to this industry. And all the Republican lobbyists agreed with me anyway."

"Well there's a shocker. Waters is not a *real* conservative. He's in a safe seat in a mostly red state, and doesn't need the funds. I make the decisions on giving to Republicans around here. Next time, you check with me before asking for money for *anyone*. We clear?"

Bozeman, Montana

Summer 2006 The Campaign Trail

A Gallatin County deputy rattled the cell door. The noise brought Nick into focus and re-awoke his sluggish client.

"How you boys feelin' this mornin'?"

"Not that great actually," Nick mumbled, feeling and looking every bit his recently confirmed middle age.

"Your friend there's quite the comedian. Had us all laughin' pretty hard last night."

"Yeah, he's a riot. Bad influence, too."

"They'll be servin' you some breakfast soon."

Kale's eyes reopened. He squinted at the sunlight filtering in the window and wiped strands of matted blond hair from his forehead. He gurgled, "Di...did he say breakthast, breakfast?"

"For fuck's sake, have you lost your hearing too?"

"What's your problem?" Kale asked.

"Well...for starters, we're in jail. I don't have a clue why. We attended a fundraiser last night for Senator Waters. We wrote him checks, and I'm on the steering committee for his 2006 reelection campaign. I spoke publicly at his event. Reporters were there."

Nick leaned up against a wall. "That event was important to my job, Kale. The election's only a few months away. The press is after him for anything he's ever said to anybody he's ever met. They're going to use this to hurt him."

"Hmmm."

"You even remember why we ended up at each other's throats?" Nick asked.

Kale tilted his head as if struggling.

"Unbelievable. I told you not to get drunk at that event."

"Hey, I do my best work when I'm drunk."

"And your worst."

Nick looked toward the metal bars. "I was about to snap your neck before that bouncer broke us apart."

"I do know why we're here though, and you don't." Kale said, smiling.

"Why are we here?"

"For driving without a license and wasting natural resources."

Nick tried to swallow but his mouth was parched. "What?"

"You wouldn't remember because you were passed out."

"And *you* were driving?" Nick asked, stunned.

"Yep."

"And you didn't get a DUI?"

"Nope. They actually kinda liked me."

"Wait a minute." Nick wiped the sleep from his eyes and exhaled. He sat up on one of the cots. "We got thrown in jail because you didn't have a license and for wasting...what?"

"First of all, the wasting resources part is what they give you for driving too fast here."

"I thought you said there were no speed limits in Montana."

"There aren't. That's why you get a wasting resources citation instead." [3]

"Makes about as much sense as you do. So, why are we in jail?"

"Well...I couldn't remember what hotel we were staying in, and you were incapable of conversation, and we had no money between us."

Nick, checking his pants pockets, "No money? Where's my cash and credit cards, and my driver's license?"

"Gave all your cash to that smokin' hot stripper from Coeur d'Alene. Thought for a minute you were going to propose. I'd respect that though. I'd marry her."

Kale coughed harshly, then spoke with a hoarse voice. "Amber I think was her name – nice girl. I must've drunk most of my cash. Not sure about any credit cards." He spit toward the sink.

"You couldn't remember where we were staying, and you had no money, so they threw us in jail? I'm certain that one day I'll be unable to return to this state because of you."

Kale crossed his arms. "Actually, *we* couldn't remember where *we* were staying and *we* didn't have any money. So, they allowed *us* to stay here."

"We weren't formally arrested?"

"No. We were invited – thanks to my tactful negotiations – to stay here for free. You can thank me later. I can't even breathe through my nose. I think it's broken. How could that be?"

"You really don't recall what happened?" Nick sat back on the cot and leaned against a metal post. "You know, Kale, most people are put in jail for committing a crime of some kind. Hey, where's my rental car?"

"Probably where we got pulled over."

"Where was that?"

"Hell if I know. You were the navigator."

"Thought you said I was passed out."

"You were. That's why I got lost. If you could still drink with any capacity, we'd been fine."

"So we're free to leave?" Nick asked.

"Yeah, unless anyone's being charged with assault. Like maybe you. But let's eat breakfast first. It smells good, and it's free."

Washington, DC

Winter 1997 The Lobbying World

The ACC's conference room doors were closed tight. It was 24 degrees in DC and snowing. The government relations staff had been watching the live landing of the Space Shuttle Atlantis – an uplifting moment in stark contrast to the Challenger disaster of almost exactly eleven years earlier. Hally Peters walked in and promptly turned off the TV. She was determined to make the coalition's 1997 winter congressional weekend in Florida a flawless success. She had invited fifteen CEOs of the coalition's member companies to attend. Two congressmen and two senators would attend long enough to play golf and have dinner, and so far, four respectable congressional staff would participate on the discussion panels. They needed one more staffer.

Hally looked at Nick, the youngest member of her team. "You know some key Senate staffers – right?"

"Yeah, of course."

"Get one of them to join us in Palm Beach and participate on our panel, preferably who deals with telecom issues. And make it a Republican. We've got too many Democrats already. Can you get that done today? We've got two days left to finalize this agenda."

"I'll get right on it," Nick said, anxious to help out with his first trip as a new lobbyist.

"I don't need you to get on it." Hally's face flashed crimson. "I need you to get it done!"

The remainder of the meeting meandered from how many hotel rooms to block off, to how many rental cars to reserve, to who would play in whose foursome in the golf tournament. The only fun discussion was about which trendy restaurant in Palm Beach at which to host dinner for their final night of the weekend.

Having been a former House staffer, Nick knew few Senate staff. He wanted to invite someone from Waters' office but didn't really know them. He contacted his oldest Hill friend, Kale, for advice. Kale called Thurlow Carmine with a heads up on Nick's call. Thurlow was born and raised in Great Falls, Montana, had a degree in geology from Montana State and a reputation as a partier. He was not exactly a telecom expert but worked for the Chairman of the Telecom Subcommittee. Nick phoned Senator Waters' office, introduced himself and promoted the trip: drinks, golf and partying in Palm Beach, all expenses covered by the ACC. Thurlow readily agreed to be their guest.

Nick flew to West Palm Beach. Driving his rented Cadillac across a bridge over the blue-green water of South Florida, he spotted their hotel. He walked across ornate floral carpeting to the front desk to check in. Once in his room, he was pleased with how spacious it was and with its large view of the ocean. His hotel room phone rang. There was already a crisis brewing. One Senator and his wife had bailed out of the trip so there was a scramble to redo the dinner seating arrangements with an eye toward not offending any Congressmen or key company execs.

Bozeman, Montana

Summer 2006 The Campaign Trail

After a breakfast of eggs, bacon, toast and coffee, Kale McDermott located their missing rental car. "Hey, it looks pretty good. See, Nick, sometimes things just work out, don't they?"

The new 2006 Jeep was parked right in front of the sheriff's building. The officers had it towed that morning and found Nick's wallet under the seat. Nick, with his head down and lips flattened into a grimace, thanked his jailers for their generosity. Kale gave them a wink and a soul-shake, and promised to buy them drinks next time he was in town.

"Well, what do we do now?" Kale asked as if beginning another vacation day.

"I need to get back to the hotel, shower and change and get on the road. Senator Waters is having a campaign meeting in Billings in three hours. I said I'd attend."

"How far is Billings?"

"About two hours." Nick had cut his teeth in his early twenties volunteering for political candidates in Flamingo Beach, Florida, and knew how important it was to show up and do some actual work.

"Hmph. Think I'll just hang by the hotel pool." Kale talked a big game of helping the campaign but other than writing PAC checks, never lifted a finger.

"Shocking development," Nick said. "I'll probably have dinner there and be back later. Try to stay out of trouble."

"Sure, gramps. Don't forget your Metamucil."

Kale was the in-house DC lobbyist for a telephone manufacturing company headquartered in California. The company was part of a former AT&T lab which had previously been part of Ma Bell when it was one, big government-run monopoly. Nick and Kale became fast friends during their early days as congressional staffers. Their respective congressmen's offices were across the hall from each other. Kale, who grew up west of Tucson by the Papago Reservation near the Mexico border, convinced his Democrat boss to support a controversial border security amendment Nick's boss had offered to the 1986 immigration bill. Nick, who had worked

13

hard on the issue, appreciated the help.

A friendly Arizonan with a wide smile, wavy blond hair and different-colored bluish eyes, Kale left his government job early and excelled at the corporate lobbying business. Drinking and socializing were his best skills, if his only. His out-sized personality garnered the loyalty of Democrats and Republicans alike, and he enjoyed attending fundraisers, entertaining Members of Congress and playing golf.

Kale's company supported a wealthy PAC so he was free to choose whichever boondoggle fundraisers he wished to attend. Aware that if the employees of most companies knew the frivolity with which their hard-earned PAC money was spent would likely demand every dime back, Kale continued to write bigger PAC checks with reckless abandon.[4] His ready access to those kinds of funds only worsened his growing addiction to any source of money which supported, among other things, his large alimony checks and seemingly never-ending indebtedness to bookies.

Nick was always up for a party with Kale, but worried more about the consequences. A native Floridian, he'd practiced law before coming to Congress and, though reluctant, returned to the private sector to prove something to someone. Uninterested in returning to the stressful world of litigation from which he'd been rescued by his hometown congressman, Nick gambled that his inside knowledge of Congress might allow him to succeed in Washington. He joined the ACC in the early winter of 1997, but left a few years later to join a high profile lobbying firm which is when Kale hired him as a consultant.

Showered and shaved with coffee in hand, Nick struggled to appear sober as he hurried through the lobby to begin his drive to Billings. Kale watched him leave from the dark of the hotel bar, where he was playing the Montana video slots and sampling his second Bloody Mary of the day.

Key Biscayne, Florida

Winter 1997 The Lobbying World

Umbrella drinks were served at tiki bars on an outdoor patio under a star-filled Florida sky. Nick felt obligated to introduce the sunburned Thurlow Carmine to industry lobbyists during cocktails before dinner. He was, in fact, responsible for the Montanan being there. Thurlow, with his full head of dark hair and cowboy-like mustache, wore blue jeans and boots despite the South Florida weather. And, although they had not really known each other during their tenure together on the Hill, he was one of Nick's former congressional brethren, so to speak.

Remembering names was never Nick's strong suit. As they sat down at their prescribed places, he did a mental checklist around the table. Senator Powers and his wife Sue were to his right, then Jane Phillips, a staffer on the House Commerce Committee, then Tom Whitaker with the East Coast Big Telco, then Thurlow, then the Senator's somewhat homely daughter whose name he never did quite catch. He repeated the names in his head while pretending to listen to small talk: Powers, Sue, Jane, Whitaker, Thurlow.

When the current chairman of the ACC, the CEO of the West Coast Big Telco stopped by the table, Nick stood up and nervously swung into action. "Oh, hey, sir (he couldn't remember his name), you know Senator Powers and his wife Sue, and this is Jane with the committee…uh…committee; and this is Thurson Carmine…er…Thurmo…I mean THURLOW!"

The CEO responded in a modulated voice, "Nice to see all of you here. Senator, great to have you and Sue join us." He squinted at Nick, and in a quieter voice muttered, "Nice to see you too, Nick." He strolled to the next table.

Sitting back down, Nick was mortified but had little time to recoup. Just after his botched introductions, Thurlow informed him, in a low western drawl that he was, "Leavin' to meet some friends at a bar in West Palm – that's cool, right?"

"Well…if that's what you'd rather do. I mean, uh…"

"Thanks man. I'll see you in the morning."

"Eight-thirty sharp. Your panel is the second one up."

Thurlow was gone.

Breakfast was at seven-thirty in a sun-drenched foyer next to the banquet hall where the ACC's discussion panels would proceed. Nick, almost late, grabbed a bagel and kept his eyes on the floor as he found a chair in the last row of the audience. Wentworth Wardley or "Wen" sat down next to him. Wen was a senior vice president of government relations for one of the most politically active Big Telcos. He was a Republican, fifty-nine years old, with prematurely white hair combed straight back and an unusual Midwest accent.

"Good mornin'."

"Good morning, Mr. War…Wah…lerly…"

"Oh, call me Wen please."

"Okay."

"So, how's it going for you at the ACC? You enjoying it?"

"Oh, yeah. You know, it's busy, but it's great."

"You guys got a sharp group of staffers here for this weekend. That's excellent." Wen commented. "By the way, are you aware that your shirt sleeves are a little long for that blazer?"

"Yeah, I think this shirt was mislabeled or something. You're right though, we worked hard on this event. I think it's going well so far."

"Right. Right. Hally's doing a good job."

"Oh yeah. She's great." Nick nodded.

"I was involved in getting her hired at the ACC. She's a real conservative, you know. Has a lot of close friends at the Greater America Foundation."

"So I've heard." Nick said.

The moderator, a vice president of government relations for a rural western telecom company, began the morning's business by talking about the need to fix the Digital Divide which was leaving rural America behind. [5] He then introduced the first panel. Everyone settled into their seats and squinted through mild hangovers listening to a debate on telecom policy.

Halfway through the first panel, Nick witnessed Thurlow from the corner of his eye managing a shaky cup of coffee as he shuffled to a lone seat on the far edge of the room. He wore new-looking blue jeans and an unidentifiable shirt beneath a dark blazer.

Wen observed the same entrance. He whispered, "Nick, who the hell is that guy?"

"That's Thurlow Carmine. He's a staffer to Senator Waters."

Yelling in a whisper, "He's one of our guests?!"

"Yeah…why?"

"He was sitting by the pool yesterday, buying dozens of drinks for three women, all of whom looked like hookers."

"Really? Wow."

"Who the hell invited him?"

"Uhmm…"

"Jeezus H. Christopher – I can't believe he's one of our guests. Looks like he's about to pass out!"

Nick felt sweat on his upper lip. "Maybe I'll go see how he's doing."

He walked over and sat down next to Thurlow. He looked worse up close. His eyes looked not so much red as unfocused. He didn't appear hungover, more like he'd been tranquilized.

"Hey, Thurlow. How's it going?"

"Great man. Great."

"So you ready for your panel?"

"Yep. Looking forward to it. Uhh…how long you think it'll last?"

"I don't know. Depends on how much people talk, I guess."

Nick quietly walked back and sat down next to Wen.

"What's his story?"

"Said he didn't sleep very well – stomach was bothering him."

"Oh. That's too bad."

"He'll be all right."

The first panel broke up and there was a ten-minute break. Hally called out too loudly to Nick from several feet away, "Hey Nick, what happened to you last night? We closed down the hotel bar around one-thirty."

Responding in a lower voice, "Oh, I crashed kind of early." He knew what bothered her was being left by herself. She was terrible at small talk and wary someone might reference a congressional process issue which was not her strength. "Tonight's the real party, Hally."

She came back in a slightly lower tone, "I also understand you did an outstanding job of introducing Senator Powers and company at dinner last night."

"Yeah, I forgot his daughter's name."

"Was that it? Remembering names is your job. You're a lobbyist – remember?"

"Right."

"Is it also correct that one of our congressional guests bolted last night before dinner was even served?"

"Oh…Thurlow has some family relations here in Florida, he wanted to visit with them."

She grimaced. "Wonderful."

After the second panel was seated and introduced, the room quieted down. Nick was relieved to see Thurlow simply make it onto the dais without physical assistance. The dazed Montanan was seated at the very end of the table just slightly away from the other perkier panelists.

An eager Democratic counsel of the House Commerce Committee's Telecom Subcommittee started off the discussion. Her voice reverberated around the room through an all too powerful microphone. Ear-plugs would have sold at a premium.

The moderator worked his way down the table to the last panelist. "Next we'll hear from Thurlow Carmine, a staffer to Montana Senator Clarence Waters for his perspective on these issues. Thurlow?"

There was silence. Hally leaned forward to stare at Nick from several seats away.

Thurlow shifted in his chair and looked straight down at the table as if reading something.

What seemed like an endless silence blanketed the room.

Nick pleaded in his head, *Just say something for God's sake!*

"Uh…excuse me."

There's a start. Nick thought, still hopeful.

"Uhm…"

Wen Wardley, shaking his head, looked at Nick with a thin smile as if to say, "You've got to be kidding me."

"Uhm…As you know…Congress…has jurisdiction over our antitrust laws…and consequently has something to say about competition issues affecting the telecom sector…"

Thurlow got on a roll for a few minutes doling out an intelligent-sounding tale about the debate around the 1996 Telecom Act and its pro-competition provisions, then shut up for the remainder of the panel.

———————

Following that afternoon's golf and cocktails, the ACC government affairs lobbyists and khaki-clad phone company CEOs with their sundress-matched wives sat down for the weekend's last dinner. They were seated at tables under an ivy-canopied patio on Worth Avenue. The white wine flowed, the yellowtail snapper sizzled and the mood was bright. After dinner the older guests headed back to the hotel, but the younger crew were game to visit at least one nightclub in West Palm. Hally was at a loss as to where to go – as was everyone else. Fortunately, there was an upside to Thurlow's absence during the coalition's weekend agenda. He'd drawn a bead on a well-connected local club.

Thurlow's recent *mea culpa* for not attending dinner on the last night of their trip included an invite, "Hey Nick, if you decide to go for a drink later, stop by a club called The SeLaSsh. I know the owner. Just tell them I sent you."

While the others peered blankly down Clematis Street as if trying to discern which recently opened club had no line, Nick stepped up, "I know a club we can hit. Follow me."

They walked single file down a crowded sidewalk looking more like escapees from the nearest prep school. All were enjoying the sights before the Florida sky let loose with a very slight but steady drizzle.

Arriving at the front door of The SeLaSsh, they encountered a line of wannabes trying to get into the club. With the rain, humidity and hair-gel beginning to stream, Nick could see Hally was fuming.

She tucked some quickly frizzing hair behind her ears and stared Nick down, "You have any bloody idea what you're doing? How are you going to get all these people in there?"

"Just hang on, Hally." A strand of curly wet hair was dangling down the middle of her forehead right between her eyes.

He maneuvered past some bizarrely clothed patrons to the front of the line. The doorman, a larger-than-life African version of Mr. Clean sported a solid gold earring. "Uh…hi. My name's Nick Taft."

"Yeah."

"Yeah. So, we're from Washington." He pointed toward the combination moistened sundresses and button-down-blazered crew.

"Thurlow sent us, said we should come here."

"Thurlow?" He looked at Nick as if he were incredibly stupid. "Wait here."

Nick looked past the smirking line of clubbers to his coalition colleagues. They appeared bewildered, hopeful and wet. Mr. Clean returned, unhooked the rope and gestured for Nick and his guests to follow. The prepsters walked by the others in line as if it happened all the time. They were ushered into a plush, semi-private room. Magnums of champagne were on ice surrounded by crystal flutes. Although Hally was smiling and clearly pleased, she appeared more as if she'd just received a lethal dose of electroshock therapy.

The music was so loud Nick had to ask her to repeat her next words, "Nice work, Nick!" Drinking champagne as the other mere patrons looked on, they continued their last evening in Florida.

After an hour of reveling in those indulgences, most of the telecom execs were ready to return to the hotel, and taxis were ordered. Having bragged on Thurlow's connection to the club, Nick decided to see if he could locate the wayward staffer. After being questioned by the Hispanic head bartender as to how he knew Thurlow, he was led down a long narrow hallway through a thick velvet curtain to the back room. There, the music was edgier, the smoke thicker and the women seemingly more available.

He couldn't see very well through the smoke, so he slowly walked the length of the bar trying not to step on any toes. He spotted Thurlow at the end of the long marble counter, who looked somewhat out of place, but was facing down the room with a very attractive woman on each arm.

"You made it. Excellent. Want to party?" Thurlow gestured with an inviting smile.

There were several intriguing if not illegal temptations on and around the back bar, "Oh, no. I'm cool. Just wanted to thank you for getting us all in. We're in the champagne room upfront."

Thurlow's eyes were wide, he wore a permanent grin, "I know. Excellent! Have fun."

With that, Nick nodded toward the women and stumbled across bare legs and feet back to the legal part of the club. While he was acquainted with very few of Waters' staffers, he was aware that most had a reputation as dedicated and patriotic. Nick knew that some were notorious for partying, but was surprised at the contrast between Clarence Waters' down-to-earth Montana style and the big-city-lights irreverence of this key staffer. Yet he was grateful that Thurlow's antics had helped entertain his industry colleagues.

As he went to rejoin his group in the roped-off room, he recognized a guy at the bar. They noticed each other at the same moment.

"Hey, Nick. I haven't seen you since law school. John Lowland. How have you been?"

They shook hands. "Wow, John, good to see you. What are you up to these days?"

"Oh, I practiced law for about a year and hated it. I joined the Palm Beach County State Attorney's Office, and I'm head of investigations now. It's a lot more interesting than private practice. How about you?"

"I worked for a firm in Flamingo Beach for a couple of years, then went to DC to work for Congressman Sandy Palmer."

"Yeah, so I'd heard."

"I'm back in the private sector now lobbying for the telecom industry. It's more interesting than practicing law too. In fact, I'm working right now – entertaining some folks from DC here for the weekend."

"That's a coincidence. I'm working here tonight as well." John said.

"What?"

"Yep. I noticed you were just behind the velvet curtain. See anything you like back there?"

"There were some interesting temptations."

"Better believe it. And more in the room behind it. Probably not worth a stint in prison though."

"Right! What an odd happenstance, John. We graduate from school together and years later we're both paid to hang out at a club in West Palm which has nothing to do with the law."

"Well, not exactly, Nick. By the way, I noticed that some of your crew cut out a little while ago. You'd be smart not to linger too long yourself. Let me ask you, Nick, is your friend behind the curtain who's so chummy with The SeLaSsh owners aware of the growing meth problem in his home state?"

"Uh, what? I don't know. He works for a U.S. Senator..."

"I know that."

"Really?"

"Yeah. This place is crawling with eyes, Nick. The attractive woman at the other end of the bar works for the FBI."

"What's going on?"

"Not sure yet. But it smells like money laundering every time I turn a corner in here. I don't think your former boss, Congressman Palmer, would approve. Here's my card, Nick, call me some time, we should definitely catch-up."

John picked up his untouched cocktail and moved to the other end of the bar. Nick returned to the champagne room and talked with a Big Telco lobbyist he'd known on the Hill before leaving to join the ACC. "Hey, let's get some Tequila shots!"

As much fun as the group was going to have was had by 3:00 a.m. There were only four soldiers left standing. Two got into a cab headed back to the hotel. But Nick, along with a fun-loving young press secretary to a California Congressman opted for one more stroll up Clematis Street. After all, it was her last month on the job, and one never knew where the evening might lead. Once they'd crossed several blocks, she spotted Nick's Cadillac.

"Hey, isn't that your rental car?"

"Yeah, it is. Wonder why it's on the street? I left it with the restaurant's valet."

"Looks like it's got a parking ticket on it."

"Of course it does."

"Let's try the valet." She said.

They negotiated the keys from the restaurant valet and walked Clematis Street critiquing the crowds on the sidewalk. His duties for the weekend over and enjoying the glow of tequila, Nick ordered another round on his ACC credit card at a sidewalk bar. He enjoyed buying staffers drinks and seeing them have fun. He was aware that ethics laws over the years had whittled away at private industry's ability to entertain congressional employees. But in 1997 there were no *real* restrictions. [6] The Californian's alcohol-induced inflection allowed her a unique voice almost as if speaking the language of a distant planet, but he understood her perfectly. After every few sentences, they would share a knowing laugh.

Billings, Montana

Summer <u>2006</u> The Campaign Trail

News at the campaign meeting, which Nick drove somewhere between the Absaroka and Crazy Mountains to attend, was not good. First, feedback from efforts on previously voter-friendly Native American reservations had been discouraging if not outright alarming. And another young Indian on the Crow Reservation had died of a meth overdose.

Clarence Waters reacted instinctively, "That's a damn shame. I need to call Big Jim at the Crow Nation and offer condolences. He tried to be supportive of my last election."

"I don't think that's a good idea," one campaign aide said.

Waters was reminded that reservations across the state were succumbing to a new scourge of illegal drugs at an alarming rate, and some tribal leaders were pointing fingers at Montana politicians.

"You kiddin' me? Some poor native girl dies of an overdose and they want to blame me?"

A campaign aide looked nervously at his colleagues but did not respond. It wasn't really his place to do so but Nick spoke up, "Sir, according to the papers, they seem to be blaming a lot of people."

"I've voted to strengthen drug enforcement laws every chance I've had! The Crow Tribe and Big Jim know that." Waters frowned. "I need to respond."

"Everybody knows your record on crime issues," the staffer pushed back. "The tribal government plans to investigate. Let them deal with it. We need to stay focused on winning this primary election."

Second, an affiliate of the *Greater America Foundation*, in a borderline violation of federal campaign law, had just pumped another $150,000 into the campaign of Senator Waters' Republican primary opponent. His opponent was a right of right conservative who was publicly bashing Clarence every day for supporting the Iraq War which he described as an illegal authorization of power that was bankrupting the country. His slick ads were, among other things, pushing Waters to urge the president to fire the secretary of defense.

"What the hell?" Clarence complained. "Those wingnuts are

23

just going to end up helping the Democrats take my seat. How many ads can he buy with that?"

Waters' staff believed the money was raised through a scheme known as "pass the hat" when a lot of cash could be collected at fundraising events where several wealthy donors might drop thousands in $50s or $100s – below the amount required to be reported to the FEC. The DC-based organization would write a check to a Montana TV or radio station for the ads and fill out the proper paper work, but nobody could tell who contributed the money. And that was no place any FEC investigator would tread nor where the FCC had yet to push the envelope.

Waters' campaign aides knew that $150,000 could buy a lot of ads in Montana, but were confident Clarence would win the primary vote in twenty days. Yet they worried about the amount of money the campaign was burning through just to fend off a nuisance primary challenger. It was money coming in from outliers in DC and pushing a common sense Republican into adopting more extreme positions which could hurt him in the general election.

Third, fearing they might end up with an ethically challenged candidate on their hands, the new chairman of the Democratic Senatorial Campaign Committee in Washington had encouraged the local Montana Democrats to make a change and support a different candidate in their upcoming primary election. That was dispiriting to the Waters campaign because the current Democratic front runner was vulnerable. The rumor was he'd investigated his ex-wife's lover while serving in the U.S. Attorney's Office – or something like that.

Compared to the scandal-ridden previous front runner, the replacement Democrat, Evan Sutter, a life-long banker, was as dull as a butter knife. New Jersey's U.S. Senator, Maurice (Mo) Kauffman, the new head of the Democratic Senatorial Campaign Committee (DSCC) in Washington wanted the Democrats to win this Montana seat in the worst way. He believed he could help his party wrest the Senate away from Republican control if he could help capture one or two unlikely seats. And Montana's was one that he and the DSCC had targeted.

As Mo recently said, off the record, "Only like eight hundred thousand people in the whole state? You kiddin' me, we get dat miny votes outta one New Yoourk borough! How hard culd it be?"

Waters seemed unconcerned about the change in horses for the Democrats. He could hold his own against whomever. But what caught Nick's eye and stayed with him was the political money Kauffman had promised from the East Coast which seemed to tire Clarence of the challenge already.[7]

"Kauffman can pump $10 million into Montana out of New York alone if the Democrats need it," Waters complained.

New Jersey Senator Kauffman, a cagey campaign strategist, first ran for Congress in 1996 against two experienced Democrats. His opponents – a New Jersey state house representative and state senator – didn't know quite how to respond to his youthful arrogance, and were shocked at the amount of money he'd raised. Kauffman won and spent two terms in the U.S. House before winning a U.S. Senate seat in a special election. He quickly became a money guy in the upper chamber by leveraging his Wall Street friends for his colleagues. He was later awarded with a leadership post as chairman of the U.S. Senate's campaign arm.

By 2006, Kauffman was poised to seek a bigger leadership position but needed to help his party win a few longshot campaigns across the country. If he did, he could get credit for the Democrats retaking the Senate. Kauffman's strategy to help the party win the Montana Senate seat was, by hook or crook, to get every Native American vote from the several reservations throughout the state, and figure out a way to garner votes from the thousands of out-of-state college kids attending universities in Montana.

The money threat by Kauffman didn't bother Waters' campaign staff. They knew how to leverage Clarence's position to raise $10 million out of DC if needed. Nick was an outsider in Montana, but loved its wilderness and people, and liked Clarence Waters. He would try to help the campaign wherever he could. He also appreciated that the sparsely populated state had only three Members in its entire congressional delegation – two senators and one representative – making it easier to remember their names.

The next morning Kale cut his Montana trip short in order to fly to California. His company called an all-hands-on-deck meeting at its headquarters in San Diego. Nick gave him a ride to the Bozeman airport. En route, Kale recounted what little he could of his previous evening. He talked of visiting several bars and eating the best steak he ever had in a town he thought was named Manhattan. Kale then jabbered on about meeting the girl of his dreams. She was the perfect combination of legs, habits and politics – "and she kissed me!" He further confided he needed some legal advice regarding a loan he had taken out earlier in the year.

Observing Kale's meal as they rode in the car, "A Diet Coke and a Slim Jim for breakfast?" Nick asked.

"It's a Montana Slim Jim!"

"It just says Slim Jim on the wrapper."

"I'm pretty sure it's a Montana one – the nice lady at the gas station told me."

A string of negative ads about Waters came through the car radio. He glanced down at the passenger side floor, "Kale, do you realize you're wearing two different shoes?"

"What? Oh, what the fu…"

"People mistakenly wear two different socks with a suit, but I don't think I've seen two different shoes."

"I'll need to fix that before I get on the plane."

On the walkway in front of a vacant terminal, Kale had clothes from his suitcase strewn across the sidewalk. He found his other brown wingtip and stuffed his things back into his luggage. Nick helped by sitting on top of the bag while Kale struggled to close the zipper.

"Kale, why is this airport so empty? A flight to California's got to be on a fairly big plane."

Kale held his crinkled ticket up close. "Son-of-a-bitch." He lifted the ticket for Nick to read. "Doesn't that look like an eleven to you? It didn't look like a one to me. Oh well, I need some coffee and to do some reading before my meeting in San Diego."

"I'll let you go old friend," Nick said. "But we're going to finish that conversation we started the other night."

"What conversation?"

"The one that landed us in jail and that frankly I wish we'd never had."

Kale shook his head, and gave Nick a big bear hug. "Hasta luego, amigo."

Turning onto the Airport Road, Nick smiled into his rear view mirror while reflecting on his friend's comically disorganized life. Kale had been like that when Nick first met him, but was getting worse since his divorce two years prior. He never seemed to yearn for his ex-wife. But Nick was reminded that of late Kale more often spoke of missing his young childhood friend who grew up on a reservation near Kale's parents' home in Arizona. His friend, Manny, had become involved with drugs and border gangs in his teens and one day disappeared. Kale became visibly saddened whenever he spoke of him.

Driving back toward Bozeman, Nick gazed out at the Bridger Mountains, the first thing he'd seen of Montana when he first flew into Gallatin Field years earlier. To him they represented optimism. The short valley that ran up to the mountains hosted no buildings or parking lots, just tall dry grass from the warm Montana summer and crystal clear creeks. With Kale gone and some free time, he decided to go fishing.

He collected what gear he had at his hotel and headed up toward the canyon that ran along the Gallatin River. It was 69 degrees under a clear blue sky. While he still had cell service near Gallatin Gateway, he called a former colleague who worked for the *Greater America Foundation* – a conservative policy and campaign network.

"So, Ms. Stark, really smooth move. Pumping money into a primary in Montana to force a good Republican to focus on that instead of building his war chest to take on the State and National Democratic Parties in the coming general election."

"Nick, you may not realize it, but there's a growing grassroots movement in this country that's going to take back our party from these country club Republicans. We have the money and our network is growing every day."

"But you're fighting against the only party that will even entertain the policies you support."

"Well Nick, if we win a few more seats of our own, then maybe your party will be implementing those policies instead of merely entertaining them. Right?"

"You're not going to win any seats. 2006 is turning out to be a tougher year than anyone predicted. All you're doing is weakening Republican candidates. We have to stay in the majority in order to implement *any* policy. Do you get that? I also understand the FEC may be looking into some irregularities surrounding the raising of this latest batch of money against Waters."

Although Stark, the vice chair of the *Greater America Foundation*, liked Nick, and was worried that a difficult primary could help Waters' Democratic opponent, it was not a good time for her to go against the grain of her conservative colleagues. "Oh rubbish, Nick. Let them look. Every dime my organization has raised has been as legal as any dime the Democrats or their ridiculous outside liberal groups have raised. Good luck out there, old friend."

Nick threw his phone onto the passenger side floor. Passing the turn to Big Sky, he stopped at a fishing shop and talked with a river guide. He bought some locally-tied flies and a sandwich. Five miles down the highway he recognized a dirt road. His jeep spun through muddy tracks weaving past golden fields of dry weeds which framed the sharp edges of the Madison Mountains. He then rolled onto a grassy knoll at a closed off truss bridge.

As Nick began his hike, the scent of lodge pole pines put him on a different plane. Water tumbled gracefully over smooth rocks where evergreen trees followed the river's edge. He felt younger in the west, almost childlike energy found him there. Montana was the one place that reminded Nick of the North Carolina mountains of his youth. He had spent every summer of his early life there at a hundred year old log cabin snuggled in a hemlock and rhododendron shrouded forest. But after his father died his family sold it and within weeks a developer bulldozed it to the ground. Among these tall western woods Nick's sense of that loss faded.

Viewing the river from the narrow ridge above, then crossing it below allowed him to smell the fresh water as it splashed his boots. In Washington, nothing was ever clear, but in Montana the water was so clean he could see every pebble. DC's buses, horns and sirens kept him from hearing anything; out West he could even hear the wind as it blew through the aspen trees. In Washington, he gazed away from strangers on the streets; in these mountains, he kept his eyes peeled to spot a bald eagle or rare gray wolf.

Finding a good place on the stream, he observed the water for a while. Not a great fisherman, he'd learned through trial and error what not to do. He chose a run just off the opposite bank for his first cast. Above it were small rapids but below a log forced the current out into the river. So, upstream was fast water but below by the bank, the water was still. Nick, certain there was a fish waiting in that calm for food to float by, cast cross-stream and below the rocks. As he suspected, a trout shot out from behind the log, took the fly and jumped a foot above the surface. As Nick had done many times, he lifted the fly rod with one hand, pulled the line tight with his other and missed the fish by a mile. The trout plunged back into the river.

"Damn it! Little bastard." He worked his way upstream grumbling to himself.

Arriving upon a waterfall where the sunlight pushed deeper into the forest, he sat cross-legged on a boulder. He took in the silence and struggled to understand how a place with so much beauty could have the same problems as drab East Coast cities. He questioned the power of the recent drug plaguing Montana – meth. He stood and threw a cast into some quiet water. A cutthroat bit the fly and Nick reeled him in. Admiring the red and yellow of the trout, he removed the hook and balanced the tired fish a second before watching it dart back into the deep crystal pool.

Hiking under hundred year old trees, he became absorbed in the woods. His rhythm improved as he caught several more trout before twisting his way down an overgrown trail back to his Jeep. Nick heard the ominous echo of distant thunder as he maneuvered the black ruts to the highway. He stopped at The Corral for a burger. From his outdoor table he could see the hard rain move across the nearby mountain landscape like a panoramic movie and feel the fresh water replenish the land. His refuge from reality almost over, he drove back to his hotel. He would return to DC the next day to continue his role in the moneyed partisanship unwittingly aimed at his country's enduring democracy.

Washington, DC

Winter 1997 The Lobbying World

Tad Larson, Hally's political nemesis at the ACC, walked quickly past her office on the other side of the coalition's CEO Mike McDuffie. Tad was trying hard to impress with what telecom policy he knew but failing by sounding like a know-it-all. The ACC had just been invited by the House Telecommunications Subcommittee to testify on issues involving implementation of the 1996 Telecom Act. Tad, still wearing his wool overcoat, made his best pitch in order to accompany Mike to the big hearing, then switched the subject to ensure that Hally wouldn't.

Tad began, "By the way, Mike, are you aware that Hally's trip to Palm Beach lost one of our congressional guests? And Nick Taft had a female congressional staffer out 'til 6:00 a.m."

"What?"

"Yes. A key staffer to a Senator has gone missing. As in *Missing!*"

"Uh, has the Senator's office contacted us about it?" Mike asked.

"I can't imagine they haven't. Hally hasn't talked to you about this yet?"

"No."

Members of Congress were tired of anything to do with the 1996 Telecom Act. They had been confused by it for years due to arguments by lobbyists on all sides. When Congress cast its last vote in favor of the legislation during the previous winter, most Members hoped to never again be asked awkward questions about antitrust law or perplexing aspects of communications markets.

For months, the chairman of the Telecom Subcommittee had been harassed by lobbyists complaining that the Federal Communications Commission was being unfair in implementing the new law. In response, he scheduled a hearing and invited company CEOs to air their complaints on the record. Along with the more established companies and associations, the upstart ACC was also invited to appear since it represented a few of the Big Telcos as well as several smaller rural phone companies

Knowing full well that anything to do with testifying in front of Congress fell squarely within Hally's responsibility as head of the government relations team, Tad was ignoring those boundaries and trying to ensure he got his two cents in with the coalition's president. He was hoping to ensure himself one of the prized seats right behind Mike when he testified – sure to be seen on C-SPAN or included in a newspaper photo.

Hally walked into Nick's office, her face bright red as she nervously rubbed her hands together. "Uh, Mike's been asked to testify at the House Telecom Subcommittee hearing next week. Tad's trying to weasel his way onto our turf on this."

Nick thought, *So now it's "our" turf?*

"You need to call everyone you know on that committee and make them aware I'm their contact for this hearing, not that wanker Larson – got it? That little shit needs to be put in his place. We've got a meeting in an hour to go over ideas for Mike's testimony. I really need your A-game on this, Nick. So, drink some coffee, or wash your face, or do some fucking thing."

The well-educated daughter of a dysfunctional Boston family, Hally was schooled in England, leaving her an oft-utilized British accent. A good lawyer who never practiced, she was bright but tactless. After a year on Wall Street and a failed marriage, she turned to politics which led her to a presidential campaign and to the ACC. She was divorced, had a child living with his father, and a brother who fought in Vietnam with whom she didn't engage. Insecurity as to why she was there, coupled with her scant knowledge of congressional process, caused her to overreact every time she felt threatened. This latest bout involving testimony to Congress through a process which she was struggling to learn increased her anxieties.

Preparation for a congressional hearing in Washington involves a multitude of tasks, the least of which is writing the testimony to be presented. No Member of Congress would read it anyway. Nick knew the real test was convincing Members to ask relevant questions of the industry witnesses so they might have the chance to actually talk long enough to persuade someone to do something. Drafting questions to be asked during hearings and delivering them to staffers is easy. Persuading staff that it's in their boss's best interest to ask a particular question on the record in front of live cameras is trickier.

Hally, who had cut her lunch short, whooshed into the conference room where the government relations team had been working. "You guys have any idea what you're doing?"

Her colleagues could tell she'd consumed a glass of wine or two at lunch and was in one of her moods. Lunches with her very few close industry colleagues or right-wing political friends were the pinnacle of her limited social life and she jealously guarded her calendar from ever interfering.

Blaine Blakley, the buttoned down government affairs lobbyist who'd been with the ACC since its inception three years prior, spoke up, "Of course we know what we're doing. We've drafted questions and are scheduling meetings with staff of the subcommittee in hopes of getting some good questions asked."

Radiating from pink to fuchsia, "Really? Have I seen any of these questions yet?"

Blaine, sliding a file down the long table, "Here's a draft set for you." He mumbled to Nick under his breath, "As if she'll understand any of them."

Vicky Bohannon, the other ACC lobbyist, waded in, "Hally, we have eleven Hill meetings set for next week, and fifteen potential questions drafted and being edited. We're on it."

Hally seldom directly took on Vicky who had served as a professional staffer on the Senate Commerce Committee for two years before joining the ACC. She had good relationships on many levels with Members and staff, a lot of institutional knowledge and a quick wit.

"Well, if you guys have it all figured out, then what the bloody hell am I doing here?"

Wasting our time was their collective thought.

"Has anyone reviewed the latest draft of Mike's testimony?" Hally asked, impatiently.

Blaine proffered, "We're waiting for the latest draft from the lawyers."

"I see. Do any of you recall that you were supposed to tell me the minute Tad maneuvered his long nose into anything we're doing? I just found out from someone outside this organization that he will be accompanying Mike to the hearing. What is it I pay you people to do? Sit around and write stupid fucking questions all day?!"

"And, Nick, I must talk with you in my office immediately." Nick began to follow Hally.

"Never mind Nick, sit back down. This involves all of us. I was contacted by Senator Waters' office this morning. Apparently, our congressional guest, Thurlow, the Senator's staffer, decided to take a few extra days off in Florida. The hotel says he checked out the same day we all did, but the fucking bloke hasn't been back to his office and no one in DC's heard from him. Can any of you tell me anything before I meet with Mike and our lawyer about this?"

Nick reluctantly spoke up, "Well, Hally, I know he was hanging around a lot with the owners of that club, The SeLaSsh."

"Thank you, Nick, really helpful," she said, cynically. "Do you happen to know any of the gentlemen associated with that club? Any names you could provide me with?"

Bozeman, Montana

Summer 2006 The Campaign Trail

The Montana sun was at its peak of the day. Nick was checked in and prepared to depart Gallatin Field on an afternoon Delta flight back to Washington when he received an e-mail on his BlackBerry from a senior partner in his lobbying firm:

Nick call ASAP – may need you to meet with potential client on a Montana issue.

You know a lot about criminal law and prison management – right?

Aware there was absolutely no connection between criminal law and prison management, Nick's stress level shot up. He had been down this path too many times with non-lawyer colleagues in his firm. He was reluctant to even reply:

I know something about criminal law and procedure, but that has nothing to do with prison nanagement which I frankly know nothing about.

I meant management.

The partner e-mailed back within 30 seconds:

Perfect. Then you're the one to meet with these guys – D will fill you in.

His stress barometer jumped another few notches. Paul Tyson's idea of *perfect* was galaxies apart from Nick's. And any time poor D which stood for Dee, Debbie or was it Diane, was asked to explain an issue, it meant that Paul had no clue what he was venturing into. Of equal concern was the firm had zero experience with prison issues, and Paul had likely just convinced a client that the firm's prison management expertise was worth every dime of a $50,000 per month retainer.

Sure – I'll talk to D.

Figuring he could buy some time before bothering what's-her-name, Nick drove to old Main Street Bozeman for dinner. He preferred older Montana-style restaurants, but curiosity pulled him into a place called Plonk. Having recently opened in 2004, it was not old but had an open front and long bar. He ordered the house special margarita and gazed around at the upscale patrons. The drink was strong and changed his attitude about Paul's e-mail.

After a second drink, he concluded the longer he could stay out west the better. And what the hell, he'd be a prison management expert if they said so.

After his third margarita, he strolled down Main Street. The Montana summer night sky was lit up and quiet music wafted from an acoustic guitar player on the sidewalk. Cell phone reception there was known to be spotty, so he could call his firm tomorrow. Instead, he phoned a woman he occasionally dated in DC, but when he got her voice mail, he hung up.

———————

Reaching Deb at his office in Washington the next day, Nick got the basics on the prison management client. Some investors had paid for and built a state-of-the-art prison near Red Lodge, but neither Montana, nor the federal government had ever actually authorized it. Now, somebody needed to manage it, and Nick's firm had been hired by a for-profit prison management company to run the traps on getting a state or federal contract on it. He called a friend at the Montana Governor's office who said he could meet with Nick the following Tuesday.

Since it was late Friday afternoon and his firm was paying his expenses, he decided to visit Plonk on Main Street again. After sampling another margarita, he recalled Kale's restaurant recommendation and hesitantly asked the bartender, "Is there a town in Montana called Manhattan? And is there a steakhouse there?"

The bartender replied, "You're talking about Sir Scott's Oasis – great old place. It's about twenty minutes up I-90 toward Butte."

He paid his tab and, out of curiosity, headed west along the interstate. Up ahead to his left were the lush green potato crops of Amsterdam, Montana. They were highlighted by the fading sun behind them. Across the highway on his right were the ranches of Manhattan where tall summer grass was shadowed by grazing cattle. There are two primary roads in Manhattan, Montana – Broadway and Main. He parked by the railroad tracks in front of the Oasis and pushed through a thick wood door. The bar to his right was not busy for a Friday night, but the red and white checker-clothed tables to his left in the dining room were all taken.

Stepping into the dark room on his right, Nick took a seat

at one of several unoccupied barstools. A classic Bob Dylan song played from a vintage jukebox on the back wall and the aroma of grilled steaks permeated the air.

A friendly barmaid with a stocky build asked, "What'll you have, sugar?"

"A cold Moose Drool."

"That I can do."

After taking a heavy pull on the local brown ale, he ordered a steak and took in the characters around the place. His meal arrived and Kale was right, it was the best strip he'd ever tasted, although the cut was so large and fries so abundant he couldn't finish either. After giving up on the sirloin and finishing his beer, he pushed his plate away and sat back.

He thought for a moment about his friends back east, and for the first time in a long while about the Texas woman he dated his first year in Washington, the only woman he ever really wanted to be with. But their close bond was abruptly severed when she was indicted for aiding and abetting her boss, a corrupt Congressman. Nick was aware of her boss's illegal activities and was forced to testify to a grand jury about them but never thought that testimony would be used to indict his girlfriend. She was tried and acquitted, but left Washington to return home to Austin. He'd often thought he could one day salvage that relationship, and for years he'd meant to track her down but seemed constantly distracted.

"You gonna finish that?"

Nick looked up. A tall, thin barmaid with long auburn hair and a sly smile asked again, "You done with that?"

"Uh, yeah – I guess."

The youthful barkeep looked more like she belonged in a New York nightclub than in a small Montana town. She walked from behind the counter and straddled the barstool next to him with perfectly fitted, faded jeans.

"You mind? I just finished my shift and I'm starved."

He shook his head, "No. I don't mind."

She slid his plate in front of her, and with his steak knife but a fresh fork began finishing his meal. He caught her looking at him as if uncertain of a question he'd asked.

She paused after her third bite and stuck out her right hand, "Ava Mueller."

"Hi. Nick Taft."

"I saw the Senator Waters bumper sticker on your car out front. I'm a big fan of his – as is everyone here."

"That's good to know. He's going to need all the help he can get."

"I guess," she mumbled while taking in a slice of sirloin. "Where you from?"

"Washington, DC."

"Get out! What do you do there?"

"I'm a lawyer...or lobbyist actually."

"A Republican lawyer or lobbyist I presume?"

"Yeah."

"Awesome. I'm a conservative too."

Her top blouse button was pulled tight across a slightly immodest chest. "I'm so tired of friggin' Democrats, they just have no common sense. Know what I mean? They're just not rational."

"Uh, yeah." Nick said, stealing another quick glance at her body.

"What are you doing way out here?"

"Came out for a fundraising event for Waters."

"Oh, cool. Where?"

"Bozeman."

"Ah."

After salting his fries, she began delicately eating them one by one. Nick was more pleased with her every time he looked. She had fine facial features, high cheek bones, deep blue eyes and a thin athletic body.

Ava was impressed with Nick in that he didn't seem so impressed with himself as were most East Coast visitors to Montana. She'd grown weary of big city visitors to her state with lots of money who looked upon Montanans as quaint or entertaining. Nick, on the other hand, seemed to talk directly to her. She asked, "Hey, want to do a shot of Jack with me?"

"What? Oh...uh...sure."

Ava ordered, and two very generous shots of Jack Daniels Whiskey and two cans of Coke were placed on the bar.

"Cheers!" She downed the shot and took a swig of Coke.

Nick did the same, except his eyes crossed when he drank and he almost coughed.

"How can I help Senator Waters?"

"Well...you have any money?"

Ava leaned away with an impatient look, "What do you think?"

"Right."

"But I do know a lot of Republicans and Democrats here. I can keep my ears open. Want a Marlboro?" She pulled out a fresh pack of Marlboro Reds and unwrapped the top.

"Uh…okay."

"So what are you, some power broker? How does someone get into that business anyway?"

"Well, I'm no power broker. I worked in Congress for a few years and left several years ago to go back into the private sector."

"So, you're not some rich DC big shot?"

"Nope."

"Good."

"And what's your story?" Nick asked.

"Oh, I'm just trying to finish school and figure out what to do next. I'm sort of on the ten year college plan at this point. I was thinking of going into journalism, but doubt I'm politically correct enough for that crowd."

"But, maybe journalism could use a little variety in its writing these days."

"I guess. I'm not really sure yet what I'm supposed to be doing." She replied.

"Whenever I say that, Clarence Waters says to me, 'Nick, why don't you get married and have some kids – best thing that ever happened to me!' He must have said it to me a hundred times by now."

"Well, I can't have kids. So that option's out."

"Oh, I see." Nick looked down.

"That's all right – not your fault. Hey, want to go down the street and play some pool?" she asked enthusiastically.

"Yep." Nick paid the bill.

As they stood to leave, a guy who'd been drinking heavily at the end of the bar stumbled up to them, "Remember what I told you, Ava, those New York gold fuckers are bad news." He leaned forward toward the door, but looked back before he exited, "Fuckin' rip-off artists."

Nick asked what that was about. They walked out a different door onto the sidewalk.

"That guy comes in every other week or so and drinks too much.

He's a construction worker who lives down in Billings. I've shut him down so many times, he finally quit hitting on me."

She tossed her cigarette into a bucket of sand on the sidewalk.

"He was on a tear tonight because he'd been expecting a payoff from some big wig company back East that hired him to make introductions to members of the Crow Tribe. He's done construction work on the res over the years so knows some of the tribal leaders there."

They paused at the corner of Broadway and Main despite there were no cars in sight.

"Tonight he told me this company promised to pay him a lot if he recommended their reps to folks on the reservation. But after initial introductions, they drop-kicked him. Told him to get lost."

"That sucks."

They reached an old wooden building in the middle of the next block. "Yeah, I actually kind of felt sorry for him." Ava pulled the door open.

The pool hall was almost empty. The bartender welcomed Ava like they were long-lost relatives. They agreed to bet a shot of Jack Daniels on a game of eight-ball. Ava ran the table as she casually leaned across each corner pocket steadying her cue with her lean arms and arched back.

"Cheers!" Another shot – another cigarette.

"One more game?" She asked. "Same bet?"

Nick was wising up. "One more, but I break this time."

"Absolutely."

He sank one ball on the break and dropped three more easy ones in the corner pockets. Then Ava, her straight long bangs tucked behind her ears, ran the table again but didn't seem to work as hard at it. Ava appeared scattered, but deceptively so. She was, in fact, a very focused woman.

Nick's cue stick slipped from his hand for the second time and slapped the cement floor echoing throughout the small bar. He was beginning to question his ability to drive back to Bozeman.

But Ava beat him to the punch, "Hey, I better get going."

"Where do you live?"

"I live up toward Three Forks. It's just down the highway – opposite way from Bozeman.

"Oh. I'll walk you to your car."

They were both parked on the street by the Oasis. "You work here most nights?"

"Just weekends and Thursdays."

"I'll be here for another few days doing some work for a client. I'll come in for dinner Sunday night. You'll be here?"

"Maybe I'll be here," she kissed him on the cheek, "and maybe I won't. And maybe you can find a way for even little old broke-ass me to help your friend, Clarence Waters."

He watched her walk away, get in her car and drive off.

Washington, DC

Having set meetings with staff to Members of the House Telecom Subcommittee on the upcoming hearing, Nick, Vicky and Blaine set out for Capitol Hill in DC. As their taxi passed the snow-crusted Jefferson Memorial, Nick wondered what that founding father might think of the lobbying industry growing like a weed around his country's government. Vicky reminded Nick that a lawyer contacted her to discuss Thurlow Carmine's disappearance on their Florida trip. Nick somberly shook his head, knowing he would be suspect number one since he'd invited Thurlow.

The first two Hill meetings were with staffers whom they knew and had hosted for drinks, dinner or black tie events several times over the past year. These meetings were very friendly – a lot of head-nodding and reassurances that their bosses were on the right side of the issue. When the staffers were encouraged to have their Members attend the upcoming hearing and ask some questions, the lobbyists were generally assured, "The boss will be there and will see these questions. I imagine we can get a question asked."

Though never a guarantee, the implication was welcomed; they could use it with other offices that those Members would attend and ask similar questions. Nick enjoyed these meetings as they were the part of lobbying he thought was useful – educating Members and staff on complicated issues. Although he understood the public had a low opinion of lobbyists and viewed them as unethical, he thought the stereotype was undeserved. He knew how helpful lobbyists were to him when he worked in Congress and had little time to learn so many complicated issues. With about 7,000 bills introduced each Congress, it was impossible to study all the subjects sufficiently.

The next meeting was with a new staffer to a Member with whom the coalition had not touched base in months. Vicky and Blaine followed Nick through a maze of circuitous hallways, elevators and escalators between the Cannon, Longworth and Rayburn House Buildings. The newbie staffer, Todd Hackelman, was nervous as he smacked his gum during introductions. They were led to a small table in the back office where other staffers and their desks barely fit.

When they walked in, one assistant quickly took his feet off his desk and put his newspaper down. Nick smiled.

A brief background of the '96 Telecom Act was in order for Todd. Blaine did a simple overview of the statute within a few minutes. They all looked to Todd for reassurance. However, in addition to the gum smacking, Todd had developed a distracting eye twitch.

Nick jumped in, "So, Tom or, uh, Todd, any of this making any sense to you?"

Todd deflected, "Well, yeah – sort of." Twitch, smack. Dead silence.

"So, you think your boss would agree with us on some of these points?

"What points?" Smack, twitch.

Nick suspected that Todd had been nodding wisely without understanding a word. Nick had sometimes employed that tactic when he was a congressional staffer, pretending to listen to lobbyists explain some complicated issue in which he totally lacked interest.

Vicky weighed in, "Hey Todd, thanks again for your time today. We know these issues are pretty boring, but the truth is rules around who controls the network that delivers our communications to us are pretty important. You think the Congressman will attend the hearing next week?"

"Uh…yeah…I think so…yeah, probably."

"Okay, good. You think you could show him these questions and see if he might be interested in asking one of them?" Vicky gave her best, doe-eyed hopeful gaze.

Todd stared directly back into Vicky's eyes. Twitch, twitch, smack. "I'll certainly try."

Vicky gave a grateful sigh. "Todd, that would be so helpful. We'll check back with you later this week."

As he stood, Todd nodded and reached out to shake Vicky's hand. The congressman surprised them all by sticking his head into the back office. The lobbyists all jumped to their feet.

"Congressman, how are you? Vicky Bohannon with the ACC. We were just bringing Todd up to speed on the FCC oversight hearing next week."

"Oh, good to hear. Nice to see you all. How's Hally doing over there?" As he walked past to another door.

"She's fine – just great." Vicky said, then rolled her eyes at Nick and Blaine. Despite Hally's occasional lack of policy smarts, Members knew her because she was good at helping raise money for conservative Congressmen like him.

During a late lunch with a fellow lobbyist at Tortilla Coast, Nick was relieved to discover that Thurlow Carmine had just been spotted in the halls of the Senate Russell Building. There were lots of rumors swirling regarding his previous whereabouts and pending legal jeopardy as a result of the past week. The bad news was that Thurlow's new Palm Beach friends, the owners of The SeLaSsh, were the subject of a recently impaneled grand jury looking into state charges of fraud and grand larceny. Thurlow was going to be lying low and working out of one of the Senator's Montana offices for a few weeks.

Helena, Montana

Summer 2006 The Campaign Trail

Clarence Waters handily won his Republican primary election and began to focus his attention on Evan Sutter, his 2006 general election opponent. With that good news, Nick drove an hour across open western landscape to the state capitol in Helena to meet with the Montana Governor's aide who covered correctional facilities. He and Nick played in a charity golf tournament together a few years before at a beautiful course near Anaconda, Montana. Their foursome had enhanced their score slightly by giving some questionable putts hoping to win some cool prizes, only to be outdone by an all DC-based foursome who'd blatantly cheated and scored way better than everyone else.

"So, Nick, what's your interest in this prison?"

"We, uh, my firm, understands that the state or federal government needs to clarify who's going to run the place. That right?"

"Whole thing's a mess. Investors who built it should have wrapped up some loose ends. Apparently there is a need for a management firm with some prison experience. The building is just sitting there now, wasting space."

"So, it's not being used for anything?" Nick asked.

"No. It needs to be managed. You guys do that sort of thing?"

"Oh, yeah, our client is very skilled. They should be able to put it to *some* good use."

"Nick, did you know Senator Waters recently sought federal funding to allow the interior work on the building to be finished? Makes me wonder whether he wants it to be privately managed. I mean if the feds are going to fund it, then it ought to be run by the federal government, don't you think?"

"I didn't realize the Senator had done that," Nick admitted.

"Nick, you know where that prison is located – right?"

"Sort of, no, not exactly."

"It's just on the boundary of the Crow Reservation."

"Is that important?"

"There's some unsavory things happening out there these days. Two men were murdered nearby just a few weeks ago. Might be meth-related."

"Murdered for sure?"

"Their throats were slit."

"Hmmm."

"It's being investigated by the local police. I also understand the Crow Tribe investigation of the young woman who recently overdosed on the reservation is moving forward at an unusually impressive pace. Did you know that?"

"No, I didn't."

"Did you know her name?"

"Uh…no."

"Jacy. She was the great granddaughter of a former tribal chairman."

"I wasn't aware."

"You might want to do some homework before your clients get out here."

"Okay. Can I bring them in to meet with you and your boss?"

"You mean your clients? With the governor?"

"Yeah."

"I'll try to set something up for you."

"Great. Just say when. I'll get them out here from New York. Thanks for your help."

Nick assumed that was a good outcome. He wasn't prepared to answer any questions on any management issues himself. He was surprised by the news of Senator Waters' involvement, and needed to investigate that. Once again, he figured he'd wait a day before calling Deb with any news. He'd just wait for Paul to ask for a report. In the meantime he'd stop by the steakhouse on his drive back to Bozeman to see if Ava was working that night.

To his dismay, once past the wireless no man's land near Townsend on his way toward I-90, his BlackBerry started buzzing with new e-mails. Nick pulled over to check them. After deleting a dozen from political fundraisers asking for money for countless reelection campaigns, he spotted three new ones from Deb – all identical.

Paul wants to know what's up with the prison client.

Nick didn't have much to report but it was positive.

Deb – I met with the governor's office today. Have arranged for a private beeting of our client with the governor - just waiting for

dates and time.

He figured that would occupy Deb for a while.

Sorry, I meant meeting

Deb responded quickly.

I'll tell Paul.

What Deb did not tell Nick was that the firm had been recommended to represent the New York prison management company by close financial confidants of Democrat Senator Mo Kauffman. Nick discovered this days later through his own digging and struggled thereafter to figure out why a friend of Kauffman's would recommend a Republican lobbying shop with no experience on prison issues to help a New York company with close ties to the Democratic Party. He knew none of his partners would question it if the money was right, but Nick began to question it every time he lifted a finger for them.

Washington, DC

Winter 1997 The Lobbying World

Any good lobbyist has at least two fundraising receptions and one dinner to attend every Tuesday through Thursday night in Washington. That is where Nick and other advocates connected the dots between formal meetings and political goals. In the late 1990s, when Congress was in session, Members were usually in town Monday night through Thursday. With most of their families living back in their home districts, they didn't have much of a social life in DC so an invitation by a friendly lobbyist for dinner at one of DC's finest restaurants was hard to resist.

After the last set of meetings to prepare for the upcoming hearing, Nick needed to make the rounds. He hoped to share drinks with staffers and see what kind of late breaking intel he could pick up. First he needed to stop by the Capitol Hill Club – a private Republican Club on the Hill to deliver a few $1,000 PAC checks at fundraising receptions. The club was conveniently located next to the Republican National Committee's offices so one was also likely to run into a campaign operative. Three blocks away sat the Democratic Club, conveniently located next to the Democratic National Committee. Democrat lobbyists would attend similar events that evening delivering checks of equal value.

Nick delivered the ACC's check to a campaign aide at the door. She traded his check for a sticky tag with his name displayed just above American Communications Coalition in big black letters. That helped identify Nick to the Congresswoman, who would attempt to keep people and industries straight during the event. It also identified Nick's purpose there. After all, he wasn't just some guy going out for drinks, he had a job to do. Nick headed straight to the bar, got a gin and tonic and began flirting with a young blonde woman who lobbied for the American Medical Association.

Working his way to the back of the room where some telecom lobbyists had cornered the Congresswoman, Nick interrupted and introduced himself. The Representative's chief of staff was standing next to her, a sharp young man whom Nick had met many times but whose name he could never recall. He often panicked at these moments so employed several tricks to disguise his terrible memory.

On this evening, he held his drink up in the direction of the staffer's name tag as if looking for a crack in his glass.

He spoke quickly, "Hey, Fritz, how's it going? Good to see you. Congresswoman Smith, good to see you, too."

With a big smile the Representative from Tennessee said, "Good to see you, Nick. How's Hally doing over there at your shop?"

"Oh, she's fine," Nick said, less enthusiastically than he should. He'd unexpectedly run into Hally earlier that day having lunch with two men at an out of the way DC restaurant. She'd later admonished Nick for not knowing who one of her guests was. She would not reveal either of the gentlemen's names but acknowledged that one was a U.S. Senator. Nick figured that a quick glance at a list of the most conservative Senators would likely reveal her lunch companion. He guessed that the other was likely a conservative would-be candidate for Congress. He was a very straight-laced looking military guy.

A brief conversation on telecom policy ensued between lobbyists and Representative Smith regarding complaints about the need for better oversight by Congress of the Federal Communications Commission.

The Congresswoman, downing her own glass of wine, obliged, "I'll tell you what, we've got to get a grip on these unelected bureaucrats. I'll do what I can, guys."

Nick dropped another check at an event across the hallway, but missed that Member due to a late vote that had just been called on the House floor. He drove through a cold drizzle to the Capital Grille on Pennsylvania Avenue, a popular watering hole for congressional staff. He was briefly held up while dozens of SUVs, limos and police cars flew by, blasting an array of sirens escorting the president somewhere. When he arrived, the bar was wall-to-wall with lobbyists and staffers.

His industry colleagues were strategically positioned throughout the long narrow room. One was at the back of the bar smoking cigars with Senate staffers. An East Coast Big Telco lobbyist, with a flair for storytelling, was near the front buying Stoli Dolis for three female House staffers. And a Southern Big Telco lawyer was holding court at a tabletop in the middle of the bar. These political advocates knew how to work a room and have a good time doing it.

Each one scrambled to pay the large bar tabs of congressional staffers with their corporate credit cards – both to curry favor and to justify their own expensive meals and drinks. Nick maneuvered his way past sharp elbows and padded shoulders to the far end of the bar where staffers to Senator Waters did shots and laughed at the expense of their host, a flabby cheeked attorney who represented some clients in the West. Thurlow was not among them.

"How's Thurlow?" Nick asked.

A junior staffer spoke up, "He's fine. In Montana for a few more weeks."

"Or Florida." Another Waters' aide said, chuckling.

"Hey, big guy, we need another round of shots here," a Waters staffer boldly snorted.

The cheeky lawyer, Dick Hanov, half-smiled, ordered and paid for another round. The Montanans clinked their shot glasses, "*Na Zdorovie!*" Hanov tried to reach in and join them but was a second too late.

"Dick, how do you make so much money representing all those Indians? Most of the tribes in Montana don't seem to have much money."

"Well, they pay their bills, and they have more money than you might think."

"Then why are you always after us to get 'em more federal funds?"

Hanov, smiling, "So they can keep paying my fees!"

A knowing laugh was had all around. One of Water's new junior staffers, feeling the vodka, blurted out, "Shots for everyone. Compliments of Mr. Hanov."

They all looked at Hanov, who within a moment's hesitation, gestured toward the bartender to proceed. Nick talked for a while with the Montanans about DC politics including some telecom industry gossip. He ignored Hanov as best he could.

Helena, Montana

Summer 2006 The Campaign Trail

Montana's state capital, Helena, was where DSCC Chairman, Senator Mo Kauffman decided he could help win Montana's U.S. Senate race for his party. That was not because of the number of Democratic electoral votes available in that city, but because of the floor votes he could pry out of the state legislature that summer to change the state's voting laws before Election Day. To implement the plan he had in mind, Kauffman convened a meeting of the Democratic leadership of the Montana State House and Senate in a conference room of a fancy hotel near the Capitol Building.

The biggest steaks and best liquor money could buy were served. Mo, East Coast born and bred, maintained a strict diet, and was not a meat-eater, but had a steak strategically positioned on his plate in front of his poached salmon.

"I'm sort of a surf and turf kind-a-guy, ya know," Mo said to a skeptical state representative seated to his right who was a fourth-generation rancher.

Having researched Senator Kaufman's idea, the state legislators believed they could pass a new voting-related law during a special session of the legislature to be convened later that month.[8] Unlike those on the books of most other states, this law would allow anyone simply in Montana (e.g., college students) to register to vote and vote on the same day. There had been no outcry from the citizens about the need for this law. In fact, most had never heard of it. Democrats who controlled the state legislature were curious if a credible record could be built for it. But Mo Kauffman promised some free public relations to help drum up support.

One wary state representative, a farmer from central Montana who spoke up, had his doubts.

"Mo, with all due respect, what makes you think these college kids from Michigan or Nebraska or wherever could care a whit about who'll become the next Senator from Montana? Many of them may be registered to vote in their own home states. Isn't it illegal to be registered to vote in two different states?"

"Ryan, you just let us worry about those details. I can assure you by Election Day, these kids will care. Keep your eye on the ball, guys. All that matters is they vote for Evan Sutter, and we beat the hell out of Clarence Waters this fall."

Official business for the dinner over and legislators enjoying swapping hunting stories, Mo Kauffman sat back at the end of the table, smiling. He was one step closer to recapturing the U.S. Senate, and Clarence Waters hadn't a clue. Over the years the national Democratic Party had moved left of mainstream Montana and had struggled to win elections there on policy arguments. If Kauffman couldn't change the votes, he would simply change the voters. With 7,000 out-of-state students attending the universities there, Mo was sure he could convince many of them to vote for the Democratic nominee.

His private charter jet lifted off the runway from Helena Regional Airport at eight o'clock sharp the next morning. Kauffman was drinking his Starbucks coffee in his oversized leather seat, reading news clippings from *The New York Times*, *Los Angeles Times* and *The Washington Post* when his bleary-eyed staff tried to commence conversation. They'd been out to several bars with the Montana legislators after dinner.

Mo looked them over, "You guys have a little Montana moonshine last night or what? Ya' look like a couple a ne'er-do-wells."

Kauffman promised some of the state senators he would *try* to meet up with them at Jorgenson's for after-dinner drinks, but instead sneaked off to his hotel room. By nine o'clock, he was happily ensconced in his king sized bed with his Evian water, watching CNN. But he was awake early the next morning listening to political operatives about a plan to lock-up votes on Montana's Indian Reservations.

The jet was headed to the West Coast to meet with the head of a new liberal grass roots political organization. The plan was to convince some Californians to move east for a while to join the Young Democrats in Montana for some campaign work. The young Montana volunteers who'd joined forces with Democratic candidate Evan Sutter's campaign were well organized, and many had recently worked together for the most recently unsuccessful Democratic presidential candidate. Since Waters had been up in the polls, these operatives were working long hours to stay ahead of Clarence's reelection effort and busy putting together an internet media campaign, the likes of which Montana had never seen.

Washington, DC

The ACC, a national coalition, had to cover the whole country, politically speaking. So it divided all fifty states up among its handful of lobbyists. Among the states Hally assigned to Nick was Montana. It seemed like an easy draw at first – only three members in the entire delegation. But Nick quickly learned that Montana's Senator Waters not only chaired the most important legislative subcommittee to his industry, he was also a senior Member of the Appropriations Committee which held the purse strings for all of Washington including the Federal Communications Commission. He was discovering, despite its size, how complicated his assignment, Montana and Clarence Waters could be.

Born in the Midwest, Clarence ventured to the Rocky Mountains to join on as a ranch hand in Montana in his late teens. In lieu of a college dorm room, he opted to work the horses and cattle throughout the day and sleep under the stars at night. During the Korean War, like so many other Montanans, despite being underage, he joined the fight.[9] He became a member of the U.S. Marine Corps and fought through the bitter winter of 1953.

Upon his return to Montana, Waters negotiated an interest in a cash-strapped ranch outside the small town of Wisdom. One day, due to a hoarse-voiced auctioneer at a cattle sale, Clarence stepped up and discovered he had a knack for auctioneering. He began offering those services around the state which also provided a platform for his advocacy on behalf of small businesses that led him into his first political race for the state legislature. Waters' self-effacing humor and common sense allowed him to win that race by a comfortable margin. His travels over the next many years as a rancher and state representative made him a household name in the sparsely populated state.

Clarence later enthusiastically engaged in a campaign against an incumbent U.S. Senator. It was a close race even after popular President Ronald Reagan came through Montana and heartily endorsed him. Clarence was no fourth generation rancher or landed gentry but he managed against the odds to win that campaign. He was unlike most Senators in almost every way: not formally educated, not wealthy, and not enamored with himself. But he proved to have a plain-spoken presence in a body of men who'd become fearful of their own words. Years later, as Chairman of the Senate Communications Subcommittee, Waters was becoming a critical person to young lobbyist Nick Taft.

Southwestern Montana

Summer 2006 The Campaign Trail

Awaiting a response from Paul to confirm a third potential meeting with the governor for their ever-absent client, Nick continued his drive from Helena back to Bozeman. The wide-open landscape invited him to ponder his life's larger questions like how to survive in DC's precarious private sector, or would he ever again see his ex-girlfriend from Texas? But as he reached the Wheat Montana building and turned onto I-90 toward Bozeman he refocused. Approaching the exit for the town of Three Forks where the headwaters of the Jefferson, Madison and Gallatin rivers converge into the big Missouri, he remembered Ava lived there. He drove through to see what the town had to offer.

Once off the exit ramp, he was surprised to see a lush green golf course along the road to his left. After passing a few weathered grain elevators, he came upon the historic Sacajawea Inn. The first noticeable building on Main Street, it was ivory white with an enormous wooden wraparound porch protected by large round pillars. He parked in front. The heavy front door was slightly ajar so he gave it a shove and stepped into an old fashioned lobby with inviting worn leather furniture, rich hardwood floors and a subtly ornate ceiling. It had a consoling feel to it as if he'd stepped back in time.

He asked the clerk about room rates which she informed him were ninety dollars per night. Nick remarked how charming the place was, and she smiled. "It's been around for a while – located here since 1910." She said that Main Street, which he drove in on, was about seven blocks long and pretty much the whole downtown. She bragged a population of twelve hundred people.

Considering how small the town was, Nick took a chance, "You don't happen to know an Ava Mueller who lives here do you?"

"Never heard of her. And I know everyone who lives here. Sure she lives here?"

"I thought so. She works at the Oasis in Manhattan – great steaks."

"Humph. You should try the steaks at The Land of Magic in Logan – best you'll ever taste."

He walked a few blocks down the sun-filled Main Street and checked out the Saddlery and the Three Forks Café. It reminded him of the small town near his family's old cabin in western Carolina. Everyone was friendly and helpful. They seemed to genuinely enjoy talking with him. He got back into his rented Jeep Grand Cherokee and headed on down I-90 toward Manhattan where he hoped Ava was working that evening. On the way, he got a call on his cell from Kale. "Hey Nick, you got a minute?"

"I happen to be driving in uncluttered southwest Montana. I've got a lot of minutes."

"Sounds nice. Hey, remember that legal issue I mentioned to you?"

"Yeah."

"Can I give you the thirty second lowdown on it?"

"Sure."

"So, I may have fucked up."

"How?"

"I applied for a decent sized loan last year. And you know my credit's not that great. I mean, it's just okay, especially since my divorce and the tech bubble meltdown."

"Uh huh?"

"So, I needed to show the bank that I had some money here and there, you know as a safety net for the loan."

"Yeah."

"And, I…sort of borrowed some money from my company's PAC."

"Oh man, Kale!"

"Wait a minute. Just hang-on a second."

Nick turned the car radio off, shifted his cell phone to his other ear and exhaled, "All right."

"I only wrote a few checks to a fake political fund that I created, then transferred some money into my brokers account and some to my savings account."

"How much?"

"Fifty-five thousand."

"Unbelievable."

"Yeah, but I did get the loan. And bet my landlord that I would – clipped him for $500 which I unfortunately had to hand right over to him for back rent."

"Then, what's the problem?"

"I was going to transfer the money back because the loan went through. But, out of the blue, I get an inquiry from the House Ethics Committee about our PAC disbursements."

"What? The House Ethics Committee has no jurisdiction over you. That committee has jurisdiction over Members of Congress. Your stupid antics may fall under the jurisdiction of the Federal Election Commission (FEC) or the Department of Justice, but not a congressional ethics committee."

"That's what I thought."

"What's the letter say?"

"Oh, it's pretty long. Can I fax it to you?"

"Sure." Nothing about Kale's story sounded legit to Nick; and it never ceased to surprise him that even though he was a lawyer, Kale had an aversion to carrying out the slightest amount of legal analysis of his own.

"There may be one connection I can think of though, Nick. You remember I was dating that woman, Sheila, this past year?"

"I remember. You said she was married but separated from her husband. You kind of kept her at arm's length. Think I only talked to her once at that horse race in Middleburg. She was a looker for sure."

"Yeah, well, her supposedly soon to be ex-husband is Utah Congressman Judd Parker."

"How did nobody ever connect those dots?"

"She was out of town a lot. You know, back in Utah. Nick, you've got to help me. I just need this thing to go away. I can't afford this. No more fuck-ups I swear. I'm also quitting…seriously cutting back on drinking. I really am."

"So, how does Sheila fit in?"

"Congressman Parker is the senior Democrat on the House Ethics Committee."

"Oh, right. Of course…and?"

"And, well, Sheila basically hates me now."

"Tell me you're not dumb enough to have told her about the loan."

"No. I didn't."

"Thank God."

"It was her idea!"

"You're a moron."

"Will you help me?"

After a few seconds, "Kale, the question is can I help you?"

"I understand."

"Let me think on it and get back to you. Fax the letter to the Montana Sunset Hotel in Bozeman."

"Okay. What's the fax number?"

"I don't know. Call the fucking hotel and find out!"

The Oasis was not quiet like it had been the week before. The bar was packed, the music louder, and people were eating, drinking and telling stories. Smoke drifted in the air – from steaks on the grill and an array of burning cigarettes. Nick wedged into just enough room at the bar to order a beer. The people there made the place seem friendly and the charming character of the place made the people seem friendly. Unlike most in DC, they appeared unconcerned about the label on their wine bottle or what others thought of them. He overheard some guys talking about trout they'd caught that day on the Boulder River. Nick asked where that was.

A sunburned fisherman next to him said, "Go up I-90 toward Butte, hang a right and drive a while. Great river."

Nick was grabbed from behind. It was Ava, "Hey, want to join me for a smoke break?"

They stepped out to a patio on the backside of the bar. Ava lit a Marlboro. "Pretty slammed tonight and we're short one waitress."

"Yeah. Place is hoppin'."

"Thursdays are usually busy. You want somethin' to eat?" She patted his stomach.

"I don't know yet, was just having a beer. You know how lucky you are to live out here?"

"What?"

"Seriously. I drove to Helena and back today, and the scenery and just the lack of traffic and crowds were awesome."

"That's hysterical. That road through Townsend to Helena is probably one of the busiest in the state.

Ava was born in California but moved to Montana with her family as a young child and was proud of her knowledge of the state and her sense of place there.

"You want to see desolate, go up to some place like Polebridge or some fuckin' place like that."

"Fewer people than your town of Three Forks where I visited today? By the way, no one there seems to know you. Can you fly fish in Polebridge?"

"I think you can fish just about anywhere in Montana, Nick," Ava replied coolly. "Better get back to my shift."

She flicked her barely smoked cigarette into a bucket and walked back inside. Nick found a barstool and watched Ava work the locals and the tourists. She had them all eating out of her hand. She only half-smiled at him once as she hurried past filling drink orders but was too busy to chat anymore. Nick finished his beer and headed to Bozeman after almost having to shout to Ava that he'd be back again to visit.

He drove to his hotel and crashed in his room. The next morning he woke to a call on his cell from Luke Lessman, one of his colleagues at his firm in Washington. "Taft, what the fuck? Have you moved to Montana permanently?"

"You tell me. They keep asking me to stay out here to help with this prison client."

"Did you hear how much that company is paying us?"

"No."

"A hundred grand a month!"

"Wow. Good client. Who landed them?"

"Paul and Buckley brought them in. It's a company with some connections out of New York or New Jersey."

"I've got to tell you though, Luke, this client is not anxious to confirm any meetings. I keep setting them up with the governor, and they keep blowing him off. Starting to make me look like an idiot. And another thing, I don't know jack shit about prison management."

Luke, laughing, "Of course you do. You're a lawyer, aren't you? Didn't you once work in a State's Attorney's office?"

"You sound just like Paul. I've tried explaining to him, but he's not catching my drift."

"Trust me, Nick, nothing our firm will be doing on that project will have anything to do with actual prison management. You should know that by now. The client knows that world though. They're one of the biggest for-profit prison firms in the country."

"That's another thing though, Luke. If they're such a well-established prison management company, why would they need to hire us to help them get a contract? We've got no history or credibility on these issues. Something seems off to me."

"Oh, relax. It's just about money changing hands. It always is. How much longer are you going to be out there?"

"I don't know. I'm waiting to hear back from Paul about another potential meeting with the governor."

"There's supposed to be a client status conference call here in DC this afternoon. You may find out soon enough. Let me know if you need me to cover anything for you while you're gone. Hey, by the way, I saw your buddy, Kale, at a reception on the Senate side last week. He *is* very entertaining. But, Nick, I have to tell you, he was hammered and frankly out of control."

"Yeah, I hear you. He could probably use some help, but I think he's getting better."

Nick had breakfast at his Bozeman hotel and pondered what to do with his day. As he was about to take a drive, his cell phone rang again. "Hey, Nick. How you doing?"

"Oh, good, Paul. What's going on?"

"Thanks for setting the table for a meeting with the governor out there. Nice work."

"No problem. Are they actually going to make this one?"

"Oh, yeah. They'll get there. I've got Buckley on the line with me here."

"Hey, Buckley."

"Nick, you enjoying it out there?"

"No complaints. Can I head back to DC now?"

"We were wondering if you could stay out there a couple more weeks."

"A couple more weeks?!"

"Yeah. Look, we know it's a lot to ask, but you could be the glue for our client out there."

"Well, if I'm staying that long, I'm going to do some work for the Waters' campaign. Okay by you guys?"

"Let me ask you, Nick, you know campaigns. You've been working them since you were young. Tell us, can Waters win that senate race? And think before you answer."

"Yes, he can. I've seen this race from the ground out here – he can win this."

"So, he'll still be one of our horses in the Senate next year?"

"I plan to keep working with him."

"Well then, Nick, no problem by us. But watch where you step. Rumor has it Waters may get caught up in some Justice Department investigation about the activities of this dimwit, Dick Hanov."

"Really?" Nick's first thought was, *Another untethered DC rumor.*

"You heard it here first. And you can be assured the media's been tipped off and is way ahead of the story. But we need you out there, so you spend your spare time as you wish."

Montana was not a preferred destination for DC's political class, but Nick thought it a beautiful place, and the down-to-earth people there reminded him of the friendly Blue Ridge mountaineers of his childhood summers. Regardless, he complained about having to be away from his girlfriend (which he didn't have) and canceling important plans in DC (which he'd never made). After some negotiating, his firm agreed to cover whatever expenses he needed and include a year-end bonus if the client stuck around. Nick was picturing a fishing hole on the Gallatin River and another shot with Ava.

Washington, DC

The hall outside the committee room in the Rayburn House Office Building was gridlocked. Everyone who was anyone in the telecom lobbying world of 1997 was there. The line into the hearing room stretched the length of the interior hallway. Most of the corporate flacks had hired line-standers who'd been there since dawn when the building opened. The Big Telco lobbyists and ACC folks had standers – guys in funky clothes with radios, who'd stood in line for hours to save places while holding makeshift signs with names on them. Lobbyists were frantically pecking at their BlackBerrys or talking into cell phones to report back the latest gossip.

Nick arrived almost late and found his spot. His stander's sign read, Rick Naft, but it sufficed. He thanked the stander, took his place in line and pulled the sleeves down on his new wool suit. He was behind some AT&T lobbyists whose names he couldn't remember – all grateful they weren't lost in the string of people wrapping around to the end of the next hall. Only half of them would get into the room when the doors opened. Nick and the corporate lobbyists would be first in the room which provided fewer than fifty chairs for the public.

Gossip in line included word about a witness for a competitive rural telecom company who refused to submit his testimony prior to the hearing due to concerns it might be shared with the Big Telcos. They all chuckled at that one despite it being a credible fear. There were more details on the death of the staffer to a freshman congressman. She was, in fact, an assistant to first year Congressman Mo Kauffman of New Jersey, and her demise was being investigated by the Jersey City Police Department. Her naked body was found in a wealthy businessman's apartment on a Saturday morning. An initial report indicated she had died of heart failure.

Once inside the committee room, seats were claimed by strategically placed briefcases and overcoats, and the schmoozing began in earnest. Lobbyists huddled by the staff table to say hello and confirm with staffers that their bosses were still planning to attend. A few Members who arrived early and took their seats on the dais were inundated with small talk and expressions of appreciation. The

Members, simply trying to get through a first cup of coffee, smiled a lot, but any keen observer could detect confusion behind their eyes as to exactly who the fawning sycophants were.

The Subcommittee Chairman arrived and quickly gaveled the hearing to order. Everyone scrambled to their seats. Before asking the scheduled panelists to the witness table, Senator Clarence Waters was welcomed for a statement. He was the Senate author of a provision in the law that impacted rural telecom providers. His statement was brief and to the point. As Waters and his staff were leaving the room, his staffer, Thurlow, recently back from his hiatus in Montana, looked at Nick with his thumb and little finger hooked to his ear, and mouthed, "Call me."

Each of the other witnesses was then given five minutes for an opening statement. The dais was mostly empty. Lobbyists were staring down respective staffers as if to ask, *Where the hell's your boss?* But committee Members slowly began to show up as the witnesses droned on about the need for the government "to provide a level playing field for all industry participants."

Subcommittee Chairman Minter was the first to ask a question – a softball to the East Coast Big Telco witness, the senior vice president of external affairs. "Mr. Davis, can you tell us, is the FCC being even-handed in its implementation of the 1996 Telecom Act?"

"Mr. Chairman, obviously Congress wants, and we all want, a robust communications market where everyone benefits. But clearly, Congress did not intend for the Big Telcos to simply give away their long-held responsibility over the networks we built and maintain. The FCC needs to step in and create some realistic expectations."

What Mr. Davis failed to mention was that his company's networks were built with the rate-payer's money during a government monopoly protected market over a sixty year period, or how very few companies, including his, controlled over 90% of all network traffic.

The next question was one Nick and Vicky had planted, but the Congressman who asked it so butchered his reading of it that the answer undermined their purpose. The hearing would eventually end as it began, with mostly softball questions and self-serving answers designed to be quoted by trade press publications. Mike McDuffie, the head of the ACC, had his moment in the sun when asked how the commission was balancing the treatment of large companies and smaller rural companies. Mike gave as circuitous an answer as Nick had ever heard, but the Member who asked it appeared satisfied with the response.

The proceeding was gaveled closed after three hours. Each industry sector applauded the chairman for convening the important hearing and all were certain it was helpful in instructing the FCC toward a more reasoned approach. In reality, as an independent federal agency which answers to no one, the FCC could not have cared less what these companies had to say. But the hearing had served its purpose: a wonkish show for the public, a feigned warning to the bureaucrats, and a win/win for the lobbyists.

The scripted postmortem of the hearing in Hally's office was all roses. "We got five of our questions asked on the record verbatim and the answers were very helpful. And Mike did a great job – so articulate." The better news was that the wanker Larson was home with the flu and didn't even make it to the hearing. While the feedback seemed to briefly placate Hally, she abruptly dismissed them all except for Nick. When just the two of them remained in her office, she laid a formal looking paper on her desk in front of him.

"What can you tell me about this?"

Nick picked up the document. It was a copy of a subpoena from the Palm Beach County State Attorney's office issued to Thurlow Carmine requiring that he testify in a case involving fraud and larceny and the owners of The SeLaSsh.

Nick shrugged his shoulders, "I can tell you it's a subpoena authorized by the prosecutor's office down there, but I don't know anything else about it."

"Well, you better bloody well find out, and I mean every single fucking thing. He was our guest that weekend. And *you* invited him, so it's your neck!" She left Nick holding the document and abruptly exited her office.

Northwest Montana

Summer <u>2006</u> The Campaign Trail

With his New York prison client having blown off yet another meeting with the governor, and not many friends in Montana, Nick had a lot of time on his hands. He called Talcott Anderson, an old Florida friend who lived in nearby Utah. Nick explained his plight and convinced his friend to come to Montana for some fishing.

Talcott or "Cotter," the only name anyone called him, once served as a staffer in the Utah state legislature but currently was in public affairs for the insurance industry. Cotter was up for the trip and booked a flight. Nick was doing his local stream homework. They'd fish the north fork of the Flathead River near Glacier Park and then head up to a lesser known stream near one of the more remote places in the state.

Cotter arrived into Glacier Park International Airport. They were both overloaded with fishing gear and Orvis attire. After picking up cold wheat beers at the local market and following directions on a map as best they could, they turned onto a camouflaged dirt road shadowed by tall evergreens. They drove up the winding gravel trail listening to old CDs and rechecking the map occasionally to assure each other it was the right road. After an hour with no indication of any civilization in sight, Nick stopped the Jeep. They hadn't passed a single car so there was no need to pull to the side.

Nick turned off the engine. The silence was eerie.

Cotter complained, "I'm off the plane for two hours and we're already fuckin' lost? Genius."

They thought they could hear a river somewhere below them but it seemed too far a distance to hike. Cotter lit a cigarette and began to tell the story of how he almost missed his plane. He'd been detained by airport security in Salt Lake for having a handgun in his fishing gear.

"Cotter, you can't bring a friggin' gun on a plane in 2006. They've cracked down big time since 9/11. What were you thinking? What the hell you need a gun for anyway?"

"I took a fly fishing lesson in Utah a couple months ago. The guy told me Montana is full of bears, especially this part of Montana. He also told me pepper spray won't do shit to stop a grizzly bear.

So, anyway, security made me buy a gun case for it, which they sold at the airport, and check it, and eventually they let me on."

"What an idiot," Nick said, laughing.

Eventually they came upon the little town of Polebridge. It consisted of a small post office, a one-room store and restaurant with a couple of tables out front and some cabins in the back. They walked through the restaurant and around back, past the cabins and toward the tiny post office. The tour was over. There were some unusual-looking characters at a table under a tree in front of the restaurant and the slight aroma of marijuana in the air. Nick inquired if there was a less high-running river to fish around there.

A barefoot guy with a faded red bandanna on his head replied, "Bowman Lake is the best. About a half hour up the road and keep drivin', you'll see it. A mile or so from Canada."

"Hmph. A lake, huh?"

"Yep. It's beautiful, man. Big trout there."

Managing another drive over rough terrain and a partially washed-out bridge, they arrived at Bowman Lake. They split a sandwich and contemplated how best to fish the scenic water. There was no sign of any human visitors – absolutely no litter, no tire tracks, not even a footprint in the sand. Cotter smoked a cigarette and studied the untouched shoreline. He determined they should hug the east edge where the sun, now just leaning to the west, was lighting up the surface. Nick had never fly fished a lake before so followed Cotter along a tall grassy trail a few feet from shore.

Climbing over a couple of fallen trees and maneuvering through some bushes, they arrived upon a sand peninsula that jutted into the lake. Cotter tied on a Royal Wulff fly and cast first – a graceful long arc that landed almost fifty feet away. The water was so still even the feather-light fly caused ripples that seemed to roll out forever. Nick moved farther down the shoreline. He threw a side-arm cast onto the shimmering water.

They cast some more then switched flies and fished different spots for two hours. Both thought they'd had several hits that felt like bites but didn't land a single fish. They eventually found themselves on the opposite side of the lake from their car – not a soul within miles. Each discussed many reasons why the fish weren't biting until they couldn't think of any more.

Cotter sat down on a log, "Well, fuck 'em. Who said there were trout in this area?"

"Nobody, except that guy back at Polebridge." Nick offered.

"Well, he doesn't know what the hell he's talkin' about. But it's just fun being out here."

They considered that as they took in what seemed like total silence until the wind became perfectly still. Out of nowhere, the cracking of sticks struck the quiet air. Cotter and Nick looked behind them. A creature, bigger than either had ever seen, had closed within fifty yards. A grizzly bear was looking the opposite direction with his nose in the air. Fortunately they were downwind from the massive beast. Nick had seen smaller black bears when hiking in Carolina, but facing this huge brute was an altogether different experience.

Speaking quietly, "Cotter, for once you were right. Get out that damn gun."

"Can't."

"Why not?"

"Left it in the car."

Nick shouting in a whisper, "Almost arrested getting it here only to leave it in the car?!"

"It's under the front passenger seat. Where's your pepper spray?" Cotter asked, anxiously.

"I didn't bring it."

"Why the hell not?"

"Because you had a fucking gun!"

The bear ambled along the shore, and closed within twenty yards. Nick and Cotter cowered behind tall grass hoping the grizzly would go the other way. To add insult to fear, the bear slapped the water hard with a big paw and pulled out a large trout just three feet from shore. After much cursing at each other in a whisper they spotted the creature again about forty yards away at the corner of the lake. He was between them and the path they'd hiked from their car, so they looped around onto a longer trail farther from the water's edge – all the while keeping an eye out for the flesh eating animal.

Grateful to be in one piece, they drove the long and winding road back toward civilization. Nick quizzed his Utah friend. "You know anything about Congressman Judd Parker?"

"Sure. His district is mostly in Salt Lake. He was a state representative when I staffed the Revenue and Taxation Committee in the State House."

"I have a good friend who's having some run-ins with him."

"What kind of run-ins?"

Nick explained Kale's predicament.

"Geez, what a crazy one he must be. Trying to pull that off with so many in Washington looking for trouble everywhere. Well, at least Parker's a Democrat and not in the majority there – right?"

"Yeah, but he's the senior Democrat on the Ethics Committee."

"Then you better hope Republicans keep control. If Parker becomes chairman of that committee, he will be ruthless."

"How's that?"

"Parker's a mean son-of-a-bitch. Some people say his wife, Sheila, makes him that way. She has affairs all the time. She's pretty ruthless too. Damn good-looking but tough as nails."

"Unfortunately, my friend's now the object of her wrath too."

"He's managed to get Parker *and* his wife pissed at him?"

"Any chance you could help find him some leverage?"

"I know a few moves he could make. Depends on what he's willing to do. But don't focus on Sheila. In another month she'll be mad at some other lover."

Nick looked at his friend. "Cotter, Kale introduced me to Montana. We've had so many great adventures out here. He's given me a lot of good advice over the years. I've got to help him."

"Let me see what I can dig up. I know who she's dating now."

"How is it you know so much about her?"

"I dated her too – a long time ago. By the way, there's only one person she truly hates."

"Who's that?"

"Former Congressman, now, Senator Mo Kauffman."

"Why?"

"Sheila's best friend from their college days in New York went to work for Kauffman right after graduation – about ten years ago when he first started in Congress."

"Yeah? What happened?"

"She wound up dead."

Washington, DC

Winter 1997 The Lobbying World

The day after the telecom subcommittee hearing, Nick telephoned Senator Waters' DC office and asked for Thurlow Carmine. He was put on hold for several minutes.

"Hey, Nick, how's it going?"

"It's going okay for me. But what about *you?*"

"What do you mean?"

"Thurlow, I'm looking at a copy of a subpoena from the Palm Beach County State Attorney's Office made out to you."

"Well, yeah. There's that."

"Thurlow, you need to tell me about this. You were our guest in Palm Beach. We paid for your travel, room and board and God only knows how many drinks. The ACC's law firm is asking us a lot of questions."

"All right. Meet me at My Brother's Place at 6:00 tonight. We can talk there."

If there was a bar in DC that looked like it belonged in Montana, it was My Brother's Place. It was a dark pub hidden off an alley on the Senate side of the Capitol. Half its wooden chairs and tables appeared to have been either used as a weapon in a brawl or chewed on by a large animal. But it was a popular place in 1997. Nick took a cab and walked in shaking off the cold night air.

Thurlow was at a corner table top sipping a dirty martini. "Hey, Nick, what are you drinking?"

"Just a draft beer will do. Thanks." He nodded to the bartender.

"Thurlow, what the hell did you get yourself into down in Florida?"

"Don't worry. It's not what it seems. Did you see the woman I was with that last night at The SeLaSsh?"

"Yeah. She was beautiful."

"Well, I got a little distracted by her."

"And, so you're being subpoenaed? Why, she married to a local judge?"

"Ha. No. She's actually a minority owner of The SeLaSsh. But her main gig is as a chief steward on this incredible yacht, a 150 foot Fed Ship – the "H.H.S. ALES." It's owned by a German company and is docked at a pier in the Port of Palm Beach. She gets paid pretty well to work the boat and the owners are never around."

"And so you got subpoenaed for what?"

"Lighten up, Taft."

A barmaid placed two vodka shots on their table, "Compliments of the barkeep."

Thurlow looked toward the bar and raised his glass, "*Na Zdorovie*!"

"So, anyway she invites me on a quick cruise to Bimini in the Bahamas. It's only like a two hour cruise from Palm Beach. We docked her at the Big Game Club, a great old marina on this little spit of an island."

"Yeah. I'm familiar with it. I grew up in South Florida – remember?"

"Right. So, we go to this cool ancient bar – The Compleat Angler. It's covered in old photos of Ernest Hemmingway and has so much character. So, we and the rest of the crew get a little hammered, close out every other dive on the island, and on the way back to the dock, decide to take the island fire truck for a spin. I mean it was just sittin' there on the side of the main road with the keys in it."

"And?"

"We drive down the main drag laughing our asses off when someone thinks they see a cop. So, we park the truck in the nearest space we can and haul ass back to the yacht."

He looked at Thurlow as if to say, *And that's it?*

"Well, the next morning we wake up a little late. The tide came in overnight, and it turns out we parked the fire truck on the down-slope of a boat ramp. Half the truck is under water, the engine was completely submerged in sea water."

"And that's why you were subpoenaed by the Palm Beach County State Attorney's Office?"

"Well, no. So, the Bahamians are pretty pissed. They don't know who drove their truck onto the boat ramp, but they have a good idea." Thurlow takes a big sip of martini. "We cast off quickly, and after a brief stopover at Cat Cay just south to drop off several dive gear bags or something, we booked it back across the Gulfstream to Florida. But when we pulled into the Port of Palm Beach, a U.S. Customs boat is waiting for us. We suspect the Bahamians tipped them off to our swift departure. They board our boat, hardly glance at anyone's passport, but they place my girl, Geneveve, under arrest."

"For what?"

"Apparently the night we were in the Bahamas, the West Palm police arrested the owners of The SeLaSsh pursuant to an indictment on criminal fraud charges, claiming they'd stolen millions of dollars. Some Special State Drug Task Force raided the club's business office the night before. She was the only one of the owners they couldn't locate, so they put a warrant out on her."

"So, why are you being subpoenaed?"

"I'm not exactly sure. But I did bail her out."

"Man, you *are* in love. How much did that set you back?"

"Well, ten percent of her $250,000 bail. So, $25,000."

"Thurlow, where the hell did you get $25,000? That's got to be about a third of your salary."

"Oh, that's a whole 'nother story, Nick."

What Thurlow did not reveal was their mutual friend, Kale, had wired the money so Thurlow could get a cashier's check to bailout Geneveve. Kale was, in fact, partially responsible for facilitating Thurlow's aptitude for partying. When the Montanan first arrived in DC to work with Waters, Kale was just beginning his lobbying career. Kale was constantly testing the limits of his corporate expense account in Washington. Thurlow, as a Senate staffer, was a willing, if not eager, accomplice in that endeavor which enhanced Kale's enthusiasm to expense *all* their drinking, golfing and lavish meals.

Thurlow had to wait a couple of days in West Palm for the money to clear, then he and Geneveve spent a few last nights together in Florida.

Washington, DC

Sid Lucas was one of the most effective if unscrupulous political fundraisers in the New York, New Jersey area. He was almost single handedly responsible for every dime freshman U.S. Congressman Mo Kauffman raised in his first successful bid for Congress in 1996. He'd also had a hand in almost every politically-related venture Mo had been involved in since they met. Mo was grateful to Sid, and like most politicians, slow to recognize the dearth of other admirable qualities of his moneyman.

Lucas was married to an attractive New Jersey woman who'd grown up in a rural area of the state well outside of Mo's congressional district. Her family was neither interested in politics nor fond of politicians in general, but she reluctantly played the good political wife for the sake of Sid's livelihood. Unfortunately, Sid's appreciation of her commitment to his work was outweighed by his eye for unattached young ladies. Sid had a knack for identifying such single DC women, and over the years had perfected his approach to them.

One of the last staffers newly elected Representative Kauffman hired to join his team in Washington was Alexandra Martin. She was a bright young liberal from Indiana determined to work on Capitol Hill. Her best friend from college, Sheila Parker, was recently married to a Utah Congressman and anxious for Alexandra to find a job and move to DC. She introduced Alexandra to a man she understood was well-connected in the money circles of DC. And Sid Lucas introduced Alexandra to freshman New Jersey Congressman Mo Kauffman.

The young Midwestern woman jumped at an offer to be a legislative assistant in Kauffman's DC office, and moved to Washington in December of 1996 not knowing another soul there. Her friend Sheila would come into town with her husband, Congressman Judd Parker, on Tuesdays through Thursdays, but was back in Utah the rest of the time helping him tend to constituents. With Sid's help, Alexandra found a unique studio apartment just four blocks from Capitol Hill that had a cool skylight across the ceiling. She began her new job the first week of January 1997.

Their relationship started innocently enough with a peck on the cheek to thank Sid for all he'd done to help her get set up in Washington. But a cold and lonely January invited a nonpublic romance between them. Within weeks it blossomed into a full blown sexual affair. Sid was twelve years older than Alexandra but seemed young for his age. Although he was, technically-speaking, married, Alexandra knew his marriage was basically over; and Sid's wife rarely came to DC. Though U.S. Congressman Kauffman was pleased with Alexandra's work, her colleagues were puzzled as to how this newbie Indiana woman always seemed to be ahead of the curve on all things connected to New Jersey politics.

Washington, DC

Winter 1997 The Lobbying World

Hally Peters despised morning fundraisers. By the 1990s fundraising had become an indispensable industry in lockstep with DC's growing special interests, and campaign-related breakfasts, lunches and dinners were an everyday occurrence. Any lobbyist who contributed money to a candidate in amounts reported to the Federal Election Commission found their contact information embedded in the databanks of fundraisers from Washington, DC to Fairbanks, Alaska.[10] Dozens of political fundraising companies would pound out hundreds of faxes and e-mails per day and scatter-blast them to thousands of people identified only by an e-mail or checking account.

Hally would do dinners but send Nick and Vicky in her stead to the early events. Breakfast events invariably involved a group of sleepy lobbyists from a given industry showing up at eight o'clock to have eggs and bacon with an overscheduled Member of Congress. PAC checks would be turned over to a caffeinated campaign fundraiser with a ready smile who would greet them at a semi-private dining room and slap a big-print name tag on them.

After standing around a creaky-floored room looking out vintage paned-glass windows onto Massachusetts Avenue, Nick and the rest of this morning's wordsmith warriors took their seats at a round, white-clothed table and began making small talk with a Senator and the staffer at his side. Wen Wardly thanked Nick for being there but subtly pointed out that his sleeves were a bit too long for his suit. After a few minutes of chit-chat and the passing around of sweet rolls, Wen, the designated host formally started the event by tapping his fork against a glass of orange juice. The room became dead quiet immediately.

"If I could have everyone's attention for just a second. You all, of course, know our guest today. Senator Jarvis sits on the Senate Commerce Committee, but I just wanted to share a few facts that you may not know."

Wen took a sip of coffee, his hand shaking slightly. "Senator Jarvis was born and raised in Missouri and practiced law in St. Louis before serving in the Missouri State House and then in the

Missouri Senate. He was elected to the U.S. Senate in 1984 when President Reagan won a landslide reelection against Walter Mondale and pulled a few good Republicans along with him. The Senator is also a member of the Appropriations Committee and has a strong understanding of the issues our industry faces. Thank you, Senator, for joining us this morning."

"Thank you, Wen. It's always good to be with you and your folks. Hope we'll have a good discussion this morning about regulations around the energy industry."

The staffer, who sat next to him, whispered in the Senator's ear.

"I meant the telco industry! Heh, you know it's early for a Thursday mornin'."

Only slightly relieved, everyone politely chuckled. The Senator, in order to avoid any complex policy conversation, quickly changed the subject to the upcoming *March Madness* basketball tournament and how well the University of Missouri Tigers were going to do.

"You know, I'm convinced Mizzou is going all the way this year. You heard it here first!"

Nick was out too late the night before to engage. He'd left the Capital Grille at midnight with a woman from the Canadian Embassy. He couldn't get her inviting green eyes or mischievous smile out of his head. Eggs benedict in a creamy sauce was served. He could just hear the words of his doctor, "Son, you're too young to have cholesterol levels like this. I'm telling you, avoid red meat, eggs, fried food and sugary drinks." He'd washed down the Grille's fried calamari and sliced sirloin the night before with several rum and Cokes. But the Canadian bacon smelled so good, he dug in while trying to think of anything intelligent to say.

After a few bites, he noticed his colleague, the perfectly turned-out Vicky Bohanan, three seats away looking warily at him from the corner of her eye and making subtle hand gestures from her chin down toward the middle of her breasts. He thought that to be a welcome distraction until he realized he'd spilled a healthy dollop of egg yolk on his dark tie. He managed to wipe it upward with his napkin and cleaned it off in one motion. Vicky was smiling while she gazed at the Senator as if hanging on his every word.

The lobbyists had heard the arguments many times before. Wen explained, "You see, Senator, the 1996 Telecom Act was not intended to *require* competition, it was meant to simply *encourage* it where a new competitive company could build its *own* infrastructure and compete fair and square for the Big Telcos' customers."

Wen took another sip of coffee, "But most of these new fly-by-night operators, rather than make the necessary investments, just want a free-ride on our networks. The FCC's got it all wrong."

The Senator began to reply but was obviously confused by the complicated issues. Nick got distracted again by his Canadian bacon. The staffer suddenly informed the group that unfortunately there was an early quorum call on the Senate floor, and with that, their guest was on his feet offering heartfelt thank yous to his hosts. They all maneuvered to shake the Senator's hand and emphasize how much they looked forward to working with him.

The refueled lobbyists funneled down the steep, narrow stairs and traded notes about their guest on the chilly sidewalk in front of the restaurant. They acknowledged that despite having collectively contributed $20,000 to the Senator's campaign, the industry had a lot of work to do on Senator Jarvis.

"Did he really not know who the hell we were?" asked an East Coast Big Telco lobbyist.

"No, he knew!" Their host, a Southern Big Telco lobbyist fired back. He was just tired, for crying out loud. You know how many breakfasts, lunches and dinners these guys do all week?"

"I don't know," another said, warily, "but we better damn well make sure he knows who we are from now on."

All agreed to redouble their efforts. The well-dressed advocates then went their separate ways, some to meetings on the Hill, others back to their offices. Nick pulled yet another pink U.S. Senate Sargent at Arms warning from his windshield, but this one had an actual DC Police parking ticket on top of it.

"Twenty-five bucks!" He said to no one. But as he drove toward his office he calculated that he was financially-speaking ahead for the month – to park in a garage cost $20 and was a longer walk. If he only got one real DC ticket per month for $25 after parking on the street 5 times for free, then he was better off. Once in the quiet of his office he called Roline Devereaux, the young Canadian woman he'd met the night before, to see if her memory of how well they hit it off was at all similar to his.

Western Montana

Summer 2006 The Campaign Trail

Nearing civilization again after their somewhat life-threatening fishing venture, Cotter commented to Nick about the political ads coming through over the car radio.

"Taft, we've been driving for only a few hours since I arrived here, but I've heard about a hundred ads blasting Clarence Waters as corrupt, a thief and all-around bad person. What the hell's going on in this state?"

"Want to hear more, just change the station. The national and state Democratic parties just began their negative ads. The worst I've ever heard."

Cotter tuned the radio until another station came in clearly, and as a country-western song ended, more political news rolled-out painting Senator Waters as an insensitive, out-of-touch Washington politician. The story recounted how Clarence had suggested to a struggling young college student that she should try to "straighten-up and fly right." It turned out that the young woman's older brother was a student pilot who had recently been killed flying a small plane. Waters had been repeatedly asked by reporters if he would apologize to the woman's family.

Nick changed the station and another attack ad blasted Waters for doling out federal dollars for political reasons.

"That's the dumbest political ad I've ever heard. Why are they blistering him for bringing millions of federal dollars into Montana?" Cotter asked.

"Since the media decided to demonize it. You should try reading the mind-bending articles in some of the local papers. You'd want to shoot him yourself after digesting those contradictions."

"Senators from Utah get rewarded for winning political battles for federal money."

"Of course they do. But in uniquely DC-orchestrated campaigns like this, accomplishments don't much matter. And these oft-repeated cynical themes tend to bleed out everywhere. Even one of his best supporters, the President of Montana State University, a school to which Waters brought millions of dollars, has turned against him. And despite the fact that the school's president and

76

his well-paid lobbyists begged Waters for those funds. Every week now it seems as if one of Clarence's previous fawning allies is eager to be the next one to publicly distance themselves."

"Talk about your fair-weather friends." Turning to another station and listening to another ad, Cotter asked, "Who the hell is Dick Hanov? Why do they keep bringing up his name?"

"He's a crooked DC lawyer, but one who contributed a lot of money to dozens of Democratic and Republican Congressmen and Senators – including Waters. If you haven't heard of him yet, you will soon enough. The Justice Department has begun an investigation into his corrupt lobbying practices."

"Is Waters close to the guy?"

"Don't know if he's ever met him, but his campaign received as much in contributions from Hanov's clients as any other candidate up for reelection this year." Nick explained. "And unfortunately, at least one of Waters' former staffers went to work for his firm."

They turned onto a highway back toward Kalispell, the Big Sky sun had set and the skyline was beginning to dim. Cotter suggested they stop for dinner. Nick mentioned that their hotel in Whitefish had a great bar and grill, but Cotter had other ideas.

"Let's just pick some dive place on the side of the road and check out the local color."

"Local color? This isn't Jamaica, fuckwad. It's Montana. And I've been here for weeks, seen lots of color."

"Oh, come on. Hey, look at that place, the Rooster something pub. Let's check it out."

As evening descended, Nick reluctantly pulled his Jeep into the dirt parking lot. They wore damp fishing clothes, but having nothing convenient to change into, just went inside. Faux Tiffany plastic lamp shades plastered with $1 bills hung from the ceiling. License plates from almost every state were haphazardly nailed up on one wall. The place was empty except for a weathered-looking barmaid, two guys playing pool and one burnout perched at the end of the counter. Next to him was a pit bull terrier seated atop its own bar stool.

"Hey, I'm the only one here tonight," said the friendly woman. "If you want food service, you'll have to sit up here at the bar."

There were only two unbroken stools left at the truncated bar: one on the opposite end which Cotter quickly claimed, and the other next to the one upon which the terrier sat. Nick cautiously checked out the dog which would be within inches of him if he took the only remaining seat.

"Go ahead, pet 'im," insisted the glassy-eyed man at the end as he dragged on a cigarette. "He's friendly."

"What?"

"He's my dawg, Choppers. Pet 'im!"

The marbled brown and black dog looked up at Nick showing shark-white teeth, seemingly daring anyone to touch him.

Nick looked at Cotter with a crooked grin. Cotter, helpful as always, "Yeah, go ahead, Taft. Pet 'im."

He sat down on the bar stool, but took a pass on befriending the dog. The terrier's eyes stayed locked on Nick.

"Aw, man, what's wrong with you? Dontcha like dogs? He's a goood dawg."

"I'm sure he is. How are you doing?"

"Just fine friggin' dandy." He let go a high pitched chuckle. "How you boys?"

"Good."

Cotter and Nick quickly ordered beers and burgers from the barkeep. She gave a reassuring smile as she took their orders. "Coming right up."

The dog owner enthusiastically asked, "Hey, what 'n hell you fellas doin' out here?"

Cotter responded, "We...uh...were fishing."

"No kiddin'. Where?" He stabbed his cigarette into an overfilled red plastic ashtray.

"Uhmm...Bowman Lake."

"Bowman Lake? Why way the hell up there? Aren't much fish up there."

Nick admitted, "Yeah, we figured that out. We didn't catch *one!*"

With that, the local fishing expert patted his dog's head and wobbled off his bar stool toward them. "What kinda bait were ya usin'?"

"We were fly fishing."

"Ohhh!" He walked uncomfortably close to Cotter eyeing his Orvis shirt and shorts. "So you're a couple of them 'River Runs Through It' kind of fellers." He smiled at Cotter. "Ha, fly fishin'. I catch a ton a trout when I go fishing. Know how we catch fish out here, Orvis?"

Cotter hesitantly shook his head.

"Here's how we do it. Two guys go downstream with a big net. One guy goes upstream, drops half a stick of dynamite in. Boom! Fifty dead trout." He stepped closer, staring at Cotter from inches away. "They's lots a folks fish like that 'round here."

Nick intervened, "You catch fifty trout?"

"Yep. You fuckers just don't know how to fish 'at's all."

Cotter changed the subject, "So what's your name?"

"Buzz. What's yours?"

"Cotter. That's Nick."

"Good to meet you guys." He laughed again.

Unnoticed until then was that the pool players had wandered over behind them. "Where you fishermen from?"

"Florida originally, but now Utah," Cotter said, taking a sip of beer. Nick did not listen to the voices behind him, instead he studied Cotter's face to see how concerned he was with their circumstance.

One of the pool players chimed in, "Florida? They got all kinda wicked critters down there, don't they? Hey, you ever seen a duck get et up by a crocilgator?"

Cotter pivoted on his bar stool, "What?"

Buzz stepped in, "Shut up, Doyle! Go back to ur game. Where in Utah?"

"Salt Lake."

"Oh, big city fella."

Buzz, looking at Nick, "And you?"

"Washington, DC."

"Another big city boy. Well...lotsa things 'bout big city people I just don't much like."

After a nervous silence, "Like what?" Cotter asked.

"First of all, big city folks don't even say hello much less take care of one 'nother. They just all concerned 'bout themselves. And, I think you've got a lot more freedom out here than in a city. Course I never lived in a big city. Don't spose I ever will neither. What do you do there?"

"I'm unemployed," Cotter answered quickly. "By the way, are *you guys* from Montana?"

Buzz answered defensively, "No, but a damn sight more so than you two fuckers. You're sure no mountain man there, Pudgawitz.

You look more like somethin' that fell out of one of them fancy fishin' magazines. For cryin' out loud, e'en a dopetard can catch *one* fuckin' fish in Montana."

A microwave oven beeped from the kitchen. Nick intervened again for Cotter, "So, you're not from here, but what do *you* do?"

"Used to make some high octane puddin' back in the north Georgia woods. But not no more." He smiled at Nick, his partially rotted teeth showing. "That's right, I was a maker. Now then, what the hell do you do, big city, big shot?"

"Uhm…I'm unemployed too." Nick said.

Their burgers arrived, and Nick and Cotter focused on their food. The locals slowly moved to the other end of the bar seemingly to allow them to eat in peace. Cotter spoke nervously under his breath, between bites, "This is starting to remind me of a disturbing movie."

Nick talked to Cotter from the side of his mouth like a ventriloquist but in a stupid voice, "*Hey, let's check out the local color.* Moron." The pit-bull's head tilted up each time Nick lifted his burger for a bite.

The barmaid asked, with a not-so-reassuring tone, "You fellas doin' all right?"

They were left to eat their meals in peace until Buzz, downing another beer, strolled back and looked closely at Nick's Rolex. "You know, that's a pretty damn fancy watch fer someone who's unemployed."

After a few moments of silence, Nick put his half-eaten burger down. He'd briefly considered just handing his whole plate over to the drooling pit bull. "Well, I'm sort of in-between jobs."

"So what *do* you do?"

Cotter, helpful once again, "He's a lawyer."

"Ohhh! We got us a LAWYER here!"

They all chimed in, "A Laaawwyer?!"

Nick shot Cotter a look, shaking his head.

"So, what kind a lawyer we got us here?" Buzz asked.

"I'm actually a lobbyist," Nick offered, trying to improve his lot. "What 'n hell's that?"

"I represent companies to the government. I mean, you know, *against* the government."

Buzz pondered that as he stared Nick down, "Hmmm."

Nick added as if talking to one of his Montana brethren, "I actually work with guys from your Montana delegation. Like Senator Waters, Senator Range, and Congressman Fields."

"Well ain't never heard a any of them fucking good-for-noths," Buzz snorted.

Having been subtly reminded of the fine line between apolitical and off the grid, Nick tried a different tact. "Hey, Bub or uh, Buzz, before this, I was actually a prosecutor."

"Oh." Buzz said, warily leaning back on his heels. "A prosecutor, huh? Guess you're pretty hooked-up there then aren't ya?"

Nick embellished. "Actually an Assistant U.S. Attorney. Have had to put a few folks away."

"Well, shee...iit." Buzz looked at the floor in silence for a long moment, patted his dog on the head, then glared back at Nick. "Well, you know what, Mr. Big? Not everyone stays in the game. You'll learn that as yer life goes on. Think yer above the fray? Maybe it's your big shot political friends you actually ought to have been a prosecutin'."

"Thanks for the heads-up," Nick said.

Cotter, sensing a break in the action, quickly asked the barmaid for the check, put some cash on the counter and whispered to Nick, "Get up slowly and walk toward the door. Don't stop for anything." They paid the tab and got up to leave.

When they were halfway to the door, "Hey, Nick!!"

Nick turned toward Buzz. "Yeah?"

"Know what yer fuckin' problem is?"

After a few seconds of silence, "No."

Buzz, standing up, "You're fuckin' weird. That's yer problem."

Nick smiled, "Have a good night, Buzz."

"Good luck fishin', boys." They all had a good laugh.

Washington, DC/New Jersey

Winter 1997 The Lobbying World

Hugh Haddad, a successful New York defense lawyer had a thirty-thousand-square-foot house in Basking Ridge, New Jersey. His private parties were well known in the circle of New York City lawyers, lobbyists and below the radar high rollers who liked to live on the edge. Hugh hosted a big party later in January of every year called the Real New Year's Bash, and a summer solstice party each June.

Sid Lucas invited his new lover, Alexandra, to accompany him to Hugh's 1997 party which was a little late this year. Alexandra had been at her new job in DC only a short time but worked very long hours to learn the ropes. She was thrilled to take the train from DC to the upscale party, and meet some people from Congressman Kauffman's congressional district.

Once introduced, Hugh Haddad looked Alexandra up and down and took a double take at her and Sid together. Hugh spoke in a deep, raspy voice, "You know, young lady, your boss Mo and I went to law school together. Better watch your step or I'll have to report back on you." He smiled. "Enjoy the party."

Sid and Hugh had done a lot of work together. Sid referred some clients to Hugh who were in need of serious legal representation. Hugh had introduced Sid to some clients who needed introductions to some connected politicians. Sid was aware that Hugh's law practice involved the representation of some unsavory characters, but Sid didn't ask a lot of questions.

After an hour, Hugh pulled Sid away to introduce him to some of his firm's clients. They reeked of old money and seemed out of place. But they were friendly and appeared especially interested in meeting Sid. Hugh explained they were in the minerals business and owners of the Slipper Gold Refining Company. He noted that the company was very successful but always looking for new ground to plow for geological mining potential. Hugh thought Sid might one day help them play a role in DC to leverage some politicians when the company needed a mining permit somewhere.

Having downed several cocktails, hob-knobbed with the guests and partaken in some mood-enhancing illegal activities – compliments of Hugh's Mexican Import/Export clients – Alexandra and Sid departed for the city. They headed through snowy streets to an apartment of one of Sid's friends in Jersey City. It had a grand view of Manhattan and the twin towers. Sipping more champagne from the fridge of the upscale apartment and ingesting some additional recreational drugs, they engaged in a long-running and vigorous romantic evening. At some point they both passed out naked on the expansive living room floor.

From his relatively brief private sector experience in DC, Nick understood that generally, there were two types of lobbyists: the heavy-drinking, back-slapping advocates who rely on their perceived great relationships; and the legislative strategy lobbyists who rely on their perceived substantive expertise. Nick figured one without the other was risky, so he tried to be a little of both. The backslappers could be found at the Capital Grille most nights, drinking and telling stories. The substance wonks could be found in their offices reading FCC filings.

When focused, Nick could usually hold his own with congressional staff during the day and entertain with the best of them into the night. The nightshift lobbyists were usually in around 10:00 a.m. reliving their evening; the pure strategists, at their desks by 8:00 a.m. debating some mundane policy memo.

He also learned that most lobbyists get hired for a few primary reasons. First, is to help a client solve a specific problem with the government. Second, is to simply hold the hand of some inexperienced government relations person in charge of the DC office of some large corporation. Third, is to create an ethical conflict for a firm to prevent its lobbyists from being hired by the opposition. Or fourth, to build a stable of in-house political flacks for a company so it will have some presence on the ground in DC to help handle political problems that may arise.

Nick's first job out of Congress that year in 1997 with the ACC was as a flack for some large telecom companies. Though he worked hard at the trade, he quickly came to realize that a lobbyist is only as valuable as his or her best political connections are on any given day. His relationship with members like Clarence Waters was becoming more of an important political asset with every week that past.

On this particular evening, he was meeting his acquaintance from the Canadian Embassy for a cocktail at the Center Cafe in Union Station. Roline Devereaux agreed – after their last encounter at the Capital Grille – to join him for a follow-up drink after he'd guilted her for the hangover he suffered through at a fundraising breakfast the next morning. She looked more fashionable than he remembered, but had the same mischievous smile. They ordered drinks in the station's restored main hall. Nick was so focused on his platinum blond date he was slow to notice that the two gentlemen seated a few barstools away were Senator Clarence Waters and one of his staff. He didn't really want to, but excused himself.

"Senator Waters, how are you, sir?"

"Look who's here, the telephone guy. How are you, Nick?"

"I'm okay. Good to see you, and you too, Thurlow," he said as he shook the hand of the Senator's recently promoted legislative director.

"What brings you here, Nick? Headed out of town?"

"No, I was just having a drink," he motioned toward his date who was looking in their direction.

"Ah, the life of a young lobbyist in Washington – must be tough." Waters smiled.

"Are you guys headed somewhere?" Nick asked.

"We're headed to New York for a breakfast tomorrow morning."

Nick knew that would be a fundraising event. "Oh, yeah? Who with?"

"A company headquartered in New York," Thurlow said bluntly, raising an eye brow.

"I see." Nick gave a hard stare back, "Been to South Florida lately, Thurlow?"

Nick had recently caught up with John Lowman, of the Palm Beach County State Attorneys Office, who he'd run into at The SeLaSsh Club in Palm Beach. John informed him that Thurlow was still hanging out with Geneveve and was still on their radar.

Senator Waters changed the subject. "Nick, are you aware of this push for a prison reform bill which includes some telecom issue?"

"A what bill?" Nick was confused. He didn't like being out of the loop on anything concerned with telecom-related legislation.

"Nothing much yet. Just some discussions with prison rehabilitation folks, but it does involve a push for more prisons to be built."

"What exactly would the bill do?"

Thurlow chimed in, "It's a bit of a mixed bag. It would require new regulations to address prison over-crowding and maybe allow the charging of higher fees for prisoner phone calls."

Senator Waters advised, "Nick, I need to learn more about the overcrowding issue – maybe we need more privately run prisons. But I don't know what to think of this prisoner phone fee idea. Sounds unfair to me. You guys might want to take a look – see where your companies are before we get very far down the road on it."

"Yeah. I'll do that. Many people involved in this effort yet?"

Clarence smiled, "Just talking to a couple folks. Hey, we better get goin', our train's about to leave. Good to see you, Nick. Better tend to that pretty young lady there before someone else gets her attention. 'Bout time for you to settle down and have some kids anyway. Best move I ever made."

The Senator and Thurlow walked past Nick's date. Waters paused, "What are you eatin' there, little lady?"

"Sushi!" She replied, enthusiastically. Senator Waters looked closer and almost flinched.

Thurlow took advantage of the moment to pull Nick aside, "Hey, we need to raise some serious cash this quarter. Can you help?"

"Glad to. And, congrats on your promotion to legislative director."

"Thanks."

"By the way, Thurlow, I was raised in South Florida and still have friends in law enforcement down there. I understand you hired a lawyer and got out from under that subpoena. But for some reason, you're still on their radar. I don't know what your ongoing relationship is with that woman from The SeLaSsh, but I'd watch my step down there if I were you."

"Well, Nick I have some friends in the conservative movement in this town, and considering your boss's involvement in their fundraising antics, I'd watch my step up here if I were *you*."

Nick's date held some raw fish between two chop sticks out toward Waters, "Want a bite?"

Waters scowled. "Ma'am, we call that bait where I come from."

As the Senator began to hustle down the stairs toward the train tracks, Thurlow paused and said quietly, close to Nick's shoulder,

"Don't worry about Florida, Nick. I can take care of myself."

Nick's date ordered another round of drinks. "Who was that character?" She asked.

"That was a U.S. Senator from Montana."

"Really? He seemed so down-to-earth. I've never been to the Western US before. I hear it's a beautiful place."

Bozeman, Montana

Summer 2006 The Campaign Trail

After a few leisurely Montana days and his friend Cotter gone, Nick decided to do some actual work for Waters' 2006 reelection. During a conversation with a staffer in the Bozeman campaign office, he was asked to help round-up some volunteers for door to door and phone bank work. The campaign was willing to pay expenses. As it was a Friday afternoon, his second thought was to check in with Ava whom he'd asked to recruit some volunteers. Nick called the Oasis, and Ava was much friendlier than during their last encounter. She encouraged him to come by for an after-shift cocktail.

He drove to Manhattan but had to park way down at the end of a long line of cars under a big tree. Many people were setting up for the beginning of the Potato Fest the next day where potatoes from the fields of Manhattan and Amsterdam's Dutch farmers across I-90 would be prepared into delicious foods. They would be sampled as a local parade wound down Main Street. When he walked into the Oasis, Ava gave him a kiss on the cheek, said she'd be done shortly. She was wearing the same painted-on jeans she wore the night they'd first met. A waitress put a shot of Jack Daniels and a can of Coke in front of him.

"This one's on Ava."

Nick stared at the shot for a few seconds recalling his precarious drive back to Bozeman after drinking with her the last time.

"You goin' to propose to it or drink it?" Ava yelled from the far end of the counter.

"Why don't you come help me?"

Ava slid down the bar, drank half the shot and took a swig of Coke. "Gladly! Hey, I'm outta here in ten. Want to shoot a game of pool down the street?"

"Yes I would. I've been practicing."

"Good! You needed to."

They began the three block walk to the same place they'd been before. People were packing up from their festival preparations and cars were maneuvering onto the street to get out of town. The pool hall was empty except for the barmaid who once again came from

87

around the counter to greet Ava as if they were long-lost sisters.

"Where you been, girl?"

"Workin' and going to school."

"Lord, woman, haven't you graduated yet?" The barkeep asked.

"No." Ava sighed with resignation. "But I doubled down on my hours this quarter. And, God willing, I could graduate in a couple months. I just have to get three Cs."

"Okay, then. Shot of Jack? It's on the house."

"Sure." Ava replied.

Nick racked the pool table and was set to break. "What's the bet?" Ava asked.

"Not another shot of Jack." Nick countered.

Ava laughed. "Okay. Winner's choice."

Unsure of what that meant, Nick broke with a strong shot but didn't sink any balls. They went to the counter to down the shots the waitress had poured. They clinked their small glasses together. Ava nonchalantly walked to the table, tucked her long bangs behind her ears, and sank four balls back to back without even pausing. Nick then sank three but scratched by accidentally sinking the cue ball. As Ava was leaning over the table with her cue stick, Nick reached under her arm through her long hair to place the cue ball on the table for her. He accidentally grazed one of her breasts with the back of his hand as he pulled back.

"Hey, nobody's won this bet yet," she said with a confident smirk. Ava sank the rest of her balls and the eight ball. "Well, let's see. What *is* the winner's choice?"

He rested against a bare concrete column a few feet back from the table. Ava came over and pushed her cue stick against him and gave him a long kiss on the lips. The barmaid called out, "Oh, puleeze, get a room."

They left the bar and walked down the quiet street toward the Oasis. As they passed through the moonlight they could see that all other vehicles were gone except his Jeep parked under the lone big tree. "Wow, this place really cleared out. Mine is the only car left. Where's yours?"

"In the shop," Ava said forlornly.

"How you getting home?"

"I don't know. How am I getting home, Nick?"

He leaned into her, her back against his car. After a long kiss he slid his hand between her legs. As he kissed her neck, Ava let go a quiet moan.

"Maybe we should go to your place," he offered.

"Yeah, but my damn roommate's there. Let's get in your car!"

He put the key in the ignition to electronically move the passenger seat back as far as it would go. Within seconds her shirt was undone and he was trying to undo her belt and the zipper to her jeans. He was half straddling her as she leaned on one hand beside the seat and pressed her bare feet against the inside of the windshield.

Ava paused, "Wow, I guess you're aware there's a large hand gun under this seat."

"Actually I wasn't. But I know whose it is."

"Ava smiled, pulled him toward her and kissed him hard. She got her left leg free of her jeans and in an attempt at leverage to lift her other leg, inadvertently put her foot on the steering wheel and pushed off. The Jeep's horn blasted loud before she realized what was happening. They both jumped and Nick hit his head on the ceiling.

"Oh, my God! I'm so sorry," Ava said with a guilty smile.

As they started vigorously back in on each other, the only Manhattan patrol officer, having heard a loud horn coming from the only car on the street, pulled over next to them. Their undivided attention, coupled with the slight interior condensation on the Jeep's windows, kept them from noticing the local policeman. He exited his cruiser and pointed a flashlight into the front windshield.

"Holy shit!" Ava screamed.

Nick yelled in a whisper, "Oh, shit. It's a cop."

Ava pulled her shirt together and rolled down the window. "Earl, what the hell are you doing?"

Officer Johnson replied, "Well, Ava, I was just about to ask you the same thing. Everybody all right in there?"

"Yeah, Earl. We're fine!"

"Well, somebody honked the horn. Made me curious is all."

"As you can see, we're just fine." Ava said with an edge in her voice. "Have a good night, Earl."

"Okay, then. You do the same. Watch your horns," he chuckled as he got back in his cruiser.

That abruptly ended their romantic interlude. Nick drove Ava to her place, an unlit garage apartment behind a two story house.

They laughed for an awkward few moments while parked in her driveway.

"Sorry about that," Ava said.

"It wasn't your fault."

"It kinda was. You still around for another week?"

"Yeah. I'll be back to see you."

"Okay." She kissed him and pulled back. "I'll be in Great Falls for a few days but back at work soon."

"All right. Hey, Ava, you ever going to round-up those campaign volunteers I asked about? If you can, that'd be great. But if you can't, don't worry about it. I'll still do a shot of Jack with you any time."

"I've got some ideas." Ava said. "By the way, I heard Senator McMahon's flying in to do a campaign rally for Waters. That would be hugely helpful. People out here really like him – especially with his military background."

"Yeah, those two go back a ways and serve on some of the same committees together. A plan for the rally is supposed to be in the works." Nick confirmed.

"They're both military vets – right?"

"Yeah, Waters asked McMahon to help him out, and I think he will. On getting the volunteers together, time's ticking, so just get me whatever you can. By the way, exactly where am I?"

They had taken a back road from Manhattan to get to Ava's apartment. "Oh, you're in Logan. Which, by the way, *is not* Three Forks. And for the record, I never said I lived there. I said I lived *toward* Three Forks."

"So?"

"So, the next time you go asking around my town if anyone's ever heard of me, make sure you're in the right town, de-tec-tive." She slammed the door and walked away.

Washington, DC

Winter 1997 The Lobbying World

Hally Peters, outfitted in a stiff dark wool suit giving her a masculine appearance incongruous with her petite frame, asked Nick into her office and closed the door. "How would you like to attend a fundraiser for a Republican Senator scheduled to take place in Colorado?"

"What do I have to accomplish while I'm there?"

"Oh, come on. Skiing, drinking and partying in Vail. Bloody hell, what's not to like?" Whenever Hally utilized her British school-days-accent, she would jut her chin out in an odd formal adaptation which unfortunately accentuated her slightly buck-teeth.

"What's the catch, Hally?"

"All I want is for you to see if our CEO Mike McDuffie's boy, Tad, is working this Senator or his staff."

"I see." It had become clear to Nick that whatever malevolence existed between Tad and Hally was never going away.

Having recently met Hally's parents, who visited the ACC's offices one day during a brief DC trip; and seeing how valiantly Hally tried to paint a loving family portrait despite its lack of connection to reality, Nick had softened toward her. Although wary of her ultra-conservative mischief and confused by her management style, he'd begun to feel some sympathy for her.

"I'll see what I can learn, Hally. But why?"

"I have my reasons. And don't bugger this up, Nick. I need real fucking info."

He landed at Vail Eagle Airport on a Thursday in the winter of 1997 and caught a shuttle to the lodge in Vail Village. The registration desk was crowded with players from DC's lobbying world. He rented his skis from a shop next door along with a contingent of familiar faces. He later met his colleagues in the bar. Nick was struggling to figure out how best to investigate Hally's suspicions of Tad's meddling without creating any personal awkwardness between he and Tad. Tad was a bright lawyer and considerably more tactful than Hally. Nick didn't believe he was any more or less ill-willed than most others in politics, just very ambitious and ever-mindful of the effective role that gossip played in DC.

After drinks they all headed to a posh restaurant in the village for dinner with Nevada Senator Jon Raines. Entering the private dining room at the back of the restaurant, he discovered that Tad Larson was sitting at the table across from the empty seat reserved for the Senator. Nick was dumbstruck.

Tad looked up and smiled, "Hey, Nick, glad you made it."

He knew Tad had good connections with the few Big Telco members of the ACC. He also knew they basically funded 80 percent of the coalition, while the smaller companies' dues were mostly perfunctory. Although Nick had to be loyal to Hally since she was his boss, he also had to be politically circumspect from a larger DC perspective.

"Tad, I didn't realize you were going to be here."

To add weird to awkward, Tad pulled out the chair right next to his and insisted Nick sit down. Instead, Nick managed some small talk with Tad and other lobbyists while he worked his way down the row of chairs and sat down at the far end on the opposite side of the table. Pre-dinner conversation meandered between ski stories about those who'd arrived the day before to details of the previous evening's drunken bar crawl.

Nick decided on the direct approach. He leaned in and looked down the middle of the table. "So, Tad, are you out here on behalf of the ACC?"

The unexpected question quieted his end of the long dining room. "Nick, of course I'm here on behalf of the ACC. You don't think I'm spending my *own* money to drink with these derelicts do you?"

Laughter was heard down the row of those seated in the private room. They all looked to Nick for a response.

"I'm a little confused. I brought an ACC PAC check with me for Senator Raines reelection campaign. But I thought we were only allowed to send one person for $5,000."

"Nick, I was here to attend the Utah Democratic Delegation ski outing which technically ended today. Just thought I'd stick around and maybe take the opportunity to get to know Senator Raines before I left. Okay…?"

"Sure. Just trying to keep it straight for the record."

"Oh, don't do that, Nick. You'll ruin it for all of us."

Much chuckling was heard again by the lobbyists who were a

few drinks into their evening. The Senator from Nevada and his wife arrived and everyone seemed to focus their attention. Nick was surprised to identify Senator Raines as one of the men with whom Hally recently had lunch at a remote DC restaurant. She'd later admonished Nick for not recognizing who he was. Raines, perhaps the most conservative Member in the Senate, was rumored to be considering leaving Congress later that year to head the *Greater America Foundation.*

Halfway through the dinner, which involved no discussion of telecom policy but lots of Capitol Hill rumors and political stories, Tad excused himself to use the men's room. Nick waited an appropriate minute, then did the same.

He caught Tad in the hallway. "Hey, Tad, I didn't mean to be obnoxious before."

"Yeah you did."

"I was just confused when I saw you here."

"You confused now?"

"So, the Utah delegation has ski events here instead of Park City?"

"As you will learn, Vail is popular for political events this time of year. I'm usually here for Democratic events. I've seldom participated in a Republican one."

"You know Congressman Judd Parker from Utah?" Nick asked.

"Yeah. His wife's on quite a crusade about the death of her college roommate. She says the woman was dating a fairly well-known New Jersey politico."

"Who?"

"She didn't say." Switching topics, Tad shot back, "I hear you're hanging pretty tight with Senator Waters' staffers these days."

"Yeah. I cover Montana for the coalition, you know."

"Right. And an interesting crew they are." Tad said.

After breakfast the next morning in the upscale resort where lobbyists fought like kids over free DVDs supplied by a corporate sponsor, Nick skied with some of his colleagues. They hung together on the slopes and coordinated their places in the lift lines. During a lunch break in the lodge, Nick caught up with his old DC friend Kale, who had arrived too late the night before to attend Senator Raines' dinner. Kale was there on behalf of the telecom manufacturing company for which he was the in-house DC lobbyist. They decided to ski a few runs together.

Simply riding on a chairlift with Kale was entertaining if not unnerving. He had a bota bag full of premium scotch strapped to the interior of his ski jacket from which he took a swig every now and then.

"Even on the slopes, Kale?"

Kale smacked his lips, then smiled wide. "Helps me ski better."

"Whiskey seems like a thorn in your side, my friend."

"Interesting observation, Nick. It's actually Thornes best blended Scotch whiskey." Kale let go a big laugh.

But on the long trip to the top of Vail Mountain, Kale had considerable difficulty negotiating his whiskey while simultaneously lighting a cigarette, and more than once barely rescuing his ski poles from dropping off the chair and hurtling toward skiers in the depths below. During the cold ride, Nick alluded to Senator Waters' staffer's blind eye toward any limitations on partying, then asked for Kale's take.

"Oh, Nick, you're starting to sound like all those paranoid DC people. There's real life happening outside of Washington, you know. Just relax and have some fun. Besides, the only staffer that truly matters in Waters' office is his approps counsel—she knows everything and is the only one Clarence really trusts."

On the second day, Nick's legs were spent. He opted for a stroll down the main drag of Vail Village before packing to leave. DC lobbyists quickly dive in and out of many places for political fundraisers and Colorado was no exception. As his plane landed that night at the recently renamed Ronald Reagan National Airport, Nick pondered how best to inform Hally of these latest developments with Tad. He was due to have coffee with her in the morning after a telecom policy briefing in downtown Washington.

Bozeman, Montana

Summer 2006 The Campaign Trail

With no actual client work to do in Montana and Ava out of town, Nick decided to once again try to find a way to be useful to the 2006 *Waters For Senate Campaign*. Congress was in recess for the whole month of August, and most well-connected DC lobbyists would be on fundraising boondoggles somewhere across the country. That is except for his evermore grumpy friend, Kale McDermott, who was busy in Washington fretting about his likely demise pending a threatened Ethics Committee investigation. Nick received a call from him every day, sometimes twice a day. Another call was buzzing.

"Nick, you've got to help me plot a way out of this thing," Kale pleaded into his static-ridden phone.

"Oh, Kale, calm down."

"I can't calm down. Everywhere I look I see Judd Parker or his investigator's face."

"Kale, you better get the hell out of DC for a while. You're losing your perspective. Why don't you come out and do some campaign work with me? You know, do some real work for your old friend, Clarence's reelection."

"Oh, I don't know." Kale moaned.

"Come on. It'll do you good. Get out here, get some fresh Montana air and maybe we'll even get in some fishing."

"Uhm...yeah, maybe that would be good for me."

"Now you're talking. Bring your gear. We'll plot a strategy while we hike the rivers."

———

First introduced to Clarence Waters shortly after joining the ACC ten years prior, Nick immediately liked the straightforward Senator. Kale had convinced Nick to attend one of Waters' fundraising events in Bigfork, Montana on Flathead Lake. They fished all day and built a bonfire under the Montana sky that night. Sipping after-dinner drinks around the fire, Kale cajoled the Senator into telling some of his old stories. Clarence spent an hour weaving humorous personal adventures into actual U.S. and Montana history. Nick was taken-in by the storytelling and impressed with the political history of the tales. They laughed well into the night swapping anecdotes while drinking the best of whiskeys.

From then on, whenever Nick was headed to Montana, he'd give Kale a call to entice him to join him. By this Summer of 2006, they'd fished their way across Montana for almost twenty years. Kale, a good fisherman, taught Nick some traditional Indian methods of reading rivers he'd learned on the reservation by his childhood home in Arizona. As the years passed though, Nick did more of the actual fishing because Kale's aptitude for rich food had rewarded him with a premature case of painful gout in one leg. That took some of the fun out of it as Kale's companionship on the rivers provided much of the entertainment.

On this particular trip, Kale, despite his diet-induced infirmities, was driven by a desire to discuss his legal problems and struggled to keep up with Nick. But as they hiked downstream on a stretch of the Dearborn River flowing beneath Highway 287 north of Wolf Creek, it was Nick who started in by lamenting their profession.

"Kale, this process has become so ridiculous. We deliver money as an industry in order to persuade or pressure Members of Congress to introduce, cosponsor or vote on legislation that will help our clients. Our opponents don't have one tenth the political money or manpower we do. We outraise and outspend them ten-to-one and run over them like roadkill."

"Yeah, and what's wrong with that?"

"We're only ensuring these Members stay in Congress so they'll vote right on our clients' limited self-serving interests. We don't engage one iota to affect their positions on the larger critical issues facing our country. We create partisan battles around non-partisan issues only to ensure a party-line vote every time so our clients can prevail. It's the height of cynicism."

"Like for-profit prison management, Nick?"

"Okay, yeah, among others."

"I know more than you think, Nick."

"You're not answering my question."

"Nick, if you were worried about cynicism, why the hell'd you go to work in politics?"

Kale downed whatever it was that remained in his Gatorade

bottle, "Nick, that's why I get paid, to focus on one industry."

Nick, slow to respond while holding his reel up high and cautiously maneuvering around a chest-high boulder in the middle of the cold river, "Just because you've been doing something doesn't mean you have to *keep* doing it, does it?"

"This country's rotting from its core, Kale, and we're a part of the problem." Nick pointed to some large rocks under the surface to help Kale see his footing. "The lobbying industry is on a self-indulged suicide mission and you're about as accurate a representation of today's endangered powerbroker as anyone I know."

A large trout jumped out of the water then darted under a log within feet of them. They looked at each other and shook their heads.

"I see what's happening, Nick. I'm not blind. But our industry happens to be one from which you and I are making a pretty good living. I represent business interests, Nick. I am what I am, I do what I do." Kale handed Nick his fly rod while he balanced on a mossy rock. "And, I'll remind you, we are acting within the law. So, for your stupid analogy it would be more like involuntary suicide. You know like involuntary manslaughter."

Nick shook his head, "That would still be against the law, Kale."

Kale broke into laughter. "Oh, please, man, you're giving me a headache."

"Kale, millions of good Americans would give anything to have dinner just once with a Senator and tell them what they think ought to be done."

"Yeah? Well, come to think of it, they *can* have that dinner if they hire you can't they? It'll cost 'em though won't it, Nicky? You know it all too well. By the way, you got something against lobbyists in general?"

"No, most of my best friends are lobbyists, including Einsteins like you. I just think our craft is bound for trouble."

"Then, we better enjoy it while we can, Nicholas." He threw a beautiful arced cast that landed just on the edge of an eddy. "Your compassion for our country is touching, Nick, but it's a weakness of yours." Breathing heavily and growing tired of maneuvering over the slippery rocks, Kale sat up on a large ponderosa pine log fallen over the stream.

"You want to worry about the soul of America, Nick? Run for

Congress. Just lay it all out there. I'll write you your first campaign check." He reeled in his line.

Nick sat down as the crystal water rushed beneath their feet. "You know what I'm saying."

"You're a little different, Nick. I get it. You care. Not my favorite trait of yours. But I will write you a large check if you run. Of course, you'll *owe me BIG!*" Kale let out a wicked cackle that echoed down the pristine river.

"After serving the people, Nick – idiots and all – when that idealism begins to weigh on you, give me a call. I'll still be here making a good living, and having more of an impact on public policy than you ever will."

After casting into a few more pools over the next hundred yards, Kale, facing down stream, slipped and snagged an unlucky trout by the tail. He held it up and yelled across the river to Nick, "Look at this beauty, eh?"

Kale then retreated to the riverbank for a nap in the shade of some aspen trees. Nick fished the next mile of the river alone. Cautiously navigating the river rocks brought back early summer memories of hiking smaller streams in North Carolina's Smokey Mountains. He caught two cutthroats, and then spotted a majestic bald eagle gliding just over the water's surface. He threaded his way back through the woods to join Kale for a premixed Gatorade and vodka. They headed through Wolf Creek on the way to their hotel in Helena.

During the drive, Nick took a deep breath and then asked, "So, Kale, tell me all the specifics of your legal troubles. Let's talk this through."

Kale, slow to respond while sifting through the mental lint in his brain, just stared out the front of the car with his head cocked slightly sideways. "Nick, is that a footprint on the inside of your windshield?"

"What?"

Kale's heavy eyelids squinted into the sun, "That's definitely a footprint."

"I...don't think so." Nick replied dubiously.

Kale ran his finger through the heel part of the print. "Yep. A woman's footprint I do believe. What the hell you been doin' out here, son?"

"Honestly, I don't know where that came from. I'll have to take it up with the rental car guys."

Nick would usually share such adventures with his old friend, but something told him to keep this one. Kale had been having a rough run with women lately, so why rub it in.

"Everyone in our business has to be a good liar, Nick. You're not. Why is that?"

"Never quite had your skill for it, I guess."

Kale, in a ruffled, off-tone, almost frog-like voice, "Silent you are, but speak you will."

"Oh don't start with your stupid voice from that movie. Just don't do it."

Kale, in the voice again, "Ah, disapproving you are."

"Do you know how immature that is?"

With a big smile, he continued, "Inexperienced *you* are, but learn you shall. The future unknown it is, but see it you will."

"I can't even understand what you're saying."

"But understand you will," Kale concluded, laughing.

Absorbing the uncompromised landscape in silence as they continued their drive toward Helena, Nick brought up a different subject, "You know Kale, everyone talks about the so-called digital divide impacting rural America.[11] Telecom companies, including some of our clients, use it as a ruse to get ever more federal money to wire so-called rural areas which never get wired anyway. But there's really a much bigger divide taking place."

"What is that?" Kale asked, in a normal voice.

"It's more than just a rural versus urban *divide*. I think federal politics and policies are discouraging people across rural America.[12] That, coupled with what feels like an ever-present cynicism is undermining the values of a lot of good people."

"Undermining how?"

"They're discouraging people who live out in the countryside, trying to push them into big cities. They make that seem like it's a cooler lifestyle with more money and no rules."

"You sound like one of those conspiracy nuts, Nick. And, just fyi, there are plenty of rules to break in big cities. Believe me, I've broken most of them."

Despite Nick's yearning to feel at home there, his usually short trips out West had never allowed him to feel the hometown rhythm of Montana. But this trip was different. "Kale, there are unspoken rules out here, like manners or a sense of respect for one another. There's still *some* understanding of right and wrong – maybe it's just western common sense."

"And that matters, why?" Kale asked.

"Well, I think most people here don't buy into the national media's constant blurring of right and wrong – they live more practical lives here, spend more time outdoors, not indoors staring at the idiot box. People here just don't abide that bullshit."

"But they are abiding *you* out here?"

"Hmph."

"So, what are your instincts about this decency divide, Nick?"

"I think the big money being spent by the hard left and hard right is undermining what common sense remains on the issues that matter."

Kale was mixing another vodka and Gatorade. "What?"

"Kale, these outside groups with their vague names and huge ad buys are intimidating anyone from saying anything that makes common sense. If elected politicians take a moderate position on anything, they're going to attract a well-financed primary opponent."

"Nick, it's a free country. People can say whatever they want and parties can spend their money on whatever political position they support."

"But, Kale, the real impact of all that money is a new insatiable level of greed in DC."

"Not any worse than it ever was," Kale countered.

"You're wrong. I remember when equity and fairness arguments still mattered – even to corporate-laden Republicans. I think they still would if we could get this money-monkey off of Members' backs."

"Oh, for fuck's sake, Nick. It's called politics. Grow up."

"Well, it's destroying our democracy."

"Nick. Let's be serious for a moment. As you know, most Members of Congress have the attention span of a goldfish. But you think they're listening to your complicated arguments about what's fair for your clients?"

Kale shook his head and looked at the floor. "You're wasting your gratitude, my friend. It's always been a mathematical calculation as to what any Member will support and it's about which industry's given more money – and it's a pox on both parties. They have no obligations outside of their top political necessity of any given moment – which is getting reelected. Hell, the Republicans are bad enough. God help us if the Dems take the House. God help me anyway."

Looking out the window at the passing ranch land, Nick reiterated, "It's the growing untraceable money, Kale. And the more of it those groups are able to raise and offer, the more they'll become the *only* path to political office. It's like watching a slow dying forest."

"That's not just a rural problem, Nick"

"But I think people in rural America are smarter, Kale. They've been able to hold on longer to their roots. Montana is the perfect place to put an end to this nonsense – relatively few people, a small congressional delegation and good old western common sense. With the amount of money going to the political ad whores these days though, I'm not sure how much longer anyone can hold out." [13]

"Hmmm."

"We're in the wrong fight, Kale. I don't think we realize back East how much of this crap is going on around us, and more frequently all the time. Before you know it nothing's particularly newsworthy – or everything is – and its meaningless dribble. They don't even know how to define it or what to call it anymore."

Kale, as if looking beyond, stared out his window at a far distant sun shining through distant sheets of rain. After a while he said, "Nick, when I was young, my little friend Manny had a pet chipmunk. He took it with him wherever he went. He would even snuggle it in his coat pocket when he went to school. He called it a munk-munk, I think because he either didn't know the English name for it or couldn't pronounce it. Anyway, one day this big brute of a teacher discovered it, took it from him, and killed it."

Nick gave Kale a hard sideways glance, threw his right hand out toward him palm up and asked, "What the hell does that have to do with anything?"

"Nick, whatever you want to call it, and regardless of whether the media deems it newsworthy, you better get ready for some brutal

East Coast moral relevance regarding Waters' campaign. It's coming and it's coming with a lot of money behind it."

As if on cue, another slew of ads poured out of the car radio blasting Waters as an all-around low-life politician. One ad highlighted that Waters had responded to a question from a troubled young voter by saying, "Well, just do unto others as you would have them do unto you." The ad's voice-over detailed that those words were from the New Testament and criticized Clarence for invoking religion to attract votes – then asked for an apology to the people of Montana.

"Doesn't it seem a little early to you, Nick, that this kind of money has been spent against Waters? The corporate pipeline has been wide open and out-raising a popular three term incumbent Senator by two to one margins for months. And money is coming in at rates irrelevant to the difference between Manhattan, New York and Manhattan, Montana."

Kale paused and wiped the corner of his eye with what he called his good luck bandana. "The National Democratic Party has had fifteen full time staffers on the ground here since April, including five regional field directors and three communications directors. Now, you and I know that media buys in Montana are relatively cheap. But the amount of money pouring into the airwaves here, and that level of saturation in a rural state like this as early as April for a fall election is unheard of."

"You know something I don't?"

Kale nodded. "And you better too if you want to help Waters."

Washington, DC

Spring <u>1997</u> The Lobbying World

The *Washington Herald* finally did a story on the investigation into the death of Congressman Kauffman's staffer, Alexandra Martin. Jersey City investigators initially believed she'd died of natural causes, but after an autopsy revealed a heavy dose of narcotics, their theory evolved into a common one of accidental overdose.[14] A theory that attorney Hugh Haddad had floated. After further inquiry, however, which involved interviews with dozens, including her college roommate, Sheila Parker, they concluded that Alexandra had no track record of drug use. Sheila, the wife of Congressman Parker, argued that foul play was involved.

Amid yet more pressure from Alexandra's family, the inquiry was quietly turned into a criminal investigation in the spring of 1997. One of the first people scheduled for an interview was Alexandra's employer at the time of her death, then young Congressman Mo Kauffman. Mo's loyalties regarding the whole affair were to his moneyman, Sid Lucas. He knew Sid was no murderer but perhaps dumb enough to have put himself in a bad situation. Kauffman was not willing to take a fall for Sid but he needed him, and therefore was willing to go to the mat for him.

Nick read the story while seated at his desk at the ACC with his feet up on his credenza. He had never met Congressman Kauffman, but had heard he was arrogant and somewhat of a bully to congressional witnesses. Nick thought, *A hit piece like this ought to soften that New Jersey slugger up a little.* But it didn't. He also noticed that Kauffman's office had declined to comment on the article. Nick considered that an interesting PR strategy.

Anyone who knew Mo Kauffman would consider him a pretty smooth operator with a cool head. So, anyone who knew him would be surprised to see him overreact in any situation. But that's exactly what the new Congressman did. Hoping to avoid any embarrassment to his congressional office or any roadblocks to his political career, Mo called an old law school acquaintance for advice – a person he thought he would never call. Although his former classmate was a criminal defense lawyer, the clients he represented were seldom innocent. In fact, everyone in New Jersey and New York knew he represented members of the mob.

The lawyer, Hugh Haddad, invited Kauffman to his law office in Manhattan. He asked questions about Mo's relationship with Alexandra. He drilled him on details of the police report. Haddad knew Mo was not telling the truth but few of his clients did. Mo was unaware that Hugh had seen Sid and Alexandra together at his party on the night of her death. But Haddad knew how to make such investigations lose their way. If young Congressman Mo Kauffman had nothing to do with Alexandra's death, the series of poor choices he made to avoid publicity about her demise led him into an indebtedness he would forever regret.

Helena, Montana

Summer 2006 The Campaign Trail

Though Western Montana had settled into its summer slumber of camping and fishing, the 2006 Waters/Sutter campaign had kicked into high gear. Kale and Nick departed their hotel in Helena after a cold beer to quench their thirst from fishing the Dearborn River. They were en route to dine at the Silver Star Steak Company. Nick gave his friend the only advice he could think of regarding his illegal PAC-fund-backed mortgage scheme.

"That's it?" Kale asked. "The best you could come up with? Put the money back, create a paper trail for a mathematical miscalculation and lay low? Are you kidding me? I seriously doubt that'll work."

"Let me do the doubting for you, Kale. They have nothing concrete, they can't possibly. Don't overreact. Don't let Parker or his investigator rattle you or believe you're worried. And cover everything on paper. The balance will be right – right?" Nick looked directly at Kale. "Tell your company and PAC board about the miscalculation and show that it's all been cleared up. Trust me, most of the execs in your company don't even have the slightest clue what a PAC *is*."

"Yes, the math will be right." Kale took a bite of his meal. "You think Waters could help me with Congressman Parker?"

"Are you kidding me? Waters could crush Judd Parker like a bug. I believe Clarence would help you. He's your friend. Just let him get past this reelection battle."

"You think Clarence will help me because he's *my friend?*"

"Yeah."

"See, that's another problem you have, Nicky. You don't get it. Allow me to free you of your illusion. There are no *friendships* in DC politics. These are all transactional relationships – understand? And if you think Senator McMahon is coming to Montana to help Clarence because he's his friend, you're stupid. That's also a purely political calculation."

"Well, friend or not, Clarence may be the only person who might help you under your circumstances."

Of late, there seemed a dark energy lurking just beneath Kale's surface which Nick tried to avoid. "And keep in mind, Parker can't get the Ethics Committee to go rogue on its jurisdiction against you unless he's the chairman, and even then, it would be problematic. Virtually no one's predicting Republicans will lose the House this fall. I'm friends with someone who knows the current Chairman of the Ethics Committee really well. We've got you covered, Kale."

"Too many contingencies, Nick." Kale ordered another scotch on the rocks.

"There are very few contingencies, Kale. Just relax. Now tell me what's going on with Waters' campaign. You know I need him to win as much as you need Parker to stay in the minority."

"One word, Nick – meth."

"What?"

"Meth – the drug?"

"I know it's a drug. What's it have to do with the campaign?"

"It's one of the reasons Waters may lose his reelection in November."

"Why?"

"Someone is providing large quantities of meth to thousands of tribal members on the reservations in Montana," Kale said. "For free."

"Why?"

"I'm not sure. But they've lured many in the tribes into the world of meth. Some suspect that it's to, among other things, guarantee they'll owe favors."

"To who?" Nick asked.

"Not Clarence Waters."

"So, you're telling me someone is handing out meth for votes? That's maybe the dumbest thing I've ever heard."

"I didn't say that. But somebody working for someone with access to a lot of money is handing out meth to Native Americans at an alarming rate. Nick, you find out who's behind these destructive moves on the reservations, and I think it will lead you to who's orchestrating this ugly campaign against Clarence."

Nick thought out loud, "It's not like there are a tremendous number of votes on the reservations, but I guess in a close race they could make the difference.[15] It still sounds pretty far-fetched, Kale."

"Nick, did you know the Crow tribal investigation of the woman who overdosed earlier this summer is looking outside the reservation for answers – and they've requested the FBI get involved?"

"No. But, frankly, the more I think about it, the more harebrained your theory sounds."

"Nick, if Republicans lose their seat in Virginia this fall which is beginning to appear likely, and Waters loses his seat, it could mean control of the Senate will switch to the Democrats. That means hundreds of billions of federal dollars will be redirected through the congressional appropriations process to different organizations and people than they are today. And that would, in part, be because Waters would no longer be a senior Member of the Appropriations Committee. Some Democrat would take his place. And that vote is worth a lot of money to a lot of people."

"So, what can we do?"

"Look, I don't know all the answers, but I have good sources. The Mexican cartels are being paid by somebody to set up the reservations with a lot of meth for a reason. And it's easy to do."

"How is it so easy?"

"Nick, the Mexican cartels have made steady gains on the international narcotics trade. America is their market, and as you know, our southern border is wide open. They've recently made inroads into the drug business here in the Rocky Mountains. To the extent you can describe the meth business as organized, the Mexicans are taking control of most of America's trade.[16] Frankly, its use in an election context is a new one on me too. But that's what I'm told and by a trusted source."

"Why don't Republicans get that out into the public domain? Why aren't they talking about this?"

"Because Hanov, the Republican lobbyist and generous campaign contributor, is all over the news since his recent indictment. The feds took him down for taking federal funds as part of his fee – money he helped the tribes get via Congressional appropriations. That's illegal. Now he's singing to prosecutors trying to finger anyone else in order to save his own ass."

"And the media's connecting the dots between Hanov's illegal activities and Clarence?"

"And others, Nick. With that partisan media blitz on all over the map, Republicans are afraid to mention the words politics and Indians in the same sentence."

"I see," Nick said with a discouraged tone. "Is the media also doing stories on how meth is increasing on the reservations, Kale?!" He pronounced his name as if it had more syllables. "And where it's coming from?"

"Look, don't get distracted by those poseurs. You're asking the wrong question. As a Republican candidate you have to power through your opponent's campaign and through the media's hostility against you too – it's just the way it is. And no Republican is going to break the Democrats' ecumenical grip on the mainstream media.[17] And, if they try, they will surely regret it."

"But, Nick, if I was working for the *Waters For Senate Campaign*, I wouldn't count on getting any votes out of the reservations in November. Or, I'd find someone who knows something about this meth business and figure out what the hell's going on out there."

"Maybe I can help expose it."

"Nick, you can't do a damn thing. You're a lobbyist, not a DEA agent."

"Well, maybe with the right people and the right plan I can help."

"Nick, there's political turmoil of its own making on the reservations these days. Don't get cross-ways with those folks. But, there are professionals in this country who deal with the likes of those cartel fuckers. You need to hire one of them – and one of the best."

"Kale, will you help me?"

"No. I don't want to have anything to do with those bastards."

"You mean, you don't want to have anything to do with them *again*. Don't you?"

"What the hell does that mean?" Kale asked, angrily.

"What your alcohol-addled brain is apparently incapable of remembering is what you told me the night we got into that fight in Teaser's bar and ended up in jail after Waters' fundraiser in Bozeman. You told me about your other money issues and how you owed a Mexican cartel money. And that's how you know what's happening on the reservations, isn't it?"

"You're confused, Nick. I was talking that night about my old friend, Manny."

"I'm not confused. You told me the whole story, Kale, about what happened near the border and your attempt to save your friend. You couldn't find Manny and for that I am sorry. But you said there was a direct money connection."

"You don't know what the fuck you're talking about!"

"Well, what do you know, Kale?"

"I know those Mexican cartels are ruthless and not to be messed with. And, yes, it's part of the reason I cannot help you. The part of the story you apparently didn't hear me tell was that I almost got myself killed dealing with them. Manny was not just my childhood friend, Nick, he was my little brother."

"But, you said he and his parents lived on the Papago Reservation near your home?"

"His parents lived on the edge of the reservation near us. But his mom and dad were killed in a terrible farm truck accident one night. My parents basically adopted him. It was a little sideways with tribal and federal law but he had no other relatives anywhere. Most folks there thought it was a temporary arrangement – not my parents. Everyone who lived on and off the res knew my family, and they knew Manny was like family to us. We both went to the junior high school near the boundary of the reservation."

"How did Manny disappear?"

"Manny loved my parents and I think he liked living in our home. He had his own room all fixed up, you know. But I don't think he truly felt like he belonged there."

Kale looked down and let out a heavy sigh. "When he was about fifteen, he started hanging out more exclusively with his native friends again. He didn't lose interest in our friendship but his interest in school dropped off a cliff. Unfortunately, some of those kids were also hanging out with the early border gang derelicts."

"Kale, you didn't explain any of this."

"Manny was not a tough kid, Nick. After his parents died, he was also not a very secure or happy kid. I think Manny wandered off with those guys because he wanted to discover who he was. He was looking for some kind of affirmation through them. I don't really know what happened. But you know there are these sorts of initiation rituals in those groups. One day he just didn't come home. We never saw him again."

"Sorry."

"It was a long time ago. I was sixteen when he disappeared. I didn't have many options then. The tribal law enforcement and local police were unable to help. But I didn't forget about him. A few months later, a retired U.S. Border agent moved in across the street from us. He was a nice older guy who had so many incredible stories. I told him of Manny's disappearance and asked him if he might have an idea what happened to him."

Kale looked down at the table and shook his head. "He had plenty of ideas. He gave me the basic background of the early Mexican gangs and how they worked people, drugs and guns across the border. He said a young Indian recruit like Manny could be very helpful on the border especially where it crosses into the reservation. He said Manny would make the perfect mule in those days. He also emphasized that it was very hard to get out of a gang alive once you're in."

"So, what did you do?"

"He was my little brother, you know – only by a year, but seemed much younger. The only brother I ever had anyway. I asked the border agent to help me. To see if we could trace Manny's steps. He was retired and didn't have anything else to do. And it was summer and I was out of school, so he pointed me in the right direction. We did some initial snooping around together on the edges – he showed me the ropes. But when he wasn't with me I'd go back and push much harder for information."

"What'd you find out?"

"I found out how naïve I was about Mexican drug gangs, Nick. They beat the shit out of me and held me for ransom. They threatened to kill me unless the old agent came up with $25,000. They broke my nose, my jaw, three of my ribs, then hung me by my feet from a ceiling rafter."

"Shit! And?"

"He paid them and they let me leave with him. I went to the hospital where I stayed for a week. I had a punctured lung."

"What happened to the border agent?"

"He made sure I got home and helped me heal up. Told my parents a wild tale so they wouldn't worry. I eventually borrowed $15,000 from a loan shark to pay the old agent back. It's all they would lend me. This loan guy introduced me to a bookie who he said could help me make the money back to pay off the loan. My retired friend didn't know about any of that. In fact, a few weeks after I paid him the $15,000, he forgave the rest of the debt but made me promise to forever stay away from the border. He was a good guy."

"So, you never found out what happened to Manny?"

"I believe he was long dead by the time we even went to look. I started way too late to try to save him, Nick. It was a terrible decision that I'll regret forever. I think about him everyday."

"How did you pay back the loan shark – or the bookie?"

"I still am. I was up with the bookie pretty big about ten years ago, enough to get the loan shark off my ass for good. Ironically if I could have just held out a little longer, I'd of been off the hook anyway. The loan shark was murdered in Juarez two months later. The bookie and I go back a long way now. He's Mexican. We're actually friends – sort of. My balance with him has been up and down. I only owe him about $40,000 as of last month."

"Where is he?"

"He's in Nogales, Mexico or Nogales, Arizona depending upon the day of the week. He's right on the border. You see, Nick, what you misunderstood me to say that night in the bar was that I was also still working a money angle with the Mexicans on the border. You just assumed the worst. You always do."

Washington, DC

As Hally and Nick knew, landing a job in DC government relations in the late 90s was almost as difficult as losing one – unless there was a merger. A politically savvy staffer in Congress who'd managed to avoid the usual Capitol Hill pitfalls could find his or her way into a Fortune 500 Company's DC office. However, if that staffer were qualified but not responsive to DC lobbyists, he or she may as well get certified as a plumber. Talent and preparation only insulate one willing to go the extra mile every day. Nick attended an ACC gathering to determine who might be offered a new lobbying position wherein the lesson was learned.

The Northwestern Big Telco lobbyist, who was campaigning for one candidate, started the discussion. "This kid from the Senate has all the qualifications to be an excellent addition to our team. He's smart, presentable, articulate and has good relationships with Members of the Commerce Committee."

The Southern Big Telco lobbyist chimed in. "That may be true, but that son of a bitch has never, and I mean never, returned one phone call or e-mail from me. He's an arrogant little shit."

The Pacific Big Telco lobbyist weighed in. "I agree, he's smart and qualified and knows our issues pretty well. But it's true, he has never engaged with us on anything. To hell with him."

End of discussion. Relationships matter in the nation's capital. Nick learned early on that the old adage rang true, "If you want a friend in Washington, get a dog." People will support you as long as someone else is supporting them – and not a second longer.

Immediately after Congress passed the 1996 Telecom Act, which allowed the big phone companies to compete once again in the long-distance industry, they began to put the old monopoly back together. The Northeast and Atlantic Coast Big Telcos merged and bought one of the biggest long distance companies. Then the Midwestern, Southern and West Coast Big Telcos all merged and bought back the mothership, Ma Bell. The U.S. Justice Department, which fought for decades to break up the big monopoly, oddly stood by as it was all re-assembled. Those acquisitions made many corporate executives millionaires, but also cost many jobs.

A lobbyist's survival in any merger can be unpleasant, but in the telecom merger wars of the 1990s, it was warfare. The hardest part about seeking help in Washington's job market is deciding who to trust and how fast to move. The longer one waits, the more likely someone else will ask their mutual friends for help first.

One young lobbyist, Tom Whitaker, from the East Coast Big Telco was given notice he would be let go. He had left the Senate two years prior where he worked for a senior Democratic Senator from New Mexico. Tom knew several well-connected people in the DC political community so Nick was surprised when he received a call from him.

"Nick, I was hoping to talk with you about my job search." Tom assumed everyone in the industry was aware of his circumstance within a minute of his firing. He was right.

They met at the Post Pub, near the Washington Post Building. Nick paused outside the front door before entering. A drizzling rain was struggling to clear pollutants out of the thick cold air and wash them down a sewer drain. A sad homeless woman leaning against the outside wall asked Nick for "just one dollar." He bent over to look more closely at her. A young professional couple quickly wove around them with a disparaging glance. Nick gave her five dollars and entered the crowded pub.

"So, Nick, thanks for coming. I'm applying for a job with the Telecom Manufacturers Association. I've never worked for an association, and thought you could give me some pointers for my interview."

"Oh, sure. Tom. As you know, the ACC is not as formal as an association, but the politics of a coalition with all the different sized member companies is similar. I assume you have some of the Big Telco folks already lined up to help?"

"Yeah. I've asked Julia at the Southern Big Telco for help and Scott at the West Coast Big Telco as well."

Nick went on to give Tom his best summary of the politics of a DC-industry coalition without going into too much detail. He talked about the challenge of balancing the interests of the smaller companies against those of the bigger ones, and explained how the interests of the bigger companies almost always win out due to the fact that they pay most of the dues to keep the organization afloat.

Nick asked, "Are any of the others who were let go because of the merger applying for this job, too?"

"All of them." Tom admitted. "Could you put in a good word for me?"

Tom did not get the job at the association. Other than Nick, none of the people he asked to help him did. Tom felt betrayed and was out to get even. He eventually took a job outside of the industry but in an organization with which many in the industry interacted. He started as a director in the DC office of the Democratic Senatorial Campaign Committee (DSCC) where he would use his hard learned lessons to master the art of winning any campaign. Tom survived for years there acquiring a lot of power. He and Nick remained friends.

Montana/DC

Summer _2006_ The Campaign Trail

By the mid-summer of 2006, Democrats realized that running against the individual who Clarence actually was would be problematic.

"I'm told we're running against a somewhat beloved Montanan," Mo Kauffman said cynically to his party's weary campaign operatives. "To hell with that. We're going to run against what _we say_ he is. Through our ads and media markets, we'll determine who he is – and that's who we'll be running against. Understood?"

Waters' penchant for giving straight-up responses without hiding his words had occasionally been problematic but mostly remained under the radar. To Mo Kauffman and the DSCC, it was a problem in plain sight. When a person in power tends to speak their mind, they may say things that are not "politically correct," and Clarence said his fair share. The Democratic Party immediately hired a video guy – a tracker – to follow Waters wherever he went every minute of the day. The tracker's recordings picked up each word Clarence spoke from the minute he stepped out of his modest home, to every interaction with a voter on the sidewalk.

Each response was edited, posted online for delivery to detractors and spoon-fed to an awaiting media. Few Americans or Montanans had yet heard of YouTube but they would soon learn how destructive the internet and its technology could be.[18] By that summer, journalists were constantly needling Waters for something he'd said to somebody somewhere. They confounded him with an awkward new question as quickly as he could answer the previous one. It was a callous strategy designed to take down an affable man. A testament to Clarence's authenticity was that the tracker and he became friends. To his opponents' dismay, the tracker ultimately defended Waters against many of the unfounded rumors floated to hurt him.

By running for reelection in 2006, Clarence had unwittingly entered a world where cracking an innocent joke or spontaneously giving time-tested advice to a young voter could be deconstructed into a ruinous political liability. These were not factually-related errors, but new politically-defined missteps subject to a constantly moving moral code, set not by local Montana mores, but by big city reporters for national publications. Regardless, Waters' every hide-bound instinct told him to engage with the voters and he continued to do so.

Eventually, though, Clarence acknowledged his liability, and as the campaign drew down to the wire, he mostly withdrew from public interaction. Sometimes the less said the better, but to Clarence, no class of public servants had responded more haltingly to political correctness than his fellow legislators – and it chafed him to no end. To Nick, that kind of inhibition away from the voters worked like a plague on the electoral process.

Over his years of visiting there, Nick considered Montana's journalists to be a distinctly talented and eclectic lot – a reflection of their unique and open western surroundings. But he was becoming more concerned everyday with the long-trusted local media's eagerness to throw in with the national press corps' rhetoricians and their unsparing attacks on Clarence. *The New York Times* and *The Washington Post* took down politicians all the time – that's just what they did. But their coarse hit pieces reiterated in rural hometown papers alongside little league baseball scores carried an unusually smug and indifferent sting.

Austin, Texas/Washington, DC

Summer 2006 The Wires In-Between

Lisa Castile, an intriguing combination of all-American Texas girl and cynical Harvard Law grad, had not thought much about Washington, DC in twenty years. She had previously served as a majority counsel on the House Judiciary Committee in Congress when Democrats dominated there. She worked on the committee for several years until she left under a cloud to return to her home town in Texas. Her boss, Representative John Staunton, lost his seat in Congress in a grueling campaign when he was accused of being involved in drug- and human-smuggling across the Mexico border. He was later indicted on those counts but ultimately only convicted of tax evasion.

Along with other staff to the Congressman, Lisa was also indicted for aiding and abetting her former boss. She was acquitted on all counts. Those days were long behind her. She had been fortunate after her acquittal, to land a job with a Texas legal aid organization. Within a few years of hard work, she became head of one of its organization's regional offices covering a rural area between Austin and San Antonio. That work helped her focus on anything but her previous Washington career and the shame she felt about it. And something else she'd kept carefully to herself, the love interest she abruptly left behind.

A rush of memories came over her on this night in 2006 when she looked at an invitation her current boyfriend received to a dinner in Washington. The card invite had photos of the Capitol Building and the Lincoln Memorial on its cover. Those images threw her back to her previous work there, her colleagues, and remorsefully, her ex-boyfriend, Nick Taft. Though they had worked on opposite sides of the political aisle and mostly against each other's interests, she had graciously taught Nick a few tricks of the trade when he arrived in Washington many years before. She had also, despite her better instincts, fallen in love with him.

Their relationship seduced her into supporting Nick's risky inquiry into a politically-connected smuggling ring on the U.S.-Mexico border. What she didn't realize until too late was that those efforts would uncover her own boss's involvement in that smuggling

117

ring. Due in large part to Nick's efforts and his sworn testimony to a grand jury, John Staunton, a fourteen-term Texas congressman, served time in federal prison. And what nobody ever expected from those endeavors was that, based in part upon Nick's testimony, Lisa would also be indicted for her tangential involvement in the same conspiracy.

Lisa had lived in Texas for the past twenty years, and the political machinations of Washington, and Nick Taft, were a distant and unwelcome memory. She had not visited Washington since. She talked to Nick only once after her acquittal in 1987. Although she'd thought of him many times, and been tempted to call over the years, she never found the nerve. Her current romantic interest, Burch Maloney, though not exactly exciting, was somewhat of a safe bet which she needed. Lisa quickly declined her boyfriend's invitation to accompany him to DC, where he would receive an award for his efforts in anti-drug programs across the country.

Burch Maloney was a lawyer who helped cities fight illegal drug dealers and their ilk. A former Texas prosecutor disillusioned by the system's inability to battle drug cartels, Burch joined forces with several nonprofit, anti-drug organizations and had become an untitled leader of their cause. He was gaining a regional reputation for his work and had been written up in some legal publications. During the dinner in Washington where he was recognized by his colleagues, he was intrigued to receive a voice message from another lawyer asking for help with a drug-related problem in the Rocky Mountain West.

After the dinner, Burch called Lisa in Austin to give her a rundown of the evening. She told him how proud she was of his work and that he was actually doing something about the illegal narcotics problem. In reality, though, Lisa was concerned about how little Burch was being compensated for his efforts. She was therefore intrigued when Burch told her about the phone call he had received.

"What did the guy say he wanted you to do?"

"He wasn't quite clear in his message." Burch said. "But mentioned he was a lawyer who had previously worked on drug enforcement issues. He mentioned something about needing help or wanting to talk with me about the growing meth problem in Montana. Said that if I could help, I'd be well compensated for my efforts."

"Wow! That would be a nice change of pace, wouldn't it?" Lisa said, a little too enthusiastically.

"Well...yeah. I guess."

"Honey, you really are becoming well known for your hard work. Good for you."

"Yeah, maybe. He said he'd like to meet with me as soon as possible and would even be willing to fly me to Bozeman, Montana."

"Awesome. I've never been there before. Can I come?"

Southwest Montana

Summer <u>2006</u> The Campaign Trail

Once Nick and Kale had settled their score on Nick's advice regarding Kale's legal challenges and Kale's advice regarding Senator Waters' Indian reservation challenges, they made their way down I-90 back toward Bozeman.

Kale mumbled into his cell phone, "Well, shit." He tossed his phone onto the dash board.

"Um, how are things?" Nick asked hesitantly.

"Oh, I'm just fucking hanging on like a Band-Aid to a cut. Down big with my bookie again. Ever make a mistake you simply can't get out of, Nick?"

"Come on, there's a way out of just about anything."

"Some days I wish Manny had never even known me, Nick."

"You don't really mean that."

Kale studied the landscape through his window, "Nick, you know me about as well as anyone. Would you say I'm a sane person?"

"Not particularly. No."

"What? Okay, I get it. Dark sarcasm. But seriously…"

"I'm not saying you're insane, Kale, just not especially sane."

"You know what I really want, Nick?"

"Not a clue."

"Just want a normal life." Kale said matter of factly.

"No, you don't. You don't even know what that is. And trust me, *you* don't want it."

"Why not? A regular day-to-day work week, steady girlfriend, whatever."

"First, you're not a normal person. Beyond that, if you had a normal life, you'd have to get a normal job where you'd actually have to produce something resembling a normal work product. You couldn't handle it."

"Hey, I do good work!"

"No, Kale, what you do is leverage someone else's money to create an illusion of power in order to influence votes in Congress. That's not a work product. Just try explaining what you do to any normal person outside of DC."

"They wouldn't understand – that's all."

"No, they wouldn't. And it's better that way for you. Lobbyists like you thrive on our society's lack of understanding of where power actually resides in Washington."

"And what about lobbyists like *you*? You're somehow different?"

"No, but I'm gonna be. I'm going to move from DC and do something different."

"Like where?"

"Like maybe somewhere where I can trust people again."

"Oh, I see, you're the lost sheep among the wolf-like lobbyists. Good luck with that one."

"No, just feel like I need to figure out where I'm really supposed to be."

"Hmm. Maybe you're just still on the potter's wheel. Still being molded by the big Guy."

"Kale, why don't you leave DC, maybe go back to Arizona? Just get the hell out of there."

"Oh, I could never go home – not to Arizona. You know what, Nick? I like being around all the people in DC, and the unpredictable chaos that lobbying and campaigns bring to my life."

"Chaos does seem to agree with you."

A Senator Waters campaign ad came in over the radio emphasizing that Evan Sutter had been endorsed by every national liberal organization in the country. Kale turned up the volume. "Finally an ad for the good guys."

"Yeah, but they're so few and far between." Nick responded. "The Dems must be outspending Clarence 5 to 1 out here."

"Hey, Nick, slow down! Did you see that sign? It said Manhattan. I knew that was the name of the town I was in that night. That's where I had that great steak."

"Yeah?"

"What was the damn name of the place?" Kale wondered out loud.

"The Oasis...?" Nick slowly offered.

"Yes. How did you remember that?"

"I found it after putting together your few hungover clues the day I drove you to the airport. And you were right, they serve great steaks."

"I'll tell you what, let's go there," Kale said, enthusiastically.

"When?"

"Now!"

Nick slowed down the Jeep and took the Manhattan exit.

"Wow. I remember this street now. Man, how I ever got home that night, I'll never know."

Nick parked in front of the restaurant. They stepped into the bar. As their eyes adjusted to the dim light and Kale looked around, he grabbed Nick's arm. "Holy shit, Nick. That's the girl of my dreams I was telling you about."

"Who?"

"Hey babe. Told you I'd come back to visit." Kale said through a big grin.

Ava looked up at Kale from the table where she had just served some meals. "Oh my stars – it's alive! Hey, good-lookin'. How are you?"

"I'm good. In fact, it's my 48th birthday. But, *you* look great!"

Ava's eyes locked onto Nick's with a puzzled gaze as Kale gave her a big hug. "Well, hey. Happy Birthday! You two know each other?"

"Yeah. I'm the one who told Nick about this bar."

"Dude, I'm amazed you can remember anything about that night. You sure lit this old place up though. Do you recall that my friends had to drive you back to your hotel?"

"I do have some recollection about that. But mostly about you."

"Oh…uh…well. Why don't you guys have a seat at this corner table? I'll get some menus." Kale and Nick both watched her as she walked away.

"Nick, that's the perfect combination of legs, attitude and politics I was telling you about. Isn't she a trip?"

"She *sure* is." As Kale smiled and waved back to some local guys across the restaurant, Nick was reminded of his near magical ability to boost the energy level in any room.

So Nick looked on almost privately during the next hour of interaction between Kale and Ava as if he wasn't there. The two of them were lit up like road flares. Kale was downing the scotch like it was spring water. Ava came and went between serving customers.

Kale gushed, "She just quoted proberbs to me. She's like an angel of some sort, isn't she?"

"It's Proverbs, you idiot. Kale, you realize the devil was once an angel of some sort, too – right?"

"I'm going to marry her!" Kale said, exuding as much optimism as Nick had heard from his old friend in years.

Washington, DC

To Nick's knowledge, Hally Peters had not been informed of Tad Larson's appearance at Senator Raines' fundraising dinner in Colorado. So far, that had proved beneficial to Nick's developing professional relationship with them both. He knew, however, that it was just a matter of time in the gossip-ridden corridors of DC before she would hear it. Nick was at his desk one evening drafting a memo on telecom policy when there was a knock at his door.

Tad Larson opened it. "We need to talk."

"What about?"

"Life, liberty and the pursuit of happiness – yours." Tad was at the office a lot, mostly to avoid his live-in girlfriend. So he was always up for a chat. "Get your overcoat. Let's go somewhere."

After riding down the elevators, they cautiously stepped over two homeless men sleeping in bundled carpet matting on the sidewalk. Once seated at Smith & Wollensky's Steakhouse, Tad started in, "Nick, Hally knows that I was in Vail at Senator Raines' dinner and she knows that you know."

"Shit!"

"She hasn't mentioned it yet – right?"

"No."

"See, that's how she works. Well, first let me tell you what I told her so our stories jibe."

"Thanks. I appreciate it."

"That's okay, you'll owe me. I told her that I was at Utah's Democratic Delegation ski trip at the request of a vice president of the Western Big Telco. That's actually accurate. I also said that *our* boss, Mike, asked me to show support at Senator Raines' dinner, and that Mike didn't know you were planning to attend. That's also true. But I told her that our paths only crossed for a brief second in the street when I was leaving the restaurant early and you were just arriving a little late. And nobody can dispute that or disprove it. I did have to leave early."

Nick paused for a second, "Well, I can give it a try. There were plenty of industry folks there who saw our bantering back and forth, though."

"Yeah, but those drunks won't remember how long either of us were in the room."

"I'll give it a try. But don't go changing your story on me, Tad. Deal?"

"Deal."

"Tad, let me ask you something. You seem to have pretty free rein to interact with Senators here in DC. Why would Hally care so much about your being at Senator Raines' event in Vail?"

"Now, that's something we really need to talk about, Nick. I guess this is as good a time as any."

"Okay."

"You ever wonder why everyone who works for Hally is always tip-toeing around. She threatens to fire people all the time. When she decides to let you know that she's aware that I was in Vail and that she knows that you know, she'll hold that over you like a guillotine."

"And?"

"So, you're going to need some leverage of your own. What I'm about to tell you is not well known in this town." Tad looked around the restaurant to see if anyone could hear them.

"I'm listening."

"Hally's an overly private person. Would you agree?"

"Yes. I assume she has her reasons."

"Nick, Hally's in deep shit because of a questionable fundraising scheme she's involved in to raise huge bucks for conservative candidates. Senator Raines of Nevada is apparently a part of it as well. And, there's an additional rumor that she and Raines are, uhm, how should I say, romantically involved."

"What? I can't even picture that. How do you *know* that?"

"That, I can't tell you. And, while not many are aware of it yet, the way this town works it's just a matter of time."

Nick didn't believe Tad, was taken aback by the destructive nature of the rumors and was hoping it was a lie. In Washington, where politics were political beyond any understanding of the word, Nick didn't trust any rumors he heard. But since Hally was his boss and the implications serious, he vowed to at least try to determine their veracity.

"So, Nick, when she comes down on you for whatever reason and trust me she will, you just keep this in your back pocket. There will be a right time to use it."

What Tad was not revealing was that he wanted Nick to wait and use that information at an opportune time in order to put Hally's job in jeopardy so that Tad could have another shot at being senior vice president of congressional affairs at the ACC. The job that, as he saw it, Hally stole out from under him.

"You'll know when the time is right."

"I see," Nick said, a little dumbstruck. "Where does she do all this back-channel fundraising?"

"Probably every day from her office, Nick. What the hell else does she do in there all day anyway?"

Nick recalled how Hally's office door was always closed. She was always on the phone to somebody and didn't like to be interrupted for any reason.

Tad was watching him closely. "Look, don't worry about it. It's her liability, not yours. But you've got a seat at the table now, Nick. And you and I have to stick together. Deal?"

Nick nodded reluctantly, "Deal."

Montana

Summer 2006 The Capitol - Helena

Senator Kauffman's private jet landed at the Helena Regional Airport at noon. There were 100 members in the Montana House and 50 members in the Montana Senate. To call a special session of the State Legislature that summer, a total of 76 members of the State House and Senate combined would have to vote in favor of a resolution to do so. Mo met with the Montana Governor in his office to confirm a plan. The governor also had the power to call a special session of the State Legislature without a vote – and that is what he did.

The governor called the session to consider changes to Montana's voting laws in order to allow anyone in Montana to register and vote in the same instance. Senator Kauffman had come through with the public relations and media support as he promised. Several papers published articles encouraging the state to allow same-day voter registration. They argued that it would be fairer to people who had recently moved to the state or who had other things to worry about than registering to vote. This change, it was argued, was about the government encouraging citizens to participate in their democracy.

The bill was debated and voted on in a matter of days.[19] Some Republicans disputed that the legislation was good for democracy, and argued it was simply about swelling voter ranks with out-of-state voters before the November elections. Democrats held sufficient majorities in both chambers. They passed the bill in the State House and State Senate and sent it to the Democratic Governor for signature with a swiftness rarely seen in State Capitols.

Mo Kauffman, who'd been at this political game for years, had prevailed on his plan. Thousands of young college students from all over the country would be able to register and vote on November 7th and affect the outcome of the 2006 U.S. Senate race in Montana.

Washington, DC

Winter 1997 The Lobbying World

With months gone through the winter of '97 and no concrete answers regarding the suspicious death of one of her oldest friends, Sheila Parker finally put the screws to her husband, Congressman Judd Parker.

"What are you, powerless? Useless? You're a fucking Congressman, aren't you? Well, do something. You help all your whiny political constituents when they have problems. Help *me*. I'm a constituent too, and your fucking wife! You're going to find a way to pressure the truth out of that Jersey City Police Department about what really happened to Alexandra."

Judd Parker had his staff make some calls and do some investigating of their own. He discovered that Hugh Haddad, a powerful New York lawyer, had been hired to represent Sid Lucas regarding the investigation into Alexandra Martin's death. He also knew that Sid was the slick money man to U.S. Senator Mo Kaufman – the last employer of Alexandra Martin.

Never one to sit still for long, Sheila continued digging on her own. She discovered how well-known Hugh Haddad was for his criminal law practice and how expensive he was to hire. Sheila was aware that Kauffman and Sid had worked on campaigns together. After all, she was the one who introduced Alexandra to Sid Lucas. But what she didn't know was what close friends they were and how indebted Mo Kauffman was to him. Sheila put the facts together as she saw them and pushed her husband further into Alexandra's investigation.

"I'll tell you what more you can do, Judd. You can call this slimeball, New York lawyer who's slow-rolling this investigation and scare the hell out of him. You're the Ranking Democrat on the U.S. House Ethics Committee, for crying out loud. Make something happen!"

Congressman Parker finally got Haddad on the phone and asked a lot of questions about the case – who he was representing and who was paying for that representation. Hugh bobbed and weaved through the questions mostly hiding behind attorney-client privilege. During their one and only conversation, Parker acknowledged that Alexandra was a close friend of his wife, Sheila. He also informed Haddad that Sheila was aware that Alexandra and Sid Lucas were having an affair. Parker let Haddad know that he also knew that Sid Lucas helped Alexandra get her job in Congressman Kauffman's office. The two men had a cordial if somewhat superficial signoff to their awkward conversation.

When Hugh hung up the phone, he immediately called then freshman Congressman Mo Kauffman and filled him in. "Mo, you encouraged me to help your guy, Sid. You need to understand that you and Sid are both still vulnerable in the Alexandra Martin investigation. So, here's your new role in this whole mess: you get this fucking Congressman Parker off my ass. We clear? Or this investigation might make some forward progress real soon."

Bozeman, Montana

Fall <u>2006</u> The Campaign Trail

Burch Maloney and Lisa Castile landed at Gallatin Field on a cool Friday morning in the early fall of 2006. They looked like any tourists visiting a beautiful part of the country. Lisa had done some reading on Bozeman and planned to check out the art galleries on downtown Main Street. She was impressed by the uncluttered landscape reaching toward the Bridger Mountains and commented that it reminded her of Texas.

Nick met Burch for lunch at a restaurant that offered sidewalk tables looking onto Main Street. He liked Burch immediately and knew his research had paid off. After sampling their food and wading through small talk, Nick pondered how much to tell Burch. He had been led to believe, per advice from some of Senator Waters' supporters that the local Republican Party or some affiliate might be willing to hire a consultant to focus on the reservations. But he wasn't sure the arrangement was one that Burch would buy into.

After a few bites of lunch, "Burch, as you may know, there's a meth problem in this state. I don't expect you to fix it. I'm looking for someone who can help us figure out why so much meth has been showing up of late on some of the Indian Reservations here."

"Hmmm…who's *us?*"

"Let me be straight with you. Primarily, it's the Citizens for a Better Montana. But the Republican Party might be convinced to help out some as well."

"Why the party?"

Nick vaguely recounted the details as explained by Kale involving the possible involvement of a Mexican drug cartel and the unanswered questions about who was funding it.

"Nick, first I want to thank you for flying me and my girlfriend out here and for your interest. But…I'm not a political consultant, I…"

"I know, Burch. But you know about patterns of drug use and drug dealers and their world. We need to get to the bottom of this and we need your help."

Burch, taking in a final mouthful of his grilled salmon, chewed for a long time, "Well, I…uh…"

"We'll pay you $25,000 just to take a hard look at it. And if you can trace the meth, another $25,000 to help us identify the source." Nick was playing a little loose with the monetary figures and knew he needed the help of Waters' one time staffer, Thurlow, to make it happen. But that was another challenge for another day.

Burch looked past Nick's shoulder down the sidewalk. "Well, there she is. How's the shopping?"

"It's great. What a cool town."

Nick half-stood and turned to extend his hand toward Burch's girlfriend. The sun fell over the silhouette of a slender woman with shoulder length hair. Her face was shaded by a very bright sun behind her.

Nick spoke before her face came into view. "Hi, nice to meet you. I'm Nick Taft."

"Hi, Lisa Castile."

Nick was so stunned he missed her hand. He could not speak.

"Everything okay, honey?" Burch offered.

"Yeah. It's fine. Nice to see you, Mr. Taft."

"Nice...to see you too."

"Want to join us for coffee, honey?"

"Oh, no. Think I'll just...keep on, keepin' on...shopping." Lisa fingered a jade necklace just inside the collar of her denim shirt. She looked at Nick and walked away.

"Okay. I'll call your cell when we're done," Burch said.

Nick watched her walk away. "Oh, we're done." Nick said. "Just let me know if you're interested. We'd like to get started soon."

"I see. Uhm..."

Nick stood up. "Please call if you have any questions. My phone is always on." He quickly maneuvered through tables on the sidewalk to pay the lunch tab inside.

"Good to meet you." Burch said with some volume, hoping Nick could still hear him.

"You, too." Nick bellowed from the bar.

Burch crosscut between some cars to catch up to Lisa and they slowly walked down the opposite side of Main Street. Lisa looked back over her shoulder, but Nick was obscured by the restaurant's shadowed interior.

Washington, DC

As Nick dodged raindrops to enter the back door of the ACC's office building one afternoon, he saw Hally slinking around to the corner of the parking garage. "Where you running off to?"

She turned, "I'm not *running* anywhere. Just late for a doctor's appointment."

Once back in his cramped office, Nick was strategizing on the best tactic to defuse Hally since she'd become aware of his Vail encounter with Tad. His office door opened. The lady who was head of HR to the ACC stood in the doorway.

"Have you seen Hally lately?"

"Uh, no, I haven't." Nick un-instinctively lied. "Why?"

"There's a gentleman from the Federal Elections Commission who's been waiting in the lobby to see her for about a half hour. Said he had an appointment."

"Really? Humph. Well, you know how over-scheduled she is, and sometimes a little spacey."

"If you see her, please have her call me. Will you?"

Nick closed his office door to think on what Hally might be up to, and the interesting facts he may have just stumbled upon. His office phone rang.

"Hello, this is Nick."

"Hey, Nick, my erudite colleague. Do you really want to read more telecom law on this cloudy spring day?"

"Oh, hey, Hally. As a matter of fact, no, I don't."

"Why don't you meet me on the patio in front of Smith and Wollensky's?"

"Thought you had a doctor's appoint..."

"It got cancelled."

Nick made his way down the hall to the elevators then up the block to the steak house. Hally was seated at an outdoor table under the awning holding a cigarette toward him.

"Want a smoke?"

"Sure." Nick lit a cigarette.

"So, have anything you want to tell me?"

Nick wasn't sure to which *anything* she might be referring, the salacious political gossip about her, the Vail dinner encounter with Tad or her most recent dodging of the gentleman from the FEC.

He took a chance, "Yeah I do. You need to get over your paranoia of Tad or grow a pair and confront Mike about him. Washington's a tough town, Hally, and everyone here has to fend for themselves. That's my advice."

"What the bloody fuck does that mean?" Her words were punctuated by the shrieking noise of horns and sirens from a half dozen police cars and firetrucks passing by. Hally covered her ears.

"Hally, Mike only hired you for congressional affairs because he couldn't hire Tad because Tad's a Democrat and the conservative Big Telco guys wanted a hard-core Republican. Tad does legal work and anything else Mike tells him and with ACC funds that are controlled by Mike. You want to put Tad in his place, take it up with Mike."

"Great. That's not really helping me. Why didn't you tell me Tad was in Vail?"

"Because I knew you would overreact and do something destructive."

"Destructive to whom?"

"Destructive to you. Every time you go off on somebody because of Tad, you just strengthen his hand. You need to use some discretion, Hally."

"Well, I need to have the relevant information in order to be discreet now, don't I?"

"I suppose so."

"Bloody hell! You work for me, Nick," Hally yelled. "I needed to know what Tad was up to with Senator Raines...or uhm... his office. That fucking Tad. He thinks he's that guy from *All The President's Men* or whatever. Sneaking around everybody's business. Bloody fucking hell!"

Nick stared blankly at Hally's overreaction.

She composed herself. "Look, I hear your advice on how to handle Tad. I'll take it under advisement. But in the future, you need to cover my back to my face, understand? And, I'll cover yours. You're not exactly indispensable around here, Nick. We clear?"

"Sure, Hally." Nick said with a confident smirk. "Nobody around here is, are they, Hally?"

Bozeman, Montana

Fall *2006* *The Campaign Trail*

Back at his hotel room, Nick was reeling from the shocking appearance of Lisa Castile in Bozeman. It was far from the chance encounter he'd hoped might one day take place. She was even prettier than he recalled from their days in Congress all those years ago. A sea of memories came over him of his best lover, best friend and most patient teacher. Yet as always, they were accompanied by confusion and disappointment. His most immediate concern though was that the one person he thought might help Senator Waters bolster his faltering reelection, and help save Nick's job, now most assuredly would not. His cell phone rang.

"Nick, it's Burch Maloney. I'd like to talk with you about some of the details of your offer."

Nick was certain Lisa would quash any further involvement between her boyfriend and him, but he agreed to meet Burch for breakfast the next day. When he walked into the Cateye Cafe the following morning, both Lisa and Burch were seated at a booth next to a tall window. The café had a wood beamed ceiling, faded leather booths and various pictures of cats on the walls. Nick shook Burch's hand and looked toward Lisa. Her cheek bones were sharper than he remembered and there were slight creases at the corners of her eyes.

"Good morning, hope you guys had a good night." As Nick heard his words he was certain he didn't mean them. Burch assured Nick they'd enjoyed the evening and their very cool room at the unique Voss Inn which Nick had recommended. A snapshot of the antique brass beds of the old inn popped into Nick's head.

"Great. So, you've given some thought to my offer?"

"Yes. Just a few questions," Burch said with a reassuring tone, but then excused himself to wash his hands and walked toward a sign that read, "Litter Box."

Nick watched him cross the room, "Lisa, what the hell are you doing?"

"What am I doing? What the hell are *you* doing?"

"I didn't know he was your boyfriend or whatever. Why didn't you talk him out of agreeing to this contract or even coming on

133

this trip?"

"Obviously, I didn't know he was coming out here to meet with *you*. Since when do you live in Montana or wear jeans and mud boots? Who the hell are you now, Jeremiah-fucking-Johnson? And listen to me, Burch is good at what he does and he's genuinely interested in this project of yours, whatever the hell it actually is. You better be straight with him."

"Yeah, like you're the expert at being straight with people!"

"Oh, please. Let me tell you…"

They were interrupted by Burch returning to the table. "What are you two discussing so intently?"

A waitress interrupted to take their breakfast orders. Burch and Nick ordered quickly, but Lisa took her time perusing the menu and asked several questions about the unique breakfast sandwiches. Finally she made a decision, but then changed her order twice while looking at Nick as if to do so would help make up her mind.

"So, Burch, what were your questions?"

"First, uhm…who exactly would be paying my fee?"

"Right. The…uh…as we discussed, the Citizens For A Better Montana. And as I indicated, maybe the Montana State Republican Party, in part."

Lisa cocked her head, rolled her eyes at Nick and looked out the window as she violently shook her Splenda package before ripping it open and dumping it into her coffee. Burch looked in her direction but acknowledged nothing.

"The Montana Republican Party? Why?"

Certain he'd already covered this subject as surreptitiously as he could, Nick tried again.

"Well, it's come to the attention of some that the government has failed to fully address the meth issue which appears to be getting worse on the reservations – and the party just wants to do its part to help ensure this problem doesn't start to involve the tribal governments or any other kind of…uhm…political entity." His voice trailed off.

Nick then continued enthusiastically, "But the real party of interest here is the Citizens For A Better Montana! That's the group of concerned Montanans that truly wants to fight…uh… this drug problem."

Lisa had heard enough. "So, Nick, excuse me for asking, and

it's surely not my call…"

Burch squirmed in the booth to his left then to his right. Nick smiled, "Oh, no problem, Liza. I mean Lisa. Please ask."

Lisa pierced Nick with a harsh stare accompanied by a frozen smile. "Thanks. I couldn't help but notice there's a high-profile U.S. Senate race shaping up out here in the Big Sky state." She paused, looking for something in Nick's face. "Could the Republican Party's interest in these issues on the reservations have anything to do with votes?"

"Now, that's an astute question. There is some concern that a substantial uptick in meth use or its availability on the reservations may be somehow politically motivated." Nick talked directly to Burch.

She snorted as if interrupting a simpleton. "Talk about disgraceful. I mean the federal and state governments are doing everything they can to beat back the use of meth everywhere, and all along it's just been old fashioned retail politics feeding its use? My, my."

Burch and Nick looked in opposite directions. Nick's mind tumbled back to the first time he'd met Lisa in an empty hallway in Congress more than twenty years prior.

She continued, "Nick, can you tell us what evidence you have or could possibly have…"

Burch leaned into the table, "Lisa, please. I need to talk this through with Nick. Nick, can you excuse us for a second?"

He stepped out the front door of the crowded restaurant to give Lisa and Burch some privacy. From a small parking lot across an alleyway he could see them through the tall window. It appeared they were having an intense conversation. Clearly, twenty years in Texas had not dulled Lisa's political instincts or passion. Before he knew it she exited the restaurant and walked directly up to him.

"I should've known anything you were involved in would have something to do with partisan politics. No doubt, due to some misplaced sense of self-survival, you're trying to save some politician's career. Am I right? Has nothing changed with you?"

"Lisa, I can appreciate that you have this somewhat warped view of me, but all this politics…it's not who I really am." Though if pushed, Nick would admit that Clarence Waters remaining in the Senate was probably critical to his continued success in DC.

A shadow crossed her face. Some new political worldliness to him bothered her immensely. "I once thought so, Nick. But you lie to Burch about what this is really about and I promise you'll regret it." She turned and walked away.

Nick returned to the table. A chagrined Burch spoke quickly. "Nick, my apologies. Lisa had no business talking to you that way. She's a Democrat and I'm a Republican. We don't always see eye to eye."

"Burch, say no more. Believe me, I understand." Nick smiled. "I hear you've been involved in party politics before."

"Oh, yeah. Cut my teeth in the Republican Party of Texas in my twenties and..."

Listening to Burch talk of his journey from volunteering with the College Republicans to working for the Governor of Texas, Nick could see some of his younger self in the Texan. Although only two years his junior, Burch exuded a more youthful passion for the fight. Nick shared his similar journey through the ranks of party politics. The two bonded over mutual disgust at their country's weak border policies and the incalculable drugs and money crisscrossing into and out of America every day. They shared fears of the Mexican cartels' predation of vulnerable immigrants, and the irrevocable damage that open border would ultimately have on their country.[20]

After a while, Nick felt secure enough to unload his and Kale's whole theory on why meth was being pumped into the reservations and the uncertainty about who was paying for it. By the end of their discussion, Burch was totally on board. The only thing Nick had to do, and in a hurry, was confirm that some third party was actually going to come through with the $50,000 figure he'd thrown out to attract Burch in the first place.

New Jersey/Washington, DC

Summer <u>2006</u> The Lobbying World/The Campaign Trail

In addition to lawyer Haddad's late New Year's Eve parties, he also hosted an annual summer solstice party every June at his palatial home in Basking Ridge. His 2006 summer bash was one of his most successful – more lawyers, more lobbyists, more potential clients. Sid Lucas attended along with a new campaign client. The client seemed impressed with the almost unlimited potential fundraising targets there.

At the celebration, Hugh reintroduced Sid to the owners of the Slipper Gold Refining Company who he'd met briefly years before at one of Hugh's New Year's Eve gatherings. They appeared considerably older to Sid, not as well-heeled as before and noticeably impatient. Hugh explained to Sid, in front of his client, that the refining company was involved in an effort to obtain a gold mining permit on the Crow Reservation in Montana.

The company's CEO further explained to Sid, "The current tribal chairman, Big Jim, or whatever his name is, has been delaying and complicating our permitting process. He is quite old and frankly, way behind the changing times."

Hugh tried to interrupt but the CEO plunged ahead. "You see, Sid, we've done everything by the book with these folks, followed every requirement to a fault. But this obstructionist is determined to prevent us from doing good work on their lands. Work, I might add that would employ many Native Americans."

Sid looked at Hugh, "I see. How can I help?"

Hugh went on to explain that the chairman was up for reelection later that summer, and that the Slipper Gold Company had aligned itself with the opposing candidate. Hugh emphasized that many frustrated folks who had an interest in the well-being of the reservation were supporting the well-respected younger Crow member challenging Big Jim. They were hopeful the younger challenger would win the election and make some long overdue changes to Crow mining policy. Hugh indicated they might like to engage Sid's campaign skills to help out but would explain in more detail later.

What Haddad did not explain was that his most lucrative

client, the Slipper Gold Refining Company and one of his other clients, BF Prison Industries, had a bit of a conflict of interest on the Crow Reservation. BF Industries was always looking for a prison to manage to make a profit; more importantly to Hugh, the new CEO was always looking for ways to entertain his young trophy wife by making a big splash somewhere. Hugh knew the Slipper Gold Company wanted a base of operation near the Crow Nation to carry out some of its campaign-related activities, and one of those potential bases was an unused prison caught up in a federal/state jurisdictional dispute.

In an attempt to kill two birds with one stone, Hugh facilitated the hiring of a high-profile DC lobbying firm under the guise of getting BF Industries a new management contract. In reality, at his direction, it was hired simply to host BF's CEO and his wife at DC black tie events. Hugh also contacted his best Montana friend and lawyer, Ace Hargrove, to figure a way to utilize that unused prison for the gold company's goals. Hugh's conflict wasn't permanent. He had every intention of helping his prison client win a management bid – just not right away. And, he would help the gold refining company impact the Crow tribal election – just not through traditional campaign tactics.

One other piece of information Hugh failed to mention to Sid was that the gold company's folks sometimes had surreptitious interaction with Haddad's drug cartel clients whom he'd managed to keep out of federal prison for years. The cartel and its henchmen had proved useful in the past when the company needed to intimidate competitors.

Washington, DC

Spring 1997 The Lobbying World

Black tie balls for charities are must-attend soirees for DC lobbyists. To Nick they had become just another work-related event at which he'd have to remember people's names. The corporations that employ lobbyists frequently buy tables to support worthwhile causes. It's the employees in the DC office who are charged with filling these expensive tables. Usually they would be partially filled with lobbyists themselves and sometimes their spouses or dates along with a congressional staffer or Member of Congress.

This humid May evening in 1997 marked the end of a long week for those in an industry which required a lot of eating and drinking. Most of them had already been to at least three breakfasts, four lunches, two dinners and four or five cocktail receptions that week. But the handsome tuxedos and fitted evening gowns helped camouflage their social-weary reality.

Nick was asked to fill in for Hally who'd ducked the invite. He and his friend from the Canadian Embassy, Roline, entered the National Building Museum on E Street surrounded by enormous billowing faux clouds hanging from the ceiling and eye-catching wraps circling enormous interior columns. At first uncertain he'd ever met a single person in the room, he guided Roline to one of the bars and noticed a familiar lobbyist with whom he wished to inquire about the latest rumors on Hally.

Upon arriving at their table, Nick introduced his date to their table's host, David Jesterson. It was obvious David was taken aback by Roline. When he stood and leaned into the table to shake Roline's hand, his eyes were fixed on her low-cut neckline and he unknowingly pushed his thick menu into his water glass which tipped over onto the butter plate of another would-be diner. "Oh, excuse me." He pleaded as he held onto her hand.

Nick had met David several times in meetings, and could tell he'd had a few cocktails. "David, good to see you. What a beautiful job they've done with this old place tonight, eh?"

"Oh yeah," David said, still staring at Roline. "Hey, by the way, Nick, congrats on becoming an associate member of the Greater America Foundation. I saw that Hally sponsored you."

"What?"

"Yeah, it was in our monthly newsletter under new members. About time you came around."

Other guests arrived as a waitress cleaned up the spilled water. There were lobbyists from the West Telco's DC office, two of whom had dates, and a woman who worked at the Democratic Senatorial Campaign Committee. Nick introduced himself and sat down next to the woman who worked at the Senatorial Committee. Though distracted by news of his unsolicited new membership which he had no idea Hally had done, he wanted to see how his friend, Tom Whitaker, was doing in his new job at the DSCC. This woman would know since she had been head of Human Resources for a decade, and would know a little something about everyone.

"Nice to meet you," Nick offered. "I understand you've worked in DC politics for a while. I think you may know a friend of mine who works at the Senatorial Committee."

But as much as Nick attempted small talk with his somewhat officious table guest, the more she ignored him and remained solely focused on three women walking between the many tables.

She stared across the room. "That just boils my blood."

"What? Uhm…what?" Nick asked. He'd forgotten her name.

"The single women who work this town these days. Fancy themselves as lobbyists. They're idiots, and remarkably immature."

Other agendas lurked the room that evening. Gossip hounds, feeling out of the loop, would for their own amusement churn the whisper wheel in DC. After a few cocktails, the perpetrators had begun to roam the ballroom eyeing accomplices. Nick's table guest frowned, "Lord knows what unfounded slander those scamps are lacing this ballroom with tonight." But he knew at least two of the women, one single, one divorced, and didn't consider them ill-willed; they just didn't have much else going on in their lives beyond attending boring meetings and fundraisers.

Nick tried again to inquire specifically as to how his friend Tom was doing at the DSCC and if he was learning the campaign ropes. But the woman continued, obliviously, "They don't actually do anything – like actually lobby anyone like we used to. They basically just hand out PAC checks, wear expensive clothes and perpetually gossip."

The alleged dilettantes had arrived in their Nation's Capital years before open to the wonders of Washington. But like others in DC, over time had fallen prey to scrambling for any relevant power which often entailed – in addition to constantly trying to outdo or out-dress somebody – the drudgery of controlling others' judgments of them. One of their few fun stocks in trade was creating and enhancing rumors.

The target of their scorn on this evening was a young lady who'd recently started with an energy company. Her first mistake was being thin and attractive. Most of the women in the rumor cabal had been in DC long enough to succumb to the *Potomac Curse* of sitting in cushy offices and overeating and drinking at too many fundraisers. Her second mistake was not being deferential enough to the dozen women she'd met that evening. In reality, she was slightly intimidated by Washington and its tightknit power players. She was from a relatively rural town in Northern California.

That was inconsequential to this well-heeled brood of scandal-mongers who'd heard little about the youthful woman other than what they'd read in the trade press. First, that she was a *former practicing lawyer* was a substantial strike against her as none of these DC ladies were attorneys and felt the lack of that degree undermined their deserved respect. Second, the Californian was given the title at her new company of Director and Counsel of Government Affairs.

"Counsel of what?" One of the plump lobbyists from the liquor industry said as she downed another vodka tonic.

"She doesn't look like she's spent a lot of time in a courtroom to me," a cable industry advocate sniffed.

"She looks too young to have had much of a career in anything," chortled another, while wolfing down her third smoked salmon and gruyere cheese hors d'oeuvre.

"A career on her knees maybe!" A hearty cackle bellowed from the ladies.

Strike three, the powerbrokers in the room were checking out the newcomer's well-toned legs below her barely acceptable DC-political-class cocktail dress. This rumor lynch mob hadn't been checked out like that in years. But when dinner was served, Nick finally got the HR lady's attention. She was brief and to the point.

"Tom Whitaker is one of the best things that's happened to the DSCC in years," she said. "He's learned every aspect of campaign tactics and fundraising. He will be at the forefront of our success in taking back power in Congress from the idiots who run your party, Nick." The old battle-axe downed what remained in her wine glass, then added, "And sooner than you think, thank God."

As the evening progressed, Nick's table host became sloshed. He was so relentlessly flirting with Roline that she was giving Nick the evil-eye. David was married, but like so many older lobbyists, had quit making his wife go to these events years prior. He was often enamored with any single woman and apparently especially with Roline. After finishing their entrees, Nick took his date for one swirl around the dance floor and they departed early. But Nick had used his time there to learn about the DSCC, its current internal politics and the growing influence of his former telecom industry colleague, Tom Whitaker.

Bozeman, Montana

Fall <u>2006</u> The Campaign Trail

They all believed Nick had clinched a deal weeks earlier when Lisa and Burch departed Bozeman for Austin, Texas. They'd signed no contract for the native reservation investigation because Nick didn't want a paper trail leading anywhere near the Waters' 2006 campaign. They had covered the terms on a handshake with a start date to begin as soon as Nick mailed the initial check from his own personal account. Nick would try to meet with a local politico and Thurlow in a few days to finalize the money details.

In the meantime, he had to hear the minutia of Kale and Ava's romance from Kale by phone and Ava in person. Their affair began when Kale and Nick visited the Oasis late that summer and came across Ava. Seeing Kale's excitement and how well the two got along, Nick took a step back. Their relationship began hot and heavy, and if Kale hadn't had pressing problems in DC, he'd have permanently camped out in Bozeman. As it was, he was burning up his credit cards flying from DC every weekend. But as with most affairs that start out fast, it was having its challenges.

Kale would call Nick every day to talk about Ava. Ava, on the other hand, who lived in Logan just twenty minutes up Frontage Road would simply stop by and knock on Nick's hotel door whenever she felt like chatting. On this crisp autumn morning, Ava really needed to talk.

"Nick, you seem to like sightseeing. Have you ever been down the Beartooth Highway?"

"Only heard of it."

"Then we should take a trip. You drive, I'll talk."

He did a lot of driving in his rented Jeep and enjoyed the scenery of Montana. "Where is it?"

"Just down the road a ways – past Red Lodge."

"Oh, yeah? You know we might just have to take a quick detour right around there."

"Whatever. It's your car."

Nick recalled that the state-of-the-art prison for which his firm's client had asked for help securing a contract was located somewhere near Red Lodge. He hadn't managed to visit it yet and this seemed as good a time as any. They drove east from Bozeman toward Billings with a plan to turn south on Hwy 212 toward Red Lodge. Unfortunately, they travelled through an area enveloped in considerable smoke near Livingston due to a wildfire that had erupted earlier and destroyed thousands of acres and several homes.

Once closer to Billings, where the air cleared up, they headed south past some oil refineries. Often confused as to where exactly he was in Montana, Nick made his best guess and detoured back east near the town of Joliet on a narrow road bordered by late green crops on both sides. Having spent hours preparing for meetings with his client, none of which had yet materialized, Nick wanted to see this empty prison for himself. Past a handful of scattered homes and over a railroad crossing, the road turned to dirt. There was little to see on either side except vacant land and a few lone aspen trees.

Ava asked where they were headed. Nick explained as much as he could without getting too specific. "I just want to see this prison building that's been sitting here untouched since its construction. My firm may have some interest in it."

"So, we're working?" Ava asked.

"Not exactly."

"What exactly do you do?"

"That's kind of a long answer. But I work hard to get paid and sometimes for fun write articles and stuff."

"Really? I got a plaque for a cool article I once wrote!" Ava bragged.

"Yeah? I'd like to read it." Nick offered.

"Oh, no, you wouldn't. It just says congratulations and then my name."

Nick just shook his head.

Approaching the Clarks Fork of the Yellowstone River, they saw a large clearing well off the left side of the narrow road. There sat a shiny newly-constructed facility complete with reinforced fencing and razor wire. The gates were wide open so they drove in and parked by what appeared to be the front entrance. They peered into a few windows.

Ava asked, "So, what's this all about?"

He offered some more details. "It was supposed to be a new federal or state prison, but it turns out no one ever approved the building or operation of it."

"So?"

"So, it just sits here empty until either Montana or the federal government decides what to do with it or how to manage it."

They walked on crushed gravel down the east side of the building to see what else they could see. To their surprise, a white van drove slowly around the opposite corner of the prison and stopped just outside the front gates.

"I thought you said this prison wasn't being used."

"It's not."

"Then who's that?"

"Maybe just a contractor finishing up some interior punch list."

As they crunched along toward the back of the building they could hear doors slamming and what sounded like another engine starting. They hurried to the far end and looked around the back of the prison. Another truck was pulling away from the distant corner. Nick and Ava trotted at first then ran toward the corner to see where it went. To their dismay, when they looked around the long wall on the west side of the building, the truck stopped just outside the front gates where a Hispanic man was chain-locking the gates closed.

Ava looked at Nick, "What the hell's he doing?"

"Locking us in is what he's doing."

They began to run along the wall in a bright sun toward the front of the prison. As the man walked back to the truck, Nick yelled toward him, "Hey, what the hell are you doing? You just locked us in!"

The truck and van sped away.

Washington, DC

Spring 1997 The Lobbying World

Part of being an effective lobbyist is raising money for Members of Congress. Part of that challenge is to have good clients and friends with deep pockets who can contribute to Senators' or Congressmen's campaigns. Nick was still fairly new at the DC lobbying game in May of 1997, but was asked to co-host an event for Senator Waters with a company involved with the ACC. Waters' next election was still three years away but fundraising had become a daily burden for Washington politicians.

The event would be hosted at a company located in New Jersey. Nick agreed to raise a minimum of $15,000 and to attend the lunch in Trenton. He immediately called every Big Telco lobbyist he knew to see how much they might contribute. Then he called every independent lobbyist who represented telecom clients to see if they would help. The reality was Waters was Chairman of the Communications Subcommittee in the U.S. Senate, and it would be shortsighted for any relevant lobbyist who could do so not to support such events.

Since it was Nick's first challenge at fundraising, he went the extra mile to raise his share. He talked up the Senator to executives of the company hosting the event and encouraged them to contribute as much as possible. He also raised a fair amount from his telecom colleagues. In the end, he raised $20,000 of a total of $55,000 collected. Waters' crusty old chief of staff had called it "quite a haul." He added that, "Thurlow said we could count on you." Nick emphasized how the folks in New Jersey were looking forward to meeting the plain-spoken Montana Senator.

The day of the event found Nick on a train to the capital of New Jersey. He took in the scenery from the haphazard expanse of blighted neighborhoods and shuttered factories east of DC to the quaint red-roofed farms along the Susquehanna River. Near Trenton, they rolled over the rusted toll bridge exhibiting the sign, "Trenton Makes, The World Takes," reflecting a bygone era when it was an iron and steel boom town. Once in Trenton, he made his way to the top floor of the tallest building near the State Capitol and arrived at the host company. The corporation's government relations director greeted Nick in the reception area.

They walked to a large-windowed boardroom where lunch would be served, and agreed that the Senator would sit at the head of the long conference table. The CEO of the company would sit to the Senator's right and other guests would fill in. The Senator's deputy chief of staff would sit at the other end of the table. They took a minute to trade notes on the latest telecom industry news and the likelihood of pending appropriations bills making their way through the process by year's end. Before they could get into many specifics, they heard some commotion coming from the lobby.

The Senator had arrived. The company's CEO and some executives had assembled in the hallway near where they would dine. Nick stepped out, said hello to the CEO and positioned himself to introduce the Senator as he came down the hall. Senator Waters ambled toward them with a slight limp.

"Hey, Nick, you got out of jail! Great news."

Nick, covering a smile, "Senator I'd like you to meet…"

But before he could finish, Waters reached out his hand, "Eli, good to see you, you old son of a gun. Thanks for putting this thing together for me."

They went directly to the buffet line to get lunch and sit down. While in line, Nick asked Waters if Thurlow was staying out of trouble. Clarence smiled and said he thought Thurlow was in love with *that woman* from Florida, adding, "that's what I'd call trouble."

He studied Nick for a moment, then added, "Thurlow needs to go home to Montana, get married and settle down. He was a pretty good bull rider in his day, you know." Though Waters was unusually candid, even casual compared to most Senators, Nick found himself standing up straighter and saying *sir* a lot when around him.

When all were seated at the table, Nick realized the sun was shining through the window slightly into the Senator's face. Clarence didn't seem to mind, but Nick noticed from that angle how tired the ruddy-faced senator appeared. It was also soon evident that the usually chipper Senator had a bad cold and was not at his best. The last thing he noticed from the angle of the sun to the backs of those across the table from him was that several of them were wearing Jewish yarmulkes.

After polite small talk everyone sampled their food. A shaky-handed waiter served iced tea in tall glasses. One of the things Nick liked about Clarence was whether at an upscale restaurant in DC or a dive diner in the country, he always graciously thanked waiters and waitresses for serving him. When most of the guests were about half done, the CEO tapped his water glass with his spoon and gave a nice introduction of the Senator. Waters reciprocated but spoke somewhat slowly.

"Thank you, Eli." Clarence dabbed his nose with a handkerchief. "It's great to be here in Trenton and I do so very much appreciate all your efforts putting this nice event together. As you know the Senate has been very busy and…"

In between sniffles and coughs, Waters gave his usual summary of what Congress had been up to and what he hoped it could accomplish by the end of the year. When he was finished, some asked a few polite softball questions about pending legislation and of the likely outcome of a Senate confirmation process regarding a liberal judge recently nominated to the DC Circuit Court of Appeals. Senator Waters, uncertain of the questioner's politics, gave an articulately vague answer.

About then, a longer than usual silence enveloped the room. Eli leaned into the Senator, and speaking softly from a seemingly more personal perspective, asked him how he was doing.

Unfortunately, Waters' response was not as inaudible or as personal. "Well, I'll tell you what, Eli. Some days you know, fighting these battles in DC…some days you feel like you're just circlin' the drain." Clarence looked down at the table as if searching for something.

Nick was unnerved, especially after asking all those people to cough up so much money. He thought, *To convey some comfort with his position of power, might a slightly different choice of words be in order here?* But the Senator continued, and with considerable volume.

"You know, some days I feel just like that spider in the bathtub struggling to hold onto anything before the whirlpool spins me down. Like I'm grasping for a little piece of soap or somethin', ya know?" Waters then coughed and wiped his nose again.

The company's government relations guy gave Nick a wide-eyed, panic-stricken look.

Everyone around the table glanced from side to side to see who might redirect the conversation. A corporate executive spoke up.

"Senator, let me ask you a question on a slightly different subject. What do you think about this talk of dividing Israel into two different states, or especially the idea of separating Jerusalem?"

Panic quietly settled in on Nick once more. He was sure Waters was not ready for that kind of question or had the right answer at his fingertips. There was a long silence.

Then Waters began, "Well...I'll tell you what."

More silence as the Senator dabbed his nose again and stared down at the table twirling his index finger on its surface. Nick turned to his right toward the Senator's staffer with a look that asked, *Does he know what the hell to say here?* But the deputy chief, chewing a mouthful of chocolate brownie, just stared back with a not-so-bright look on his face.

Waters began again. "I'll tell you what...that Jerusalem is a...a...beautiful city, and a place of great historical significance. And...I'll tell you what...I have visited there."

Silence enveloped the room again as he paused. Nick could feel his heart beating. The look on Waters' face was that of a man trying to figure out what not to say.

Clarence continued, "I think...no, yes, you know it would be a shame to precipitously change the historic fundamentals of that place."

An almost audible exhale swept across the room. "Thank you, Senator. I agree with you. There's no way they should ever divide Jerusalem."

That's not exactly what the Senator had said, but everyone appeared happy. With that, lunch was over and everyone thanked everyone for their part. Nick, with wet armpits under his suit jacket, caught the next train back to Washington. He was proud to have helped host the luncheon and raise considerable money from his new peers. It was to be the first of many events Nick would co-host for the Senator between this spring day in 1997 and the fall of 2006.

Bozeman, Montana

Fall 2006 The Campaign Trail

Ava and Nick inspected the padlock securing the fence that sealed them inside the new prison grounds. "What the fuck?" Ava asked.

"I don't know what that was all about."

"The guy in the van had to hear us – right?"

"I think so."

Ava looked at the gate. "How the hell are we going to get outta here? I have zero coverage on my cell phone."

"Yeah, me too," Nick added. He began to walk toward the back of the prison. "Let's look around the building and see if we can find something that might break this chain."

They scavenged through old wood boxes and unused barbed wire. Ava found what looked like a crowbar. "Will this help?"

"It might. Let's keep looking."

Nick found a weathered UPS envelope with some old papers in it. They were not shredded but most were torn in half. He noticed the top half of one stained letter was written on official U.S. Senate stationery. It was addressed to the head of the U.S. Bureau of Prisons. He began to search for the bottom half of the letter to see who sent it. A torn section of the second half was buried in a box. It was signed by Senator Clarence Waters. Nick was familiar enough with Waters' signature to know that someone other than the senator had signed it.

He could only read the first and last sentences. The opening line included a common congressional introduction: *It has come to my attention that a prison is under construction in Montana…* That is the introduction that says: I'm not seeking this out, I don't have any vested interest here, this information just sort of fell in my lap. The remainder of the sentence was partially torn away and illegible. The last line of the correspondence read: *It would be much appreciated if your office could reply as soon as possible to these specific inquiries.*

It was not unusual for a staffer to sign a letter by a senator. In fact, relatively few letters from a Member of Congress are signed by the Member. But Nick was curious which staffer was behind this one and for whose benefit. He stuffed the two scraps into his jeans pocket and continued looking for some makeshift tools. Ava found a second piece of metal that looked like a thick door frame. They collected their tools and returned to the fence.

After a quick examination, he admitted, "We're never going to break this chain with these tools."

Ava agreed. "Right. This fence and lock are brand-new."

"I've got an idea." He twisted the crowbar through what loose chain was left hanging from the lock and turned it until it was taut. "I'm going to ram it with the Jeep."

"Nick, that's going to tear the front of your car up, big-time."

"It's a rental."

As he pulled the Jeep around, Ava stood back. Nick floored it and was going 40 miles per hour when he hit the target. Neither the lock nor chain broke but the gate snapped off its hinges on impact and whipped around onto the hood of his car. Nick jumped out to assess the damage. Other than a dented and scraped bumper and some scratches on the hood, it was minimal.

They got back in the Jeep and headed down the road.

"Nick, why did those sons of bitches lock us in like that?"

"Don't know."

"I've sure learned some important things today."

"Like what?"

"Like never go joy ridin' with you again. For crying out loud, we haven't even started the fun part of the trip yet. Hang a left at that sign and drive toward Red Lodge."

If not for struggling to tune out Ava's complaints about men in her life, and Kale in particular, his drive on the Beartooth Highway would have gone down as one of the most beautiful of Nick's lifetime. It soared from 5,000 feet near Red Lodge to over 10,000 at its peak in Wyoming, then dropped into a vast tiered valley reflecting sun-lit dark greens, and shimmering bright rusts and yellows, bordered by the Absaroka Wilderness.

"Wow, Ava, it is truly beautiful here."

"Oro y plata."

"What?"

"Gold and Silver – that's Montana." She put her feet up on the dash board and hung her arm out the window. "By the way, I got my three Cs. I get my diploma in a few weeks."

"Ava, that's great! Congratulations. What's your degree in?"

"Journalism." Ava said, proudly.

"Good for you. What are you planning to do with it?"

"I'm trying to get a job at this paper near Kalispell doing whatever – and hopefully some writing there one day. I've heard through the grapevine they won't reject me just because I'm a Republican."

"An agnostic paper in Montana. That would be a smart move for you, Ava. Good luck."

"And, one other thing. Thanks for not telling Kale about our previous little escapade. I consider that an admirable act of friendship." Ava looked directly at him.

Nick looked straight ahead. "I consider it an act of mercy."

"Say, speaking of that, why aren't you married?" Ava asked. "You got some stuff going on. Where's the woman in your life?"

"I don't know. I dated a woman once in DC a long time ago. She's the only one I ever clicked with. It went south for a lot of reasons. I haven't really felt the same since."

"So, where is she?"

"She lives in Texas. I thought to call her many times and actually dialed her number on a few occasions. But never left a message."

"Nick, just call her. What if she's been waiting all these years for you to reach out to her?"

"Well, as of late there may be more to the story. I made a big mistake years ago by swearing to tell the truth, the whole truth and nothing but the truth, which almost destroyed her. But, I may have a reason to talk with her again soon."

"Oh, man, I can see it in your eyes. You still care…"

Nick cut her off. "Enough about me." He reluctantly reintroduced the subject of his friend. "So, what the hell's gotten between you and Kale? I hear more from you two about you two than anything else in a day's work lately."

After taking in the landscape for a minute, Ava opened up. "So Nick, what's Kale's problem? He comes on like gangbusters and is so much fun. One of the few men who can keep pace with me, and we laugh so hard. But he's unhinged somewhere, Nick, and it doesn't stay dormant for long. We'll be having a great time, and then it's like his inner peace will get captured by some other place or time." She put her feet on the floor. "There's a self-destructive nature to him that's wearing pretty thin on me. I think we get along better when we're not together."

"Ava, you guys have only been seeing each other for what, several weeks? And only a couple of days per week at that."

"I don't know, Nick. He may be just another one of my mistakes. Sometimes I think he should be fitted for a straitjacket – if he hasn't already. You know what I do like about him though? He's not one of those East Coast nitwits who just seem to mean what he says. He really does mean what he says."

Nick thought that an odd take because most politicians and lobbyists in DC were masters at seeming to mean what they say rather than actually meaning it, and Kale was one of the best.

"Maybe just back up a little. Give each other some space. From what I can tell, you guys talk like every half hour."

"Not anymore."

Working their way along the northern edge of Yellowstone Park in Wyoming, silence overwhelmed their drive. Nick soaked in the post card-like scenery but was thinking about Ava's critique of his friend, *There's something really wrong inside him, it's why he drinks so much.* It was, at least, partially true. Unfortunately since drinking, mostly with Members of Congress, was much of what lobbyists got paid to do, it was hard to recognize it in Kale as an addiction.

After Kale's divorce, lobbying became his life. The problem was his taste for Scotch became braided into his work routine. He was often half-lit by lunch, and few noticed how he struggled between afternoon Hill meetings. By the time dinner with a Senator was done, he was hammered. But it didn't interfere with his work, it only enhanced it. He was respected as an advocate to Congress because he would say anything to make a point. He didn't really care what people thought of him, and the less he cared the more successful he became. When sober, he was effective, but when drinking he was brilliant and entertaining, if not unpredictable.

Wrapping up their drive, they swung back around into the changing light and exited the park near Gardiner, Montana. Winding north past Chico Hot Springs, they headed west toward Bozeman into the smoke continuing to linger from the Livingston fires. Ava turned on the radio and another slew of political ads against Waters poured out but using unusually broad language indicting all Republicans in the country with the usual shop-worn slurs: racists, selfish, rich and *intolerant.* A news broadcast followed blistering Waters for using a non-media-approved term to describe America's military enemy in Iraq.

Washington, DC

Spring 1997 The Lobbying World

Due to the information from Tad, Nick began to see Hally through a different light. He wasn't a fan of rumors or those who spread them. But in the nation's capital of 1997, one could never completely dismiss a rumor, both for the kernel of truth it might contain or its impact regardless of its veracity. Nick's impression of Hally was that she couldn't care less what the rumor mill was grinding out on any given day. She had a view of who she was and who she wasn't despite what people may think. That might be a good mindset for an elected politician, but maybe not for a high-profile lobbyist caught up in the daily riptide of information flowing around Capitol Hill.

Out of the blue on a Friday morning, Nick was called into the ACC's HR office. The head of Human Resources was a tough-minded but seemingly nice woman whom Nick had spoken with maybe twice since he started his job there. She quietly shut her office door.

"Nick, how are you doing? Do you like working here at the ACC?"

"Yeah. Yes, I do. It's an interesting job."

"You work pretty closely with Hally. Do you enjoy working with her?"

"Uhm...yes. We get along pretty well."

The HR woman shifted in her chair. "So, let me get to the point. Nick, you're a lawyer, correct? A member of the DC Bar, right?"

"Uh...yes. Yes, I am."

"Okay. Are you aware of Hally being involved in any extracurricular fundraising activities outside of the ACC?"

"Uhm..."

"For particularly conservative candidates, for instance?"

Nick was thrown off his lobbyist-acquired indifferent response. He answered a little too quickly, "No! Uhm, no. I'm...I'm not aware of any such activity by Hally in *any* regard like that for that matter."

"Okay. Great. Would you be willing to testify to that under oath in a Federal Election Commission investigation, should one arise?"

"Uh...well. Yes, of course."

"Good. I knew we could count on you. Now, then, let me ask you. Nick, are you involved in any such fundraising activities?"

"Me? No. I'm not."

"Okay, just one more question then."

This time, Nick shifted in his chair.

"Nick, have you heard anything regarding Tad's personal involvement in a Democratic candidate's Presidential Exploratory Campaign Committee - regarding fundraising perhaps?"

"No. I haven't."

"Well, it's my understanding that it's illegal to provide any type of in-kind contribution for such campaigns including personal time – if it's not reported to the FEC. So, if you do hear of anything, you'll let me know. Right?"

"Yeah. Yes, I will."

"Good to hear. And, please keep this strictly between us for now." She opened a desk drawer and pulled out some printed forms, then looked up. "That's all. Thanks."

Nick walked back to his office, shaken. He knew the law on political fundraising was a bit unclear and sporadically enforced. He figured what Hally or Tad were up to may not be by the book, but doubted they were violating federal law any more than anyone else across the country. The wiggle room between the use of tax exempt 501(c) 4s, 501(c) 5s and 501(c) 6s to 527s, to direct mailings, to in-kind contributions, to the political use of offices and phone banks, to the paying of campaign consultants by unnamed organizations, was vast – and that was just a sampling of the devices used to raise hard money, soft money, or untraceable cash.[21]

However, Nick had little time to absorb what he'd just heard. It was a Friday, sometime after 12:00, and Hally nonchalantly strolled into his office, plopped into a chair and put her feet up on another chair. "Hey, Nick, it's pretty slow around here today. Want to grab lunch?"

They walked several blocks in perfect spring weather to Old Ebbit Grill near the White House. Old Ebbit was a popular lunch spot for White House staff and downtown lobbyists. After being situated in a somewhat private booth, "So, Nick, you've been around the ACC long enough to get some perspective. How do you like working there?" Hally asked.

Nick thought, *Here we go again.* "Oh, it's all right. You know, I've learned a lot."

"Yeah? What have you learned? Who *not* to associate yourself with in DC, like those crazy Western friends of yours?"

Hally liked Nick but was almost persuaded by Tad and others that, in fact, Nick might be the one in bed with the Palm Beach miscreants. Tad consistently reminded Hally of the unflattering attributes of Nick's close friends, Kale and Thurlow. Hally defended Nick by reiterating to others that Nick covered Montana for the ACC and it was his job to befriend Senator Waters' staff. But Tad asked Hally one question that tested her loyalty: did she ever actually see Thurlow Carmine at The SeLaSsh that night in West Palm, or was it really Nick who got them into the club?

Nick responded, "Well, Hally, I have learned to be careful with whom I associate in this town, but it's not the Montanans I'm worried about. Some of them like to party, maybe too hard, but for the most part, they're a very decent and patriotic group of people."

Nick had recently called Roline at the Canadian Embassy to see what she might discover about the H.H.S. ALES. Thurlow showed Nick another photo of the yacht, and though he'd been told it was a German vessel, Nick noticed it was flying the Canadian flag. Roline, via a maritime agency, informed Nick the yacht was a Canadian flag vessel registered in Vancouver and owned by Emptor Entertainment of Quebec. She said shareholders of the company included an investment firm out of California and several individuals, including Victor Purchase, Charles Mann, and a woman, Geneveve Purchase – all U.S. citizens. She added that it was the subject of an asset forfeiture proceeding initiated by the Palm Beach prosecutor's office.

A waiter interrupted and took their orders.

"So, Hally, what's your plan? You want to stay in this industry?"

"I'll tell you, Nick. I never imagined how dysfunctional this town was going to be before I got here. I'm frankly stunned this country's still intact. And, from what I can see it's just going to get worse."

"Oh, come on. You just haven't been around long enough. You'll see how it balances out."

"You know, Nick, everybody keeps telling me that like I'm stupid or something. 'You just haven't been around here long enough.' Considering its implication, I'm not sure I want to be around here *long enough*."

"But seriously, Hally, are you going to stay at the ACC?"

A tray of glasses shattered on the floor behind the bar, quieting the room. "Well, one thing I've learned Nick," she spoke quietly, "is that you've got to be involved on the campaign side of this town to be effective. Raising money and getting people elected is where our power comes from – right?"

"I'd have to agree with that." Nick drained his water glass. "So, Hally, with that in mind, what are you going to do next?"

"Actually, I'm thinking of running for Congress. And, I'm going to need the support of people like you."

Nick, stunned, looked across the room as if to see who else was hearing this bizarre information. He stared back at her trying to think of a response.

"What? That's an odd take for someone who thinks this town is so dysfunctional."

"Maybe I can make a difference. If you can't beat 'em, join 'em – right?" Hally chuckled.

"Oh, great." Nick shook his head. "From what congressional district, Hally?"

"From the district I live in, of course, right there in Maryland."

"Hally, you've only lived there for like a year. How could you have a political base in that district?"

"Nick, I have access to *a lot* of conservative money. Plus, I can practically self-fund my own campaign anyway. If I can convince the local Republican Party folks that I'm a viable candidate, and they won't have to raise a dime for me, trust me – they'll be thrilled. And if I happen to win, I won't owe anybody anything."

"Hmmm…I see. When are you planning to do this?"

"Oh, I don't know. Just thinking about it for now. Either that or maybe throwing in with the folks at the *Greater America Foundation*."

"Hally, do you really think you fit in with that conservative crowd?"

"Yeah, Nick, I do! And, don't worry I terminated your membership there. You'll understand one day that I was doing you a favor.

The Republicans who took control of Congress a couple of years ago are already feeling a little too comfortable with their power, Nick. They don't want to rock the boat anymore. With enough money, we could win primaries against every one of those establishment Republicans."

"Hally, you've only been in DC a couple of years. You've only seen what it's like around here with Republicans *in power*. You might stick around and get some perspective first."

"Thanks for the advice, Nick. But frankly, you sound like one of those country club Republicans yourself."

"Hally, I worked in Congress for several years. I know a few things you ought to consider before jumping off a cliff into a congressional campaign. Like what it's like here when Democrats *are* in control."

"Don't worry, Nick. Not planning anything at this point. Just thinking on options for now."

On their walk back to the office, Nick thought, *Was she just deflecting? Maybe planning a back-up strategy in case the illegal fundraising schemes or the Raines affair came hard aground?* On Pennsylvania Avenue they stumbled upon a homeless man who was selling pamphlets on the sidewalk for $1.00. Hally gave him $50. "That could be your own brother one day, you know?" She said, matter-of-factly.

En Route

Kale McDermott finished a Dewars and water in his peanut-strewn first class seat and looked out the window of the Delta jet. He was streaming toward Montana at just over 500 miles per hour and just above 31,000 feet. A distant silhouette of the mountains of Colorado was coming into view, and the flat lands he'd gazed down upon would soon be running into the first folds of the Rocky Mountains. He was looking forward to seeing Ava and hoping they could get past whatever their latest spat was about. It seemed to him they got along a lot better when they were together.

The flight attendant served him his third drink, and as he sipped it, his thoughts reluctantly returned to his predicament with his company's PAC and Congressman Judd Parker. Kale was aware of his limited options. He had put all the money he'd illegally borrowed back into the PAC account, as Nick had advised, and explained to the general counsel that an accounting error had temporarily unbalanced their budget. The company appeared to not have cared less but he was given a heads-up by a friend at headquarters that some corporate downside was yet to come on that front.

His pessimism lifted a bit as he thought about how Nick's advice had at least initially worked. Maybe that kind of resourcefulness was all he really needed. He sipped at his scotch and smacked his lips. Kale's mood perked up again when he looked out onto the last of the perfect green concentric circles on the ground 30,000 feet below. This was the final stretch of farmland that lay east of the mountains. He thought to himself, *if farmers can persevere against all the elements they faced out here, maybe he could too.*

His unknown was what Parker was capable of. More Republicans suffering ethical challenges made Kale nervous they might lose the House in November. No one was predicting it, but if it happened and Parker became Chair of the Ethics Committee, Kale would be in grave danger. He wouldn't admit to anyone that he couldn't afford to fend off a congressional investigation.

He broke from his thoughts to look out the window. As they chased the sun west he could not tell if there was rain or fog between him and the lush green land below. They were an hour from Salt Lake where he would board a smaller plane for a short trip to Bozeman. When the seatbelt light dinged, he chugged the rest of his scotch, hopeful that Nick would have some good news.

Bozeman, Montana

Fall 2006 The Campaign Trail

No good news awaited Kale. First, the National Republican Senatorial Committee, the Senate's campaign arm which gave millions to candidates, had pulled its support from Waters. His poll numbers were dropping, cash on hand negligible and the party needed funds for other races. It was a psychological blow to Clarence's team right when the Democrats' onslaught of negative ads was peaking. Second, Nick's suspicions of a Waters' staffer nefariously involved with the construction of the unauthorized prison had been reinforced. Nick discovered this while attending an upscale fundraiser at a multi-million dollar home.

The Yellowstone Club, a private ski and golf resort with incomparable views of the Rocky Mountains, cost more to join than most people make in a lifetime. The tee boxes for its golf course stood at 7,000 feet, and the very few people who ever skied or played golf there were a testament to its exclusivity. Nick was certain the people there lived in a frighteningly unrealistic bubble, but equally certain they would not like to be reminded of it. While at the fundraising event, Nick came across Waters' former legislative director, Thurlow Carmine. Thurlow and Nick's political paths had crossed so many times they finally trusted each other.

Thanks to Waters' new deputy chief, Thurlow, who had helped Clarence in previous campaigns, had been mostly ostracized from the Senator's reelection effort. The new deputy chief, Zach Gerkin, was brought in by Clarence to help "clean up the loose-ship chicanery" of the DC office and was considered to be squeaky clean. Raised in Wyoming, he was not well known in Montana's political circles, and while enthusiastic, knew little of DC politics. Yet he was dropped into the middle of a powerful Senate operation about to come under siege from every quarter.

Nick decided to take a risk and tell Thurlow of the pieces of the letter he'd discovered while rummaging through boxes at the newly built prison. Thurlow's ears perked up. First he made Nick explain what he was doing at the prison, and Nick vaguely explained his firm's involvement. Thurlow raised his eyebrows at that news. He warned Nick to trace his firm's steps as to how they were introduced to the prison client. Once Nick deflected most of those questions, he pushed Thurlow on who in Waters' office might have an interest in supporting the building of the prison.

Lines at the edge of Thurlow's face tightened and he slowly shook his head. He still wanted to help Clarence wherever he could, but didn't want to jeopardize the campaign. "I can look into it a little, Nick. But we're going to have an ironclad agreement about this conversation."

He took Nick by the arm and led him out onto the vast deck that wrapped around the exclusive custom log cabin. Once out of earshot of the other guests, Thurlow began, "Nick I don't know who it is, but I'll tell you one thing, this Zach Gerkin kid is not as squeaky clean as everyone wants to think. The fact is I think he may be even more deceptive than Waters' previous deputy chief.

There was little love lost between most of Waters' recently-departed senior staffers. Thurlow checked himself and looked around to ensure once again that none of the other guests was within earshot. He continued, "Were you aware that Clarence had no idea he'd even gotten the appropriations earmark for that prison until a reporter asked him about it last week?"

"What?"

"Swear on the Bible. Waters denied it to the reporter's face. Then the journalist shows Clarence the printout of the appropriations rider with the monetary amount written in the margin with 'per Senator Waters' written right there. And then he asks Clarence why he would get money for a prison that houses no prisoners."

"What the hell?"

"Now, Clarence is on a jihad to find out how it got in there under his name."

"Who in his office could have pulled that off?"

"A couple of folks, Nick. But I think this is not only a ballsy move by a staffer, it also strikes me as a rookie mistake. And who's the young rookie in Waters' office?"

"Zach Gerkin. But do you think maybe Waters just forgot he'd agreed to it?"

"Nick. Ask yourself why Clarence, looking at a tough reelect, under any set of circumstances, would involve himself in a local prison dispute which has – I don't know – how many different interests involved on each side?"

"Okay, but why would Zach care enough to brazenly sneak money into a federal spending bill like that?"

"Well, we need to do a little homework. I'm guessing there's a link somewhere."

"I'll see what I can learn." Nick offered. "By the way, Thurlow, please tell me you're not still involved with those characters who own and run The SeLaSsh in Palm Beach."

"Why?"

"In the past few years, they've changed their corporate name several times, barely skated out from under some fraud indictments at the state level and two of them have now served jail time on federal charges. I understand your old girlfriend is still mixed up with that cabal."

"And?"

"And, they may have recently stepped into some federal nets down there. I have friends in the U.S. Attorney's office in South Florida. I hear things. Thurlow, you like the woman. I get it. But stay away from those SeLaSsh guys. By the way, you know what initially snared you into that investigation years ago? It was the paperwork you filled out and signed for some lowlife bail bondsman in order to bail Geneveve out in Florida after you guys returned from Bimini."

Thurlow nodded. "I've learned my lessons down there, Nick. Trust me, they're yesterday's news."

Before he could bring up the issue of money for Burch's Indian Reservation investigation, Thurlow clinked his crystal tumbler of bourbon with Nick's glass, "Just watch your own back, Nick." He hustled back inside to join the wealthy Montana contributors.

While there, Nick wanted to talk with Waters about his for-profit prison client. He waited his turn while the big donors were listening to Clarence educate how Republicans in Congress were trying to overcome a Democratic attempt to defeat the pending Secure Fence Act legislation. The bill, if allowed to pass, would require 700 more miles of reinforced fencing along the U.S.-Mexico border.

"For crying out loud, it was practically a party line vote in the House with over two thirds of Democrats voting against it!"[22] Waters railed. "I don't understand how Democrats continue to fight for an unguarded border. One of them argued during the House debate that us reinforcing our border was tantamount to building a Berlin Wall."[23]

The odd thing to Nick was the money for the event had already been collected – all Clarence had to do was walk around the room and shake hands.

But Waters continued, grabbing one of the guests by the arm for emphasis, "That's nonsense. We're not trying to keep people from leaving this country like the Germans did, we're simply saying, if you want to *come into* our country, you must do so pursuant to a manner and process which our laws require. You guys need to know this stuff!" Clarence looked away as if distracted, then back at his guests. "Every sovereign country has the right to do that. And most do. We just may end up prevailing by a bigger vote in the Senate – but only because it's an election year."

After a break in the conversation, Nick stepped in. Once he'd reviewed the background of the prison issue, he said, "Senator, we need to get this prison up and running, right?"

"Absolutely, Nick. No need to have an empty prison just sittin' there. Being on the boundary of the res, maybe the tribal police could use it to lock-up criminals there instead of having to drive hours over to Sheridan every time they make an arrest."

"My firm's client, BF Prison Industries, is one of the best prison management companies in the country. They could help get it up and running," Nick said.

"What's the holdup, Nick? The state not helping?"

"We haven't had a formal sit-down with the Governor yet. But we need either the state or federal government to contract them to run it."

"I've got my own set of issues with that God-forsaken building these days, Nick, but let's see if we can look into it a little. Be aware though, the Crow Nation has got some infighting of their own going on and with a lot of money involved."

"Whose money?"

"Open pit gold mine money. The tribal chairman opposes those miners and has managed to stop their latest efforts to date. His election challenger is in the pocket of the gold miners. So, as you might imagine, he's got some extra money and energy behind him. They're working it fairly hard for him and trashing the current chairman pretty good. The tribal election's not far off now."

"Who owns this mining company?"

"A bunch of New Yorkers, of course." Clarence said with a smirk.

Nick's mind raced back to the forlorn barfly he saw the first night he met Ava at the Oasis. "I see. Thanks for letting me know."

"Sure. Now let's see what we can do on this prison thing, Nick. Let's get 'er done!"

"All right."

"Call my deputy chief of staff, Zach."

"Uhm...okay." Waters had a tendency to measure those under him with a perhaps too trusting or impartial code. Nick believed that trait did not serve the Senator well.

But Water's noticed Nick's reluctance, "You know what, Nick, call my state director, Cody, instead, and let's keep this conversation between us for now." Stranded in his words was a message about where Clarence's new deputy chief really stood with his new boss.

Back in his car maneuvering around the plush homes of the Yellowstone Club, Nick called Ava to see if her heavy-drinking construction worker had been in lately. She didn't answer so he left her a voice mail.

Montana/Washington, DC

Fall 2006 The Wires In-Between

Thurlow's warning to Nick to watch his step made him all the more curious about his firm's so-called prison management client and Senator Waters' role in the project. He was unsure of where to turn, but decided to call his old DC friend Tom Whitaker. Nick had not talked with Tom in more than a year but thought insights from his powerful perch at the Democratic Senatorial Campaign Committee might prove helpful.

"Hey, Nick, it's been a long time. How are you?"

"Tom, we've traveled a few miles since our Big Telco lobbying days haven't we? You've managed to stick it out at the DSCC for a while now. Good for you."

"Well, I've paid my dues here, Nick but I'm only around through the end of this campaign cycle. I've had enough."

"I see," Nick said, sympathetically.

"So what's up?"

"Tom, can you level with me about something that may involve your boss, Senator Kauffman?"

"I can try."

"My firm may have put me in a difficult position, maybe involving ethical or legal conflicts. Can I trust you to keep this conversation between us?"

"Wow, Nick. Sorry to hear that. Look, you're the only one who helped me years ago when I was in a jam. I'd like to help, but it depends."

"Okay, understood."

As he began to relay the story of the unauthorized prison in Montana, Tom interrupted. "Nick, let me call you back on a different line in about an hour. Okay?"

Nick spent the next hour considering how much he should divulge to someone who was working for an organization trying to end Senator Waters' career in the upcoming election. But he desperately needed any kind of inside information. His cell phone rang.

Nick went on to tell Tom the history of the project and the continual no shows by the high-paying client. He also told of how

Senator Mo Kauffman had recommended Nick's lobbying firm to the New York prison client.

"Tom, first, why do you think Kauffman would recommend a Republican firm in DC which has no prison-related experience to a prison management company headquartered in New York? And why would that company pay my firm $100,000 a month and then back out of every meeting we set for them?"

Nick paused for a second to gather his thoughts. "And look, I know Kauffman is focused on defeating Senator Waters out here in Montana where I've been camped out for a while. I understand that's his job as head of the DSCC. But this ancillary prison-related matter just seems a little more than odd to me."

There was a long pause. "Nick. I don't know the whole inside deal, but here's at least some of the political backstory. When the Democratic leadership gave Kauffman the chair of the DSCC last year, many in the party were not happy. You know, he's pretty brash and has a huge ego. One of those New Jersey egos. You know?"

"Yeah."

"So he had Members griping from the get-go about him taking over the task of getting Democratic senators elected all around the country. And, unfortunately for Kauffman, one of the first ideas he brought to the party elders to win back the Senate was to take down some Republicans who most people considered to be in pretty safe seats. The first target he brought up at their very first meeting was Clarence Waters."

"Wow."

"Yeah, and Nick this was early last summer in 2005. There was not much of a Dick Hanov story then, and Waters was about as popular as any sitting three-term Republican Senator."

"What do you think made him target Clarence's seat?"

"I don't know. At least I didn't. I mean…he was my new boss here, right? I had to be careful what advice I gave. I wanted to keep my job."

"Understood. So, what happened?"

"First of all, when Kauffman informs the rest of the Democratic leadership that Clarence Waters of Montana is at the top of his list to defeat in order to take back the Senate, he practically gets laughed out of the room."

Tom pauses, several blaring sirens pass him by. He apologizes and continues.

"Members who were against Mo getting this chairmanship, including the most recent past chair of the DSCC, practically ridiculed him. They said he was going to waste the party's campaign money. They were like, 'Montana? Are you crazy?'"

"How did Kauffman handle it?"

"Well, this is where I first got a snapshot of how prepared Mo always is. He doesn't take the bait. He slowly and methodically goes through the numbers on Waters' last campaign in 2000, how close it was, and how much the Republicans spent defending his seat. He's got it all laid out. Then he criticizes the former DSCC Chairman right to his face for not putting more money into that race that year, and goes on to make the case for how Democrats could have defeated Waters back then. I swear, Nick, he had a precinct by precinct breakdown of the entire 2000 Montana Senate race in his head."

"Hmph. Pretty impressive."

"Yes, it was. And keep in mind, this was just supposed to be their first general kind of get together with the new chairman meeting. Well, when Kauffman is done with his meticulous diatribe, you could have heard a pin drop. His detractors tried to breeze past it and one said, 'So what else you got?' But Mo knew he had won that battle."

"Tom, I wonder though, especially under the circumstances last year when Waters looked fairly safe in a red leaning state, why Kauffman targeted him out of the other twenty-two Republican Senators up for reelection this year? And I still can't figure where this for-profit prison client fits in."

After another long pause. "Well, there is one other connection, Nick. I'm reluctant to even discuss this, and if you repeat it, I'll deny it. We clear?"

"Yes."

"Kauffman does have an arms-length relationship with a New York lawyer who represents some mining interests around the country, and I think in Montana. And I'm only privy to this info due to being in his office or car when short phone calls occurred, okay?"

"Okay."

"From the bits and pieces I've heard, there seems to be an

association between that client and that dormant prison. And Kauffman seems none too thrilled about Senator Waters desire to get that prison open – for whatever reason."

"Really?"

"That's all I'm saying on the subject, Nick. Period. End of story. And, honestly, it's all I really know. Again, don't repeat it."

"I won't Tom. I promise. It is a bizarre relationship between Kauffman and Waters though, isn't it?"

"Yeah. Frankly, Nick, I think maybe there's something more personal between the two of them. You know, you couldn't find two more different people in the entire Senate. A high school-educated, conservative rancher, from as rural as rural gets, Wisdom, Montana, and an Ivy League-educated liberal lawyer, career politician from as urban as urban gets, Newark, New Jersey. And I just don't think they personally like each other – at all."

"I think you're right on that."

"But I'll admit, Nick – and this is also off the record – there is something more driving Kauffman about that Montana seat. It's the first race he asks about every morning. We've spent as much money, relatively speaking, against Waters as any other candidate. And Mo's been very involved with political advice to our challenger out there – he's even had personal in-put on his campaign ads."

"That explains why all the firepower out here on Clarence seems so well-orchestrated at the federal level and through the national media. I doubt our founding fathers would be thrilled – a U.S. Senate election in the mountain West run and paid for by political architects in Washington.[24] Anyway, Tom, thanks for your help. I promise to keep this between us. I may call you again though if it's okay with yo…"

The phone went dead.

Bozeman, Montana

Fall 2006 The Lobbying World / The Campaign Trail

Postponing his trip back to DC so he and Ava could make-up from their most recent spat, Kale scheduled lunch in Bozeman with Nick to catch-up on the latest campaign and DC news. But when they met at the Rocking R Bar on Main Street, Kale had an unusually somber look about him.

"Well, old-timer, how goes the stormy romance?"

"Oh, forget that, Nick. My assistant, Jamie, received another letter in the mail today at my DC office from the House Ethics Committee."

"What did it say?"

"Said they wanted to see my company's PAC records for the past three years!"

"What? Who signed it?"

"Congressman Judd Parker."

"Look, Kale, Parker has no business unilaterally initiating a committee request like that from a private company. It's just not how it works. He doesn't have that authority."

"But he did it anyway, Nick. The letter is dated October 4th, 2006 and is addressed to me. But, it was also copied to the CEO of my company and our General Counsel."

"Holy shit, Kale."

"I know!"

"Kale, you've probably got twenty-four hours to get someone in your San Diego office to intercept that letter."

"That's a great idea. I know the CEO's assistant pretty well. And, my best friend in the company works for the general counsel's office."

While Kale was busy contacting his colleagues in San Diego, Nick decided it was time to see if his old fly fishing friend, Cotter from Utah, had learned anything helpful about Judd Parker. He reached Cotter on his cell, "Hey, you in Salt Lake?"

"No, I'm in Jackson Hole, Wyoming."

"What are you doing there?"

"Wanted to get out of town for a few days. Okay?"

"Look, I need anything you can provide regarding what I asked you about Congressman Judd Parker. It's getting down and dirty."

"Hmmm. Where are you?"

"Kale and I are in Bozeman."

"I do have some info to share that might be helpful. You guys going to be there tomorrow? You're just a few hours' drive away."

"Yes. Come visit. We could use any encouragement."

Cotter, chuckling, "I'll see you tomorrow."

The next night, Kale and Nick met Cotter for dinner at The Mint restaurant in Belgrade just outside of Bozeman. After detailing his precarious drive from Jackson Hole, how he'd had a few beers and been pulled over by a Wyoming State Trooper, he thanked his lucky stars just for making it there. He was lectured vigorously by Kale, "Cotter, never ever blow into one of those breathalyzer machines. If you do, they have the evidence on you and you're fucked. Trust me, I speak from experience." Fortunately, Cotter was not asked to take a breathalyzer and had talked his way out of trouble.

Then, Cotter started in on Kale, "So, tell me again how you left it with Parker's wife last time you saw her."

Kale, rolling his eyes, "Well, she caught me out for dinner with a young woman. It was pretty obvious it was a date."

"Oh, that sucks."

"Yeah. But, for crying out loud, she was married. And traveled back out to Utah every other week with her husband. But I couldn't even go on a date? What the hell?"

"Ha! Okay. Whatever. So she's still pissed at you? How long ago was that?"

"Oh, many months ago now."

Cotter responded, "I just can't see her being your actual problem. She's got too many other irons in the fire so to speak."

"But Congressman Parker knows about our affair," Kale complained.

"How do you know that?"

"Because she told me that she told him. And she was still mad when she told me that, and I think she did it intentionally just to piss him off."

"Okay. So, here's the information I have." Cotter said. "And don't freak out. I was just trying to help. I ran into Congressman Parker at a fundraiser in Salt Lake a couple of weeks ago. I've known him for years. He started talking about the Washington, DC lobbying world and how lucrative it had become. He mentioned the names of several lobbyists and how much money they were making. So, I intentionally brought up your name."

"Are you crazy?" Kale said indignantly.

"But hang on. Here's the deal. He didn't even flinch. He asked me to repeat your name, twice. He had no idea who I was talking about. Either that or he's one hell of an actor."

Kale sat back in the booth, "How could that be?"

"I'm just telling you what I said and how he reacted."

Kale with a raised voice, "But he signed the damn letter!"

Nick looked up at the ceiling. "Well…are we sure about that?"

If you ever thought Larry, Moe and Curly were incompetent boobs, you'd never seen Kale, Nick and Cotter try to unwind a mystery.

"Okay, so regardless of who signed the letter, we know someone on the Ethics Committee with access to Judd Parker's committee stationery did – right?" Cotter asked.

"Yeah." Nick nodded.

"So, how do we get Parker's office to realize there's a downside to them messing with Kale?"

Nick's eyes narrowed, "What kind of downside?"

"Political, financial, whatever. Parker's got to have an Achilles' heel out there somewhere."

"You mean, other than his wife?" Kale asked.

Cotter pivoted, "You know what I'd do if I were you? Host a fundraiser for Congressman Parker and write a big fat check from your company's PAC. You do that, and he accepts your check – and we all know he will – then this inquiry disappears overnight."

Kale, surprised by Cotter's suggestion, "You really think he'd accept a PAC check from me?"

"Look, these guys are all liars and cheats. Money is all that matters to them. He'll take your money."

Kale paused. "I don't know. I just don't know."

"You ever contributed any money to him before?" Cotter asked.

"No. He's on the Ethics Committee. That doesn't exactly do my company any good. But I've certainly contributed plenty to his wife in expensive dinners and five star hotels!"

Cotter slapped Kales' arm. "Hey, wait a minute. That's it."

"What?"

"Maybe that *is* our key here. We have to figure out her angle in all this."

"I thought we knew her angle." Nick said. "She's pissed at Kale. She told her husband she was sleeping with him. And now *he's* messing with Kale."

Cotter interrupted, "But I told you, Parker didn't even know Kale's name. And like you indicated, Nick, maybe one of his staffers signed the letter."

"So?"

"So, what if Sheila is the one messing with Kale?" Cotter explained, "Sheila knows all of Parker's staffers. Trust me, they're all afraid of her and she manipulates them for her own benefit. Let's just say she really is still mad at Kale. What if she got one of the staffers to send that letter?"

"What are you talking about?" Kale said.

"Think about it. Why would Sheila feel the need to *tell* Kale that she *told* her husband about the affair? Because she wants Kale to believe that Parker is after him. Why would she need to do that if Parker really was after him?"

Nick chimed in, "You think Sheila's pulling the strings of some staffer, and got them to send this letter to Kale on congressional stationery? So, if Kale's company sends information back to Parker's office, as your theory goes, that staffer will then have to carry on this charade of an investigation?"

Kale, looking at his BlackBerry, blurted out, "Oh, thank God. Neither the CEO nor the General Counsel has seen the letter yet. At least I've bought some time."

Cotter continued, "That's perfect. Now, if my theory is correct, and Kale's company never responds, what's the staffer going to do?"

Nick exasperated, "Look, if Sheila's really behind all of this, someone just needs to talk to her."

Kale reacted, "I'm sure as hell not talking to her. She hates me."

Cotter deflected, "Well, I can't talk to her. She doesn't particularly like me either."

"Why not?" Nick asked.

"I never really called her again. You know, after dating her."

Cotter and Kale looked at Nick. "But she's not mad at *you*. She doesn't even know you." Cotter and Kale winked at each other when this idea was floated.

Nick held his hands up, palms out. "No way! I've got enough troubles of my own right now. I'm not getting anywhere near this woman. You know what, though? If any of this is accurate, we need first to just find out which staffer is involved."

Kale excitedly, "I know. Nick, you call Parker's office and tell them you represent me and want to discuss a letter that I received from the committee signed by Parker. Then whoever they put you through to, just ask if they're the staffer you need to deal with."

Nick thought for a moment. "Wait, why me?"

Cotter responded, "Kale's right. Kale can't do it, they might know his voice. And I can't do it. I'm too involved in Utah, and his wife knows me and I know the Congressman."

Nick, shook his head in resignation. "You two are...you know what? Fine. I'll make the call, try to get a name and then hang up. But that's it. Then I'm done."

"Perfect!"

Montana

Fall 2006 The Campaign Trail

Proving to be worth every dollar Nick had promised to pay him, Burch had been busy studying the Montana Indian reservations. It turned out that Kale was right about a couple of things. Addiction to meth on the reservations in Montana had almost doubled; in fact, by late 2006 it was overtaking alcoholism. The primary source of the meth was a Mexican cartel, and the cost of the meth to the Indians was zero. Nick returned a call from Burch to his home in Austin, Texas to discuss his latest report.

"Hello."

"Oh, uhm, is Burch there?"

"Oh, hey Nick. Sure I'll get him for you." Lisa said in a somber tone.

Burch told the story of what he and his investigator had discovered on a recent trip to Montana's reservations. They interviewed distraught families and relatives of users and spoke with some of the tribal council members. The good people on the reservations, who already had enough to worry about, were devastated by the scourge of meth in their communities. He also indicated there was a tribal election pending on the Crow Reservation and that the increase in meth had become a topic among the tribal members.

"Nick, I've been working these issues for years. I've never seen anything quite like this. We talked to dozens of people and saw proof with our own eyes. The only potential lead we got though was on the Crow Reservation where some people believe they've seen the same van coming and going a lot."

"Burch, how does a Mexican gang from below the U.S. southern border manage to infiltrate the drug trade of a state as big as Montana over 1,600 miles away on the Canadian border?"

"Nick, last year Montana outlawed the sale of meth's key ingredients. The US-Mexico border is wide open – they bring the final product or its precursor chemicals up through Albuquerque to Denver and into Montana. With the large quantities involved on the reservations, it's possible they're mixing the components close by. All they need is a secure, remote place within proximity of the reservation to make it. But, Nick, as big and vast as Montana is,

I wouldn't know where to begin to look. We could try to follow a vehicle after a delivery, but we would need a lot of manpower, several vehicles, and a lot of luck to pull that off."

"I understand. Let me think on it. When are you headed back here?"

"Next week."

———

Senator Waters' mission to find out who from his office put the prison money in the appropriations legislation kept getting sidetracked. His volatile campaign operation was floundering, and congressional business was keeping him distracted. But the reporter who asked the initial question about the federal money wouldn't give up. After his repeated calls to the Senator's press secretary, he was finally put through to Waters' new deputy chief. Zach Gerkin, who'd been worried about Waters discovering his misdeed, was suddenly in the catbird's seat.

Zach spoke at length with the reporter and covered his tracks well. He sent the eager journalist on a wild goose chase back to the House Appropriations Committee. All Zach needed was to buy some time. The prison project, which had been faltering as investors' money was running out, had stopped paying its contractors. Neither the state nor federal government had authorized the project; nor had the federal funding bill through which Zach requested the prison money been passed by the House yet or signed by the President.

No one was getting paid, including Zach's fiancée's father, who was the general contractor for the prison. One of the reasons Thurlow couldn't link the prison funding and Zach Gerkin was because he thought Zach was married to his live-in fiancée whose name he knew as Mrs. Gerkin. In reality, Zach was only engaged to the attractive woman who wore an expensive ring. Her maiden name was Polaski, as in Polaski Construction Company out of Idaho. Polaski Construction was owed $600,000 by the prison's financial backers for the final exterior work and the interior punch list which was in the process of being completed.

Zach, who adored his wife to-be, was afraid of her father. Their relationship had warmed after Senator Waters' earmark for $1 million was passed by the Senate which Zach took full credit for.

His would-be father-in-law seemed momentarily impressed. But with every passing week, Zach found himself having to explain the congressional appropriations process and why the money wasn't quite available yet. In the interim, Mr. Polaski, who was out $600,000, owed his subcontractors a total of $400,000. Everyone involved was getting desperate and each time Zach stumbled through another convoluted explanation of Congressional Process 101, the more displeased they all became.

Fortunately for Zach and the prison investors, a short term rental offer on the prison property came their way. It was from an Arizona company that manufactured camping gear. They were represented by a gentlemanly lawyer from Billings, Ace Hargrove, and were willing to pay a generous monthly rent until they completed their own facility in nearby Red Lodge. The investors jumped on it.

Washington, DC

Spring 1997 The Lobbying World

It would be hard to argue that a young lobbyist's life in DC is boring. In contrast to the often sleepy fundraising breakfasts with Members of Congress, there were also lively dinner fundraisers at upscale restaurants all over the city every night. It would also be hard to argue that all Members of Congress are uninformed on complex issues.

On this welcome spring evening, Nick and some of his Big Telco colleagues were gathering in a plush private dining room at Kincaid's. It was a popular new restaurant off Pennsylvania Avenue that opened in the mid-1990s. Their guest was a senior Member of the House Telecommunications Subcommittee who had seniority despite his relative youth. He'd been around long enough to learn communications-related issues well and was himself part of the legislative history of then existing federal law.

The best of wines were served along with rich appetizers. A partially stained glass door to the dining room prevented other patrons in the restaurant from seeing who the private guests were. After some initial niceties, the Congressman vetoed the idea of the usual formal introduction and jumped rather abruptly into the issues. He started to question each lobbyist as he went around the table beginning with the Southern Big Telco representative sitting to his left.

"What the hell are you guys doing trying to derail the regulations that will allow this new telecommunications law to work?"

"Congressman, you know…we're not stalling, we're just trying to make sure…"

"Nonsense. You're doing everything you can to keep this law from working. Look, it took ten years for us to get the '96 Telecom Act passed and you guys were the ones who pushed it because you wanted into the long-distance industry. And now you're spending millions of dollars in attorneys' fees to screw it up. What's the point?"

Nobody responded. A waiter divided the tension in the room asking one of the cohosts to sample a bottle of expensive French Bordeaux ordered for the table. After a sip of wine, the Mountain

West Big Telco advocate spoke softly. "Congressman, of course you're right, we agreed to this legislation." The lobbyists were on mental tiptoes now, careful not to overreach in their advocacy. "But I think you understand that we didn't abdicate our ability to fight for the best rules we could get out of the FCC to implement it."

The Congressman shot back, "You're wrong! You didn't just agree to this legislation, you guys made it happen." He continued around the table asking each lobbyist a different question. Nick, no longer quite a novice, quit eating his salad and sat up straighter in his chair waiting for his turn.

The seasoned legislator finally got around to Nick. "Well, you're the newcomer. You worked on this law when you were in the House. What do you think? You think you guys are entitled to stall the process at this agency forever?"

Nick spoke up, "No sir. And, I don't think that's anyone's intention. We are trying to ensure that our rights as providers are protected as we open our infrastructure to new competitors pursuant to the law."

"Your rights? Are you kidding me? You own all of the infrastructure and have for over sixty years, which I might add was paid for by the rate payers when you guys were all protected monopolies. The only ones who need rights here are the competitors who are starting from scratch. And, by the way, I hear odd rumors lately about some among your midst questionably raising money for ultra-right candidates. What's that all about?"

Nick, hopeful the walls weren't closing in just yet on Hally, ignored the fundraising landmine. "Sir," he said flatly, "I think we're just trying to make sure we're still in business too after all the dust settles." He felt somewhat reassured when he heard affirming chuckles around the table and saw the nodding of heads.

"Still in business? For crying out loud you guys control ninety-five percent of the market. Give me a break. You've basically been cut loose of the market safeguards you operated under when you were certified monopolies. Your newly reassembled control over all these networks will one day allow you to determine who goes over what network at what speeds and under what prices. If competition doesn't flourish to keep your power in check, there will never be anything approaching a competitively neutral relationship over this behemoth we've allowed you to create."

The congressman, who seldom drank, said, "You know what, I better have some wine." Several waiters interrupted the conversation as they brought in combinations of Chateaubriand and grilled lobster. The subject changed to the Boston Red Sox.

Bozeman, Montana

Fall 2006 The Campaign Trail

As a seasoned if not doggedly patient lobbyist, Nick finally arranged a meeting with Senator Waters' state director in Montana to talk about the prison issue. They met at one of the Senator's state offices in Gallatin County on the coldest autumn day so far of 2006.

"Cody, thanks for taking the time."

"No problem, Nick. The Senator is curious to see if we can help get this prison open."

"Right. My firm's client, BF Prison Industries, has indicated an interest in managing this project. You familiar with them?"

"I've heard of 'em. They don't manage any prisons here in Montana."

"Right. So, any help you guys can be in straightening out who's in charge of this place would be helpful. Seems to be some conflict between federal and state authority."

"Nick, I understand you've scheduled them to meet with the Governor. How's that going?"

"Actually, they haven't made it out here for a meeting just yet."

"Why not?"

"We seem to keep running into scheduling issues."

"On who's end?"

"Ours, I'm afraid." Nick admitted.

"Hmmm. You know, Nick, I think Clarence would like to help you. But let me warn you of a couple things. One, part of your state/federal jurisdiction issue is due to the fact that the developers built that prison right on the boundary line of the Crow Reservation. Two, many of these characters involved in the private prison industry have a few conflicts within their own ranks. And some of their close allies might have some ideas of their own about opening that particular prison."

"But, Cody, they're paying us a lot of money because they apparently want us to help them get the contract to manage *this* one."

"They pay a lot of money to a lot of people for a lot of reasons. You ever ask yourself how your firm got hooked-up with this prison company, Nick?"

"Cody, I appreciate you trying to help, but I'm having a little trouble reading you."

"Nick, you know where your client's business is located – right?"

"Yeah, New York."

"Their corporate headquarters is in New York, but their offices are located in New Jersey."

"Okay."

"Did you know that only one person inquired to our office about why Clarence got the appropriations earmark for that prison?"

"No. Who?"

"The chief of staff to New Jersey Senator Mo Kauffman."

"Was he in favor of it?"

"He didn't say."

———————

Nick drove an hour west of Bozeman to buy a late lunch for Thurlow Carmine at a small diner on the outskirts of Butte. "Interesting choice of restaurants, Thurlow. How more in the middle of fucking nowhere could we get? You hiding from a bounty hunter or what?"

"Very funny. It has great food."

Thurlow had previously given Nick some good intel on the prison funding. Nick had not yet connected all the dots, but was hoping Thurlow might provide a few more clues. First and foremost, Nick needed to discuss the matter of funds to pay Burch Maloney. Nick knew he was out on a limb on that one but figured Thurlow might want to help after hearing of the situation with the meth and the Indian Reservations. Nick meticulously laid out his case, unaware of the intensity with which Thurlow was listening.

"Nick, you guys want to investigate the use of meth on the Crow Reservation and have the State Republican Party pay for it? Have you two lost your fuckin' minds?!"

"Uhh…We're just trying to help Clarence on the reservations," Nick said, defensively.

He went on to explain in more detail Kale's information and theory, and the things that Burch had discovered so far. It didn't hurt that Kale and Thurlow were old DC drinking buddies. After several minutes of explaining and reviewing the calculations regarding potential reservation voter turnout, Thurlow's stance seemed to soften.

"If you and Kale are even close on your theory, it may be worth looking into, but I can damn well guarantee you the Republican Party will not be paying for it."

Thurlow hesitated. "Let me think on it. I may have some sources we can tap into."

"That would be great. Thanks."

"You didn't tell them the Republican Party would pay for it did you?"

"Oh...uh...No, no." Nick insisted.

"Good."

"I actually mentioned the 'Citizens For A Better Montana.'"

"That was smart. We just might be able to get them to kick in a little cash."

"That would be really helpful, Thurlow."

"Taft, I appreciate your wanting to help but you need to watch what the hell you're doin'. Do you know anything about the Crow Tribe, the biggest in this state?"

"No."

Thurlow shook his head. "Well, you should just know their tribal chairman is taking a lot of heat for the increase in crime there. You and Kale may be on to something but you need to understand the landscape you're dealin' with. And be careful not to mention anything about Waters and Indians in the same sentence. The trail of rhetorical debris the media is floating around to connect Clarence to Dick Hanov is out of control. We're doing everything to keep it from getting worse. So, don't go making it easier the for media whores."

"Okay, I hear you. But you think you could help us find some funds for this investigation?"

"Nick, do you know that agents for the Bureau of Indian Affairs, the Tribal Police and the FBI are all working together now on the case of the young Crow woman who overdosed on the res a couple months ago?"

"Yeah, I've heard."

"Did you know she was related to a former Crow Tribal Chief?"

"I had heard that too – yes."

"Did you know she had an older sister who managed to get off the res and who works part-time for a Billings law enforcement-related rehab center?"

"No."

"Well, kind of important. Because she's on the hunt for the dealers who sold the unusually strong meth that killed her little sister. It's not often that a Crow woman with such strong tribal ties will leave the reservation permanently. But, in part, due to that fact, and her job, she's got some law enforcement credibility of her own."

Thurlow looked all around the room, then took a long sip of cold beer. "Within days of her sister's death, she went hard after the Tribal Police and the BIA agents. She implored them to look for the source of the powerful drugs that killed Jacy. She's a bit of a loner but is dedicated and respected in the Billing's legal community. Her efforts might actually turn out to be helpful to your search for who's supplying meth out there."

"I see."

Nick, you guys have got a lot to learn before you go charging headfirst into the Crow Nation."

"I appreciate that. But you think you can help?"

Thurlow smiled. "I'll talk to some of the bigger donors and see what I can come up with. But I'm going to need to meet this Burch fella myself!"

———————

On his way back down I-90 toward Bozeman, Nick contemplated stopping by the Oasis to see if Ava was around. He decided to call first. The hostess put Ava on the line.

"What's up?"

"Thinking of stopping by for a drink."

"Come on by. Beer's on me."

"Hey, have you seen that construction guy from Billings lately?"

"Right in front of me. Not sitting very straight but still upright."

"I'll see you in a few."

Nick entered the bar at the Oasis and Ava gestured him toward a guy in jeans and a red checkered shirt sitting alone. Nick sat on the bar stool next to him and ordered a beer.

"How's it going?" Nick offered.

"Just fine. How you doing?"

"Just all right."

"Only all right?" The Montanan asked.

"Yeah, I've had better days. Just got stiffed on a job I was doing. Bastards didn't pay me after I finished some work." Nick said.

"Trust me, I know the feeling."

"How so?" Nick asked.

"Oh, it happens from time to time. I'm in construction work. When a project goes south, it's always the workers who get stiffed. Ya know?"

"Yeah, I understand."

There was a silence after they both took a swig of cold beer.

Nick tried again, "You know what pisses me off the most, is these fuckers from the East Coast who have plenty of money, but stiff you anyway. It's like they enjoy it or something."

"Bub. I know all about it. By the way, my name's Ben Candler, friends call me Benny."

Nick reached out his hand "Nick Taft. Nice to meet you. So, what is it you were saying?"

Ben downed his beer and ordered another. "These New York guys hired me a while ago. They asked me to introduce them to some folks I've worked for on the Crow Reservation. Agreed to pay me pretty well. I figured what the hell? You know?"

Ben's beer arrived. He downed half of it and seemed to forget what he was talking about.

"How did you meet these New Yorkers?" Nick asked.

"Well…my lawyer in Billings actually put us in touch."

"Your lawyer?"

"Yeah. He represented me in a DUI case several months ago. The second one he'd helped me get out of. I find it difficult in Montana to not drink and drive. Hell, it takes a half hour to drive anywhere to do anything in this state. Know what I mean?"

"Yeah." Nick nodded.

"Anywho, these big shots with some gold mine company contact me and offer to hire me to introduce them to some Indians on the Crow res. They offer to pay me. So I do."

"What kind of guys were they, generally speaking?"

Ben downed the rest of his beer. "New York guinea, wop fuckers. Threw a lot of money around, and liked to eat. Didn't exactly blend in on the res if you know what I mean?"

"So, what happened?"

"So, the next day I ask who else they want to meet. They say no one. Here's your money, now fuck off. Not in so many words but that was the message. Know what I mean?"

"Yeah."

"So, they paid me about half what they owed me. So, I make a stand on it, you know…cause that's bullshit!"

"Yeah it is."

"So, they threaten me and I threaten them. But I got no more money out of 'em."

"Did they say why they wanted to meet these tribal members?"

"No."

Ben wobbled around the corner of the bar to the men's room. Ava stood across the bar in front of Nick. "Guy can put 'em down, can't he?"

"Yeah. Looks like he's had a few."

"Nine beers since one o'clock."

"Huh, seems like a decent guy though."

"He's all right." Ava smiled and moved down the bar.

Ben returned and sat down hard on his bar stool.

"So, your lawyer's a good DUI guy, huh?" Nick asked.

"Oh, yeah. The best."

"And he introduced you to the New Yorkers? What's his name? Never know when I might need a good DUI lawyer."

"For sure. You REALLY don't. His name is Ace Hargrove. Office is in Billings."

Nick wrote the name on a paper napkin and put it in his pocket. He paid his and Ben's tab and headed to his hotel in Bozeman.

Washington, DC

Spring 1997 The Lobbying World

Wearing his new Brooks Brothers suit and tie, Nick hurried across DC traffic to meet a lobbyist for lunch at Bullfeathers on Capitol Hill. This guy was one of the more connected DC conservatives in the telecom industry and always in the loop on the latest rumors. Nick got there early and took a table on the front patio bordering First Street looking toward the Cannon House Office Building. Spring leaves were in bloom so plenty of shade covered the tables. While waiting for his guest to arrive, a string of black SUVs escorted by some police motorcycles drove by headed toward Pennsylvania Avenue. He thought he recognized a friend in the front passenger seat of the lead vehicle.

Nick called his friend's cell, "Hey, Big Les, what are you up to?"

Big Les or, Leseur Horsrong, who was part French and part American Indian, had worked for a U.S. Senator for several years in the 80s then joined one of the first successful Republican lobbying firms. But by 1997, he was becoming a pretty decent player on his own. Short and stout, Big Les loved to eat and drink and had good connections on the Hill.

"I'm doing advance work for Mugabe."

"Who?"

"The President of Zimbabwe – you know, used to be Rhodesia."

"What kind of advance work?"

"Really just riding shotgun with his security detail. We're headed to the Senatorial Campaign Committee to see the Chairman. We were at a private fundraiser earlier. This guy contributed like a half a million bucks to the party. You should see all the guns and ammo his security guys carry. We could take out a small town if we had to."

"Your firm represents him?"

"Yeah. Him or his government."

"Is he one of the guys taking land from all the farmers in the countrysides of Africa?"

"Whatever. A lot of negative stories, but who knows. They pay a lot, Nick. They're not my client, but my firm pays me. Know what I mean?"

"A pretty high price to pay though, Les."

"About $250,000 a month!"

"No, I meant for you."

"What price?"

"Like a clear conscience?"

"Oh, buddy, I'd 'a left DC a long time ago if I was worried about that."

"Les, how does a foreign leader give money to a U.S. political campaign committee?"

"Some third-party did it for him then got reimbursed, back-channeled it, you know. Hey, we're at the back entrance to the building. I'll call you later."

Nick hung up the phone shaking his head. His lunch guest arrived.

"Hey, Kent. How are you?"

"Good, Nick. And you?"

They ordered food and nodded to familiar faces crossing the patio to enter the restaurant.

After a bit of small talk, Kent asked, "So, Nick, what did you want to talk about?"

Nick laid out a hypothetical situation involving "maybe" someone they both knew. He was hoping to draw Kent out regarding Hally's involvement with the alleged illegal fundraising.

Kent didn't bite. "What exactly are you asking me?"

"Uhm, okay, one, is Hally really as hooked up in the conservative movement as she wants everyone to believe?"

"I think, to say the least, she's finding her niche there – yeah. Look, Nick, you're smart to be concerned about it. I'm sure you want to be loyal to her – she hired you, right?"

"Well, yeah."

"Just don't let her ambitions become your problem."

What Kent was not ready to divulge, but what a handful in DC knew, was that Hally had been summoned for an interview with the Federal Elections Commission's investigators. She and others were barely skirting the edges of federal campaign finance laws. But every time she was set to talk with FEC lawyers, she would suddenly have to be out of town for business. She'd also hired the best and most expensive campaign lawyers in DC who were thus far keeping her one step ahead of any legal peril.

"Okay, thanks for the advice. Kent, one other thing. Are you aware of any rumors about her being involved with Senator Raines in a, uh…romantic sense?"

Kent chuckled. "Can't say that I have, Nick. But some of us do our best not to hear crap like that. I guess Hally can do whatever volunteer political work she chooses to do in her spare time. But, you should just know, Hally's been on more than a few dates with someone I know, Patrick Stark. He's a good guy. He lives in Boston, her home town. Had you heard *that* rumor?" Kent smiled.

"No."

"Maybe you should just tend to the DC rumors about yourself, Nick."

Utah/Montana

Fall 2006 The Wires In-Between

Sheila Parker, the playgirl wife of Congressman Judd Parker and once best friend of Alexandra Martin, finally returned the call that Nick had forced himself to make. Frustrated at a lack of answers from Congressman Parker's staff regarding the apparent investigation of Kale's company's PAC, Nick decided to go straight to the potential source of the Ethics Committee shenanigans. Once he finished explaining the background and reason for his call, Sheila responded.

"And where exactly do you fit in? I know the other two dilweeds all too well, Kale and Cotter. But you sound rather intelligent. Explain to me again your involvement."

"I'm just trying to help my old friend, Kale. Look, I know he's not a perfect person. I've known him a long time. But who is? What *might* be going on in Congressman Parker's office may be a serious crime. Can you help us figure this out?"

Sheila perked up at the thought of her estranged husband's office being involved in a crime. "So you think someone could go to jail?"

"Well, first we have to figure out who's behind this." Nick said.

"And you think one of his staffers might be?" She asked, an edge to her voice.

"Can you think of anyone in his office who would do this to Kale?"

After an awkward silence. "There may be one taint-faced little shit who would try to pull something like that off. But, I'll have to explain later."

What Sheila wouldn't share was that she'd encouraged one of Parker's sycophantic staffers to scare Kale with the Ethics Committee letter. Sheila had fallen harder for Kale than she usually did during her occasional trysts, and got her feelings hurt. This was about revenge. At some point, the staffer dared to question the propriety of what she had him do, but she'd brazenly threatened his job. Thereafter, he kept his distance from her but had put things in motion he could not easily reverse. This lonely staffer didn't have much of a life in DC, and Sheila knew how to play him like a violin.

"Let me see what I can learn," Sheila said with no conviction whatsoever.

Nick then played the only card he had. "Listen, Sheila, you

should understand that Kale and I are working hard to re-elect a Senator in Montana, Clarence Waters. And the one person who wants to see him defeated more than anyone is Mo Kauffman. You help Kale out of this and you're helping Kale hurt Senator Kauffman. Understood?"

"Wow, Nick, you're quite the little machiavellian player, aren't you?"

"I'm just trying to help my friend. The fact that your help will undermine Kauffman is purely a coincidence."

"Well, Nick, are you aware of the murder of Alexandra Martin, a former staffer to then Congressman Mo Kauffman in 1997?"

"Yes, I am. Whatever happened with the investigation around that?"

"The case was never solved. Or should I say, the police were distracted from pursuing it. But you may want to know that Mo Kauffman's money man, Sid Lucas, was a prime suspect in that case. Do you know anything about Sid Lucas – who some refer to as Slimevester Lucas?"

"No, I don't." Nick admitted.

"Unfortunately, I do. And unfortunately I'm the one who introduced him to my best friend from college, Alexandra. She was a beautiful girl and good person. And, I think Sid is responsible for her death."

"Sorry to hear that."

"Well, Nick, considering your interest in Kauffman's affairs, you might want to know that Senator Kauffman is the one who introduced Sid to the New York mob lawyer, Hugh Haddad. And, *he* is the one responsible for having that case buried somewhere in the bowels of the New Jersey justice system."

"I see."

"Nick, if you're being straight with me that helping Kale will somehow hurt Kauffman, then I'll help."

"Sheila, I'm telling you the truth. Please help us in any way you can."

"I'll see what I can do. But in the meantime, try to find some better friends than those two fuckwits. More importantly be sure to let me know if you're coming through Salt Lake for any reason. Maybe you and I should have a further conversation about this whole thing *in person*."

Montana/Washington, DC

Fall 2006 The Campaign Trail / The Lobbying World

It wasn't long before the subcontractors finishing work at the prison near the Crow Reservation began commenting on the comings and goings of the characters who occupied a small wing of the building. It was none of their business who else was working there for whatever reason, but something seemed out of place. In the past they had seen evidence of someone using what they thought was a padlocked portion of the new structure, but lately the usurpers had become more brazen.

When the investors got word of these observations, they advised the contractors to mind their own business. When Waters' deputy chief, Zach, got wind of the news, the only question he asked was: "Are they paying their rent in full and *on time*?" One thing no one expected was that the new renters might end up living in the prison. But it had electricity, a kitchen, plumbing and five hundred beds, so it was hard to make a case against it.

In fact, with the rents being shelled out by the new camping gear company, the contractors were getting paid again and complaints ceased. They also paid in cash, so everyone's tax circumstances improved, and soon nobody was concerned if that prison wasn't open. Back in DC, however, once Waters accepted the fact that someone from his office was responsible for the million-dollar earmark for the dormant prison, he began trying to get it opened. The longer the whole legislative process was taking, the more Waters' staffer, Zach, was determined to keep the prison closed.

Without informing Zach, Clarence scheduled a press conference and announced that he'd requested the Senate Leadership authorize an investigation into how the wayward Montana prison was built without state or federal authorization, and why it wasn't open or housing any prisoners. Without telling Waters, Zach had written the letter under Waters' signature to the Bureau of Prisons requesting it be authorized. That letter gave the investors in the project credibility with a local Montana bank to get a short term extension on their sizable construction loan.

Waters' investigation request not only caught Zach Gerkin off guard, it attracted the attention of certain criminal defense lawyers who have a general bias against prisons, but who had a particularly personal interest in keeping this one closed. Within hours Mo Kauffman received a call in his Senate office from his old law school friend, New York lawyer, Hugh Haddad. Hugh had helped Mo ten years prior to effectively shut down the Jersey City police investigation into the death of his staffer, Alexandra Martin.

Haddad got right to the point. "So, Mo, you're part of the Senate Leadership now, right? You're doin' pretty good down there in DC."

"Well, I'm actually just head of the DSCC – the campaign arm. It's not really…"

Haddad interrupted, "Have you seen this request by some Senator from Montana to begin an investigation into why this prison out there isn't up and running?"

"I'm aware of it."

"He asked the Senate to look into it – right?"

"He requested the Senate Republican leadership to authorize an investigation. They're in the majority. You understand that my party is not in the majority. And the majority leadership could not care less what I…"

"I'll tell you what I understand. You need to stop that investigation and do it fast."

"Hugh, what the hell do you care if some prison in the middle of Montana is open or not? Didn't you ask me for a referral to a firm regarding a for-profit prison company? Didn't they hire that firm without blinking an eye?"

"Let's just say it's best you don't know everything. Okay, Senator?"

"Well, Hugh, you should just know, I don't have the power to tell the Republican Leadership in the Senate what to do."

"Well, Senator, you should just know, if that investigation moves forward, you're going to have even less power than that. Have a nice day."

Two days later the *Washington Herald* headline read, "Origin of Illegal Prison Questioned." The story went on to describe the construction of a prison in Montana that was never authorized. The reporter sought responses from every member of the Montana Congressional Delegation but received none. Mo Kauffman and his consultants had been working the storyline.

Senator Kauffman figured he could kill two birds with one stone. On behalf of his lawyer, Haddad, it might intimidate anyone trying to open the prison. On the other hand, it would focus more attention on Clarence Waters for irresponsible conduct. He'd wait another few days to clarify who in the Senate sought federal funding for the dormant jail house.

Within an hour of the story breaking, he got a call from Hugh Haddad in New York.

Mo picked up the phone, smiling, "How did you like that story, Hugh? Figured that might scare off anybody thinking of opening that prison."

"Mo, are you responsible for that story?"

"Let's just say, I did my part."

"You idiot. We don't want a lot of attention focused on that place! We just want it kept closed."

"Hugh, your paranoia is beginning to concern me. And don't tell me I don't need to know. I'm the one who referred you to the DC lobbyists trying to open that facility. You asked for a firm with no prison-related expertise. I kept it all low key like you asked."

"Mo, trust me on this prison matter. It happens to be important to another client of mine. Okay?"

What Haddad would not disclose was that he was on retainer to the Slipper Gold Refining Company which was trying to persuade the Crow Tribe to allow the opening of a new mine on the reservation.

"What's the client's interest, Hugh?

"I can't talk about the work I do for other clients. You know that. Now, you just keep doing...whatever you do down there in Washington and leave well enough alone."

Haddad slammed the phone down.

Bozeman, Montana

Fall 2006 The Campaign Trail

Nick was surprised when he arrived at the Bozeman airport to pick up Burch Maloney to find him accompanied by his investigator *and* Lisa.

"Hey Nick, thanks for the ride. This is my investigator, Manuel Sandoval, and you know Lisa. She just wanted another visit to Montana."

He shook Manuel's hand, "Nice to meet you." He nodded at Lisa, "Welcome back." She looked leaner and more fit than during her last visit.

He drove them to an off-airport rental agency to lease a four wheel drive pickup. They followed him to the Sunset Hotel. After settling into their rooms, Burch and Manuel met Nick in the hotel restaurant to discuss their latest findings. They had learned more through various contacts around the country and wanted to confirm them in person. One fact was that based upon the trail of cash flows back into Mexico, they believed that an East Coast connection was involved with the uptick in meth on the reservations. Although the meth was free to the Native Americans, somebody somewhere was paying for it.

Without a doubt, the meth trade had its unique aspects and networks. But Burch's anti-drug advocates and law enforcement colleagues throughout the country gathered a lot of unique information. Burch's olive-skinned investigative partner, Manuel, who was of Pascua Yaqui native descent, grew up along the Arizona-Mexico border. He knew a great deal about border gangs and their methods. Their plan was to travel in and around the Crow Reservation and try to acquire some meth in order to interact with a supplier.

"Burch, look I really appreciate your help. And I'm all in on this endeavor – in fact up to my eyeballs – and want no distractions. But I don't want anybody getting hurt or killed on this venture. By the way, that's the largest reservation in Montana. It's over three thousand square miles, how do you even know where to begin?"

"Don't worry," Manuel clapped Nick on the shoulder, "this is not our first run at such operations. These gangs need to be taken seriously and they need to be taken down."

About then Nick and Manuel were distracted looking past Burch to the hotel lobby. Lisa had appeared in a taut bikini with a hotel towel draped around her tanned body.

"Hey, honey. I'm going to take a Jacuzzi and swim a few laps in the pool. Just wanted to let you know where I'll be."

With that, she turned and sauntered toward the pool. Nick watched her walk away. He couldn't help but stare. Manuel caught Nick staring and smiled at him.

Burch interrupted, "Sorry guys, she insisted on coming. She'll only be here until day after tomorrow."

Anxious to change the subject, Nick asked, "So, when will you guys go to the reservation?"

Manuel responded again, "I think tomorrow. Tomorrow night might be a good opportunity. Dealers like doing business in the later part of the day or at dusk so they can commute back in the dark to help make sure they're not followed."

"I see," Nick nodded. "Well, be aware. The Crow are apparently having their own disputes about meth these days. The current tribal chief is being accused, perhaps unfairly, of letting crime and meth get out of control there. Watch where you step."

"I know that turf too, Nick," Manuel said confidently.

After some discussion, Nick found himself studying Manuel's near palpable intensity. There seemed to be something deeper driving him than just the Crow Reservation meth problem. Once they began plotting out travel plans and tactics, Nick left them to finish their coffees. As he walked past the front desk toward the elevators to return to his room, Lisa materialized by the hotel receptionist asking for an extra room key. She was dripping wet.

"How's the water?"

"Oh, hey! It felt great."

Nick continued to the elevators. The front desk attendant handed Lisa a new card key, and she walked to where Nick was waiting for the doors to open.

She stood next to him. "So you're staying at this hotel too?"

"Yes, I've been here for a couple of months."

"Why?"

"Working for a client."

"You mean the *Waters For Senate* campaign?"

"No. A management company out of New York. Has to do

with a prison project."

"I see."

The doors opened. Both stepped in.

"You look good, Nick." Lisa said, unconvincingly.

"So do you. You been working out since I last saw you?"

"Me? Oh, no. No time."

"What's keeping you so busy?"

"Work. Texas legal aid work. Actually helping people who really need help."

"I see."

The doors opened on the third floor. They both stepped out.

Lisa smiled, "I hope we're not across the hall from each other."

"I didn't know you were joining Burch or I would've put you guys up in different hotel. Thought it was just work."

"Oh, sorry. I'm only here for a couple days. I like it here."

"Yeah. Me, too."

Nick nodded indifferently and began to walk toward his room. But it was no use. He could feel her watching him. He stopped and turned around. "Lisa, you going to be around tomorrow afternoon?"

"Yeah. Why?"

"Thought maybe we could have a cup of coffee and, you know, talk."

"I'd like that."

Montana/New York

Fall 2006 The Wires In-Between

Hugh Haddad picked up his office phone. "Ace Hargrove, to what do I owe this rare call from Big Sky Country? You still keeping drunks out of jail in Billings?"

"When I'm able. It's still beautiful here, but maybe too quiet for a busy New York lawyer."

"What can I do for you, Ace?"

"Hugh, we've worked together on a few things. We've helped each other out – right? I just thought you might want to know something."

"Okay."

"Remember you asked me to have my construction worker client introduce your guys from New Jersey to some tribal leaders?"

"Yeah."

"Well, he did. And, first of all, they stiffed him which really isn't cool to do to hardworking people in Montana. But more importantly, my guy, Benny, tells me that what he's hearing on the reservation is that your boys are telling people some things that don't make sense."

"Don't make sense to whom, Ace?"

"Don't make sense to most anybody, including me. I can tell you for many reasons, Hugh, that Clarence Waters is not responsible for the increase in meth on that reservation."

"What? What did you say?"

"Now, I've heard stupid politically motivated rumors about Waters being involved in a lot of things. But I hear this meth connection talk, and I know it's bullshit. At first I figure it's just usual election year nonsense like we always have. But when I hear the rest – that Waters is involved because he's backing the gold mine company candidate for tribal leader, then I know there's some intentional bullshit going on. One, I know that Clarence and Big Jim, the current Crow Tribe Chairman, go back a ways. And two, I can't see Clarence supporting any New York company on anything like that, especially in the middle of his reelection campaign – just makes no sense."

Haddad sighed heavily. "What the fuck?"

"Look, Hugh, I don't know what it's all about and as you're aware, I don't need to know. But you might want to consider reining in your guy out here before somebody else does."

Western Montana

Fall 2006 The Campaign Trail

Manuel drove the pickup down I-90 toward Billings as Burch talked by cell with local law-enforcement about recent meth activity. Burch and Manuel decided to investigate potential Crow Reservation-related transactions near Billings as it was the closest large city and a likely place for a dealer to try to blend in after a deal. The Crow Reservation is vast and bordered by Wyoming to the south and the Northern Cheyenne Reservation to its East. The Big Horn River runs north through the middle of it, and it encompasses over 3,000 square miles – a lot of ground to cover.

After coffee with a Billings detective, they drove past a local theater where the movie, *The Hills Have Eyes* was playing. Burch and Manuel both looked up at the marquee, neither spoke. Once on the reservation, Manuel talked with some men hanging around a deserted store, but they offered little information. Burch drove them to an abandoned gas station where some teenagers were milling. Manuel asked about any meth activity in the area. Two of the boys nodded when pressed. One said he knew of some meth-heads who he'd seen come and go, but didn't know who they were. After a few more stops, Manuel suggested they visit the nearby town of Crow Agency, where the tribal headquarters was located.

Around 3:00, Nick phoned Lisa's hotel room to see if she was up for a cup of coffee. When he got no answer, instead of leaving a message he just hung up. It was, after all, her and Burch's room. He decided to go hangout in the lobby and check e-mails. As soon as he sat down, Lisa walked in the front entrance.

"Hey, Nick."

"Oh, hey, Lisa."

"You still want to get together?" Lisa asked.

"If you have the time."

"Yeah."

They meandered toward the hotel bar, but Lisa asked if there was somewhere else close by they could go. They walked across the parking lot to The Old Chicago restaurant. It was a perfect fall afternoon, so they sat at an outdoor table. Before the waitress could hand them their menus, Lisa spoke quickly, "I'll have your house Pinot Noir and a glass of ice water."

Nick thought for a second, looking at Lisa, "I'll have the same. Thanks."

"Nick, Montana is a cool place. I can see why you like it here. Reminds me a little of the town where your family's old mountain house is."

"Was."

"What?"

"After my family sold it to a developer, it was bulldozed."

"Wow, Nick I'm really sorry. You loved that old place."

After a few seconds, "But you know what? I've always liked it out here. It's my next best place. Or as the local saying here goes, the last best place."

"How long have you been in Bozeman?"

"A couple of months now actually. This client project keeps going on and on."

"Where do you live?"

"I still live in DC."

"I presume not the same studio apartment I once knew?"

His thoughts dove under her words to their romance twenty years prior. "No, I gave it up. I bought a townhouse looking out over the Potomac, down by the Georgetown waterfront."

The waitress put their wine on the table and disappeared. They both took a big sip.

Lisa, said, "Hey, that's not bad is it?"

They both took another big sip. Nick asked, "You want to order lunch or anything?"

"Not for me. Thanks." Lisa replied quickly.

Nick started, "So, how have you been, stranger?"

"Oh, I've been doing okay."

"It's been a long time, Lisa."

"Seems like a long time. It was so bizarre to see your face on the street a few weeks ago. I can't believe one of us didn't overreact."

"I know! Lisa, I was so shocked. I didn't know what to say."

"Me, either."

There was a drawn-out silence. Lisa put her empty glass down, and leaned forward,

"Nick, were you never going to call me?"

"C-c-call you? Lisa…I thought about calling you a thousand times."

"Why didn't you?"

"I wasn't sure you wanted me to, and frankly I wasn't sure what I would say."

"I guess I can understand that," Lisa said.

"And, you?"

"Nick. I thought to call you many times."

"But?"

"But, just couldn't. I really wanted to talk. We left so many loose ends."

The waitress interrupted. "You two know what you want yet?"

Lisa held up her wine glass, "I think we'll both take another one of these."

Nick hadn't been hurt by Lisa's departure in 1986. She hadn't left him. She'd been indicted by a federal prosecutor, and returned to Texas to defend herself. And Nick had not left her. He'd been abducted and hospitalized by thugs associated with Lisa's then boss – a congressman who was indicted for drug smuggling. It was the chaotic departure, the awkward legally-imposed distance, the loss of friendship they once shared, and consequent curiosity about it all that had stayed with them both for so many years.

The waitress walked away. "Loose ends? Lisa, there were more loose ends than a shooting comet. One question though, why did you leave DC the day I was abducted?"

"The Justice Department made me! Their chief investigator called me and said he had a ticket for me to fly to San Antonio."

"Why?"

"He believed you and I were both in danger and wanted me somewhere safe."

"They never told me that, Lisa."

"Why didn't you tell me you were going to testify against me?"

"I never testified against you. I was subpoenaed to testify to the grand jury about your boss, Congressman Staunton's dealings. It was all about him. Occasionally I was asked if Lisa Taft was with me or aware of what I was doing. I never brought up your name or offered anything culpable about you. I would never have done that!"

"You just said, 'Lisa Taft.'"

"What? No I didn't. I said I was occasionally asked if *Lisa Castile* was aware of what I was doing. And I told them unequivocally, no."

Lisa covered a smirk, then offered a long smile.

Nick rolled his eyes and looked away.

"But, Nick, I was told that your testimony was part of the basis for my indictment."

"Then they used my words out of context. Lisa, I was trying to protect you."

Her eyes began to tear up. "Nick, I was in love with you. I felt so fucking betrayed."

The waitress placed their second round of wine on the table. "You folks doing okay?"

"Yeah, thanks." They said in unison.

"Lisa, all I can tell you is I was asked questions strictly about Staunton's activities, and what I had observed. They never asked me about anything you had ever personally said or done."

She sighed, "Well, somebody lied to me." Lisa had often discounted Nick's kind words in the past but at that moment, would appreciate even a few syllables.

"Lisa, you don't trust me?"

"Nick, I wouldn't trust you if you parted the Red Sea. I still think about you, though – a lot."

Nick nodded without looking. "I...I...always thought we would meet again."

"That's it? The best you've got?" Lisa said, laughing.

"Look, Lisa, you were not just my girlfriend, you were my best friend. I appreciated everything you did for me and taught me in DC when I arrived there. Like everyone who gets to that town with no experience, I was somewhat naïve, and you helped me tremendously."

"Somewhat naïve? You were such a babe in the woods, I didn't know whether to advise you or burp you. Unfortunately, instead, I fell in love with you."

"But, Lisa, this is complicated. Your boyfriend's my client!"

"My boyfriend? Give me a break. Guy changes his mind like every day. You dating anyone?"

"Uh...no." Nick said, distracted.

She stared at him. "So, you're happy going it alone?"

He shrugged his shoulders, "No. Not really."

"I so wish you had called, Nick. Just once. I had so much to tell you. And now, I'm sitting here wondering what to say – can't think of any of it."

They both drained their second glass of Pinot.

Burch and Manuel continued their quest to the town of Crow Agency. The wide open plains stretching east into central Montana disappeared into the horizon. Crow Agency was located about an hour from Billings. It was the site of the Bureau of Indian Affairs headquarters for the entire Crow Nation and the seat of the Crow Tribal Council, the governing body of the tribe. Not far away was the Little Bighorn Monument which memorialized the overwhelming defeat of General George Custer and the U.S. 7th Cavalry in their attempt to take on the Lakota, Northern Cheyenne, and Arapaho Tribes in 1876.

They exited I-90 at Crow Agency, and after circling a gas station and local mercantile store, parked in front of the building that housed the tribal government. There were several grand old trees separating the sidewalk from the building's entrance. Manuel knew their interaction would be limited. They were outsiders. An employee exited the front door as they approached. They stood on the front steps of the building and exchanged polite introductions. He seemed wary of their intentions.

They assured him they just had a few questions. Others in the building partially opened their window shades to see the strangers to whom the tribal employee was speaking. After some back and forth, the staffer acknowledged that meth had become considerably more prevalent on the reservation and was becoming a big problem for everyone.

He was angry and seemed discouraged by that reality. "Yeah, and some are trying to pin those meth problems on my boss, the Chairman, so their candidate can beat him in our upcoming tribal election."

"Who's trying to pin it on your guy?"

"The open pit gold mine assholes."

"Why?"

"Because our chairman won't give them a permit to put one of their polluting mines on our land. The crazy bastards. There hasn't been gold successfully mined near here in forever. [25] I even heard one of their henchmen say it was Montana's federal politicians causing the meth increase."

Manuel and Burch looked at each other warily. Manuel asked if there were specific geographic regions where usage was worse or had recently picked up. The staffer pointed west and indicated that southwest of Crow Agency there had been some dustups with outsiders. But as he began to elaborate, his boss pulled up in a truck and walked toward them. The staffer introduced him, summarized their backgrounds and explained their inquiry.

The stone-faced man replied, "What do we look like, the DEA? We don't answer to strangers about alleged activity here. And we don't need some Texas Ranger snooping around trying to help us. If we want your help, we'll ask for it. Have a nice day." He walked inside the building and slammed the door.

With that, Manuel and Burch thanked the staffer, retreated back to their truck and were on their way.

After their third glass of wine and much conversation dancing just short of the truth, Nick walked Lisa back across the parking lot to their hotel. Once out of the elevator, they began to part ways again, but Lisa stopped and gave Nick a hug.

"I'm glad we at least got a chance to talk, Nick. Thanks."

Touching her briefly and smelling her hair was intense, but he felt no warmth in her bearing. "Me, too, Lisa. Take care of yourself," he said a little too coldly as he moved toward his room.

Lisa walked the hallway down to her room, but turned around. "Hey, Nick. You don't happen to have a Band-Aid, do you? These shoes have given me a terrible blister."

"Sure. I should have one."

Lisa followed him to his room. Nick slid the card key in and held the door open. "Don't look too close. I've been living out of this place for almost ten weeks."

"Wow, what a mess." Lisa laughed, "They do have maid service here – right?"

He turned on the light in his bathroom and fumbled through his dopp kit looking for a bandage. The only chair in the room was overflowing with dirty clothes. Lisa sat on his bed.

"This isn't a bad hotel" she offered. "In fact, it's kind of nice."

"Yeah, it's pretty comfortable. I'm actually beginning to feel at home here." Nick mumbled from the bathroom.

He came out with one crinkled soggy-looking bandage. "Sorry, this is all I could find. But I think it might still work."

"That's the most pathetic excuse for a Band-Aid I've ever seen."

"Yeah I guess. But let's give it a try. Where's your blister?"

Lisa kicked off her shoes. "Well, there's one on both heels. Take your pick, doctor."

She put her right leg up on the bed. Nick sat on the foot of the bed and lifted her leg onto his knee. As he did, her denim skirt hiked up her toned thighs a couple of inches. Nick was surprised when he looked at her heel. She had a serious blister. "That looks kind of painful."

"Not really. Just annoying."

He peeled the bandage, wrapped it around her heel, and smoothed out the edges. "How's that?"

"Better. Thanks. Now what about my other foot? Is there another sickly looking bandage in that scary kit of yours?"

"Let me look."

Lisa lay back on the bed.

He walked into the bathroom again rummaging through his toiletries. He stared into the mirror and instructively shook his head at himself. Finding another bandage, he returned to the bed. Lisa had her head on his pillow with her tanned legs slightly bent. As he sat back down, she extended one foot forward and brought the other back, bending her knee and exposing most of what her skirt was concealing. He lifted her heel with his hand. She briefly scratched her calf with her other foot which required she shift her hips. Nothing she was doing was making her any less tempting. He rolled his eyes at her.

"What?" She said defensively.

He looked the other way. "Look at me, Nick."

His eyes came back to hers.

"Do you really think I came out here to go shopping?"

"I...I don't know."

She sat up close to him. "Since I saw you a few weeks ago, tell me you haven't been thinking about us."

"I have."

"And, why do you think that is?"

"Because of the way we left things. How awkward it was."

"And why else?"

"Because there's strong chemistry between us. It's hard to deny."

"It's hard to deny, Nick, because it's so real." She put her hand on his and lifted it to her chest. "Feel how fast my heart is beating."

They embraced and held a long kiss. Then groped and kissed some more as if deprived of oxygen. After twenty years, the familiarity was uncanny. Her skin, his feel, her taste – it took them back in time. She wrapped her arms and legs around him. Their clothes came off sporadically as their lips remained together. Then he was inside her. She would not let him lean away, wanting to kiss him endlessly. Eventually he felt a familiar shudder and her body let go. Although it was all over within a half an hour, it felt like an eternity to them. Both were spent.

New Jersey

Fall 2006 The Lobbying World

Senator Mo Kauffman attended a fundraiser for a young congressional candidate in rural New Jersey. His moneyman, Sid, had raised a significant sum of money for the young politician for the upcoming 2006 congressional elections. The event was crawling with lobbyists. When the candidate spotted Mo, he thanked him for introducing him to Mr. Lucas and bragged about the great job he had been doing raising money for his campaign.

"Just one thing, Senator. Does Sid just drop off every now and then?"

"How do you mean?" Kauffman asked.

"Well, we were talking like every other day for a while. We had a lot going on with the campaign. And, I know he was headed out West on a trip but I haven't heard back from him in at least two weeks."

"Where out West? On what trip?"

"I thought he said Montana."

As a criminal defense attorney, Hugh Haddad had to tolerate many things. But one thing he could never abide was a double-cross. It didn't take long for him to put it together once Ace Hargrove informed him of the unexpected message being spread on the Crow Reservation. Sid owed Hugh a lot, and Hugh believed he could count on Sid to hire the right people and carry out a fairly simple task.

So, sometime previously, Hugh had laid out the whole plan against the Crow tribal leader.

"Sid, meth is all over that reservation. It's a disaster for the Native American community." Hugh conveniently left out some of the details as to how so much meth got out there. "The current chairman's dismal record on crime and drug enforcement is a joke. Your task is to hire a couple of jamokes, get out to Montana and help convince voting members of that tribe that their leader, Big Jim, is to blame for the meth problem. Got it? Keep it simple – one plus one equals two. Get in, get out, and come back here and give me a report."

Sid owed Hugh a lot, including making the Jersey City Police investigation of Alexandra Martin's death go away. Sid was convinced that Hugh was the only person alive who knew that he may be guilty of involuntary manslaughter. But in reality, if Sid had not gone to Senator Mo Kauffman for help, and Mo hadn't brought Haddad in on the case and indirectly helped pay him, Sid may well have ended up in jail. Consequently, whenever Hugh said to Sid, "You owe me," what Sid heard instead was: *You owe Mo Kauffman.*

———————

The Slipper Gold Refining Company's stake in the Crow Reservation tribal election was huge. The company's numbers had been upside down for two straight years – not due to any lack of effective mineral extraction, but to incompetent and greedy management. Their geological research convinced them there was gold to be extracted on the Crow Reservation. The company's executives were putting heavy pressure on Haddad's firm to influence the outcome of the Crow election. The company needed the tribe to approve a gold mine permit, and they needed it soon.

Once Sid accepted the job Hugh asked him to do, he did some homework on the Big Sky state. One of the first things he realized was that the nasty U.S. Senate race out there was close and coming down to the wire, and he knew how critical it was to Senator Mo Kauffman's success as head of the Democratic Senatorial Campaign Committee. Sid didn't know much about Clarence Waters or his relatively unknown opponent, Evan Sutter, but he knew they were in a tight race and that every vote would count – even the relatively lower percentage of votes on the Crow Reservation.

So, instead of spending his time out west helping Haddad spread rumors about the Tribal Chairman, Sid decided to help the person he owed more – Senator Mo Kauffman. Sid and his cohorts spent their time trashing Senator Waters and blaming him for the growing meth problem instead of the Tribal Chief. Sid figured, who in New York would ever know what was being said in the middle of bumblefuck nowhere on the desolate Crow Reservation?

What Sid didn't know was that Hugh had some very tough

people working that reservation for various unscrupulous reasons. He also wasn't aware Hugh had a resourceful criminal lawyer, Ace Hargrove, in nearby Billings who knew and heard a lot. What Sid also didn't know was how in the hell he got hung up by his feet at the end of a chain in a very cold room in the middle of bumblefuck nowhere.

Crow Reservation, Montana

Fall 2006 The Campaign Trail

Burch knew that one reason it was easy to commit crimes, or distribute illegal drugs on the Crow Reservation was that compared to its physical expanse, there existed scant law enforcement. The handful of police there have limited and conflicting jurisdictions. On most reservations, the tribal law enforcement, which sometimes contracts officers from the Bureau of Indian Affairs, has jurisdiction over Native Americans but cannot arrest non-native people. The Montana State and local police have jurisdiction over non-native people, but not arrest authority over Native Americans within a reservation. And though the FBI has jurisdiction over all major crimes, the total number of officers of any kind is miniscule compared to the size of the Crow Reservation.[26]

That challenging mosaic made it easy for dealers to move in and out of the near three million acres of the Crow Nation and easy for cartel meth to spill into the reservation directly from Mexico.[27] It also left Burch and Manuel basically on their own. But after covering a lot of ground southwest of Crow Agency, Burch was hopeful they were on the trail of a potential meth distributor. Two shy Crow women in the small town of Saint Xavier, both mothers of high school children, had confided that men in a van had been seen around that afternoon not long before Burch and Manuel showed up.

Considering their recent unfriendly encounter with the senior tribal official, they requested the women not mention their conversation to anyone. They headed west out of town on Route 91 in the direction the suspicious vehicle had apparently exited. Since Manuel and Burch believed they were onto their only decent lead, they decided to stay the course through the night if necessary. According to their map, the closest town, Pryor, Montana, was dead ahead near the western edge of the reservation.

———————

When Lisa put down the phone after hearing the news from Burch that he would not be returning that night, she was ecstatic. Nick got the same call in his room from Burch about the day's events and their potential lead along with the news that they would likely not be back until the next day. Nick was relieved on the one hand but regretful on the other. He and Lisa had parted company only an hour earlier. Their encounter had not seemed right or wrong at the time, mostly just an affirmation of how much they'd genuinely missed each other. But as he put down the phone, he was looking at things through a slightly different prism.

Nick's hotel phone rang again. "Nick, Burch and Manuel are staying over by Billings," Lisa enthusiastically reported. "My flight home to Texas leaves tomorrow morning. Will you take me to dinner at that cool old Montana steakhouse you were telling me about?"

Nick was caught off guard as a jumble of conflicting impulses left him little room to think. "The…Oasis?" After a painful pause, "Uh, I guess. Sure. Why not?"

Nick regretted the words as soon as he hung up.

That evening, Lisa and Nick took a slow drive out Frontage Road west of Bozeman. They rolled into Manhattan at 7:30 and worked their way to a corner table at the Oasis Steakhouse. It felt somewhat like a perp walk for Nick, who was relieved to see no familiar faces. Lisa excused herself to use the ladies room but took her time looking around into other parts of the restaurant and at the plain-framed fading cowboy art on the walls. The casual nature of the place left her unaware that they were the much admired western landscape prints of the iconic Charles M. Russel.

As Nick was looking at e-mails on his BlackBerry, a waitress came by to offer menus and take drink orders.

"Who dat?" Ava asked with an enthusiastic smile.

Nick looked up, startled. "Oh, uhm, hey, that's, uh…a friend of one of my clients."

"You sure?"

"What's *that* supposed to mean?"

"I don't know. You guys just looked kind of familiar with each other, that's all."

Nick had hoped Ava would not be working that night. His

blissful post-reunion haze was quickly fading. "Oh, yeah. I've known her for a while."

"Okay. Want a drink?"

"Maybe some wine. I'll wait for her to come back."

"All right. By the way, Kale's due here any minute."

"What?! Kale's in town?"

"Yeah. He didn't call you?"

"No."

"Says he wants to settle what's been goin' on between us 'once and for all.' He's driving me nuts. I think tonight will be the final curtain."

"Oh, Ava. Why can't you guys just get along?"

"You tell me. But your friend, Kale, is plumb crazy. That's my conclusion."

"When do you expect him?"

"One never knows. I thought he'd be here by now. I'll be back to check on you guys."

That was a bad development. Kale knew Lisa all too well from their past days back in DC. He also knew the personal history between them too well. Nick had not told Kale about unexpectedly crossing paths with Lisa. He didn't want to hear Kale's lecture. Kale never trusted Lisa when Nick was dating her in Washington years before. Kale believed Lisa was working on behalf of Congressman Staunton all along and had sabotaged Nick's efforts regarding the congressman's illegal activities. Nick was scrambling for a plausible excuse to leave the restaurant.

Lisa sat back down at the table. "What a cool old place, Nick. I love it here."

"Yeah. Pretty cool, huh."

"What's the matter with you?" Lisa asked.

"Nothing."

"Nick, are you feeling weird about today?"

"Uh, no. It was just an unexpected development, you know?"

"Yeah."

"Oh my God, am I seeing a ghost?" Kale yelled from the dining room entrance. Other restaurant patrons turned his way. He walked to Nick and Lisa's table. "Lisa Castile, as I live and breathe. What the hell are you doing in Montana?"

"Oh, wow, Kale." Lisa stood and gave him a big hug. "Well, that's a long story."

"I'm all ears. Nick, you dawg. How is it that your two worlds have crossed again?"

"Hey, Kale. I didn't know you were in town. Why didn't you tell me?"

"Oh, last-minute decision. Wanted to see Ava, you know."

"I know."

"But, what the hell! I haven't seen you two in the same room in twenty years. What gives?"

Nick began, "Oh, well, unbeknownst to me, Lisa does some work with a client of my firm. And they asked if I could connect some dots for a colleague of a client. And imagine our faces when she showed up at...at...this restaurant tonight where I told them to have us meet. I didn't recognize her name...because...she's married. Can you imagine?"

Lisa looked at Nick with her eyes and mouth wide open, but was grateful for the lie. "Wow, that's quite a story. Well, Lisa, nice to see you again," Kale said looking at Nick from the corner of his eye. "Mind if I join you?"

Nick reacted, "No, not at all."

Lisa added, "That would be great."

Kale said, "Let me just get a drink from the bar first." He walked away.

Lisa looked at Nick, "What a raft of bullshit that was, Nick. You and Kale still close?"

"Yeah."

"What's he doing out here?"

"Lisa, that's long story. But you know what, I better tell you."

One of the things Nick had to do well as a lobbyist was tell complicated stories with most of the necessary facts within about sixty seconds. He went on to recount the history of Senator Waters' and Kale's friendship. He also explained about the campaign and the votes on the reservations – and of it being Kale's idea to hire a drug dealer expert. He clarified that Kale was not aware that Nick had hired someone from Texas – and that he would not be made aware of the specifics around it. He also provided a quick footnote about Kale and Ava's romantic history conveniently leaving out his own prior dalliance with Ava.

Lisa was almost speechless. "Okay."

"Look, let's just have a drink with Kale and get outta here. I don't want our whole night to get bogged down with all of this. I know another cool place just up the road."

She offered a generous smile. "Nick, your life's always complicated. But can I try one of the appetizers before we leave?"

Kale returned and joined Nick and Lisa in the dining room. Ava stopped by the table to take orders. Lisa ordered a steak appetizer and a glass of wine. Nick ordered wine and indicated they would hold off on an entrée. Kale held up his glass and winked, "I'm good. Thanks."

To Nick's surprise, Kale did not begin to cross examine him or Lisa. Instead he offered a toast to old friends, and then went on to describe his distraught state of mind over his and Ava's situation. "Lisa, I'm glad you're here, I'd like your advice, as a woman, as to what's going on with me and Ava." He was fidgeting like he'd sat in itching powder.

Kale gave a rather lengthy history, which was surprising to Nick since they'd only been dating about six weeks. After that, Kale looked down at the table with a discouraged gaze.

"I'm pretty lost here. She makes me constantly live in my head."

Lisa spoke up, "Look, Kale, considering what you've described, it seems like you need to just put your cards on the table. Ask her what she's thinking. You're torturing yourself because you don't seem to know where her heart is. Just ask her."

"Really?" Kale said with a dubious tone.

"Yes. It's the only way at this point to find out. If she's worth her salt, she'll be honest."

"I don't know if I want to hear the answer."

"Then you probably won't. But you need to make a deal with yourself. Whatever she says, you'll take it at face value and you won't second-guess her."

"Yeah, I hear you. What do you think, Nick?"

"Oh, for crying out loud, Kale, all you and I talk about anymore is Ava. I agree with Lisa. Just ask her and put an end to this never-ending drama."

"You think that'll end it?!"

"No! But at least you'll know where you stand."

"Right. Okay. Thanks, guys."

————————

Just after dusk, Manuel and Burch rolled into the small town of Pryor, Montana near the western boundary of the reservation. They believed the suspect van was at a gas station at the town's lone intersection. Burch struggled to see through binoculars so he could e-mail the plate numbers of the van to colleagues in Texas to run through a national data base. He doubted he had enough cell service to transfer the data. They hadn't seen anyone enter or leave the van. The small station had a single windowed store front but no visible door. There was an out of order sign on the gas pump. Burch and Manuel remained in their rental truck at what would be about three blocks away if the non-sprawling town had anything resembling a city block.

While Manuel was describing what he wished he had to eat, two men appeared from behind the small building and got into the van. A thin film of smoke from distant wildfires had blown into that end of the reservation obscuring their already challenged vision. The van traveled west out of town. Manuel started the truck and followed far behind. Burch checked the map. They were headed in the direction of the town of Edgar located just outside the edge of the reservation.

"Burch, where the hell are these guys going?"

"Don't know."

Before long the van took a hard right and pulled off the road out of sight. Since their truck was the only other vehicle on the remote road, they held back and turned off their headlights so as not to be seen. Unfortunately, as soon as Manuel killed the lights, pitch blackness surrounded them. Manuel eased to the side of the road.

"Now what?"

"Where the hell did they go?" Burch asked.

"I thought I saw their headlights into the woods ahead on the right. Turn on just our parking lights and move forward slowly. Let's see if we can get a glimpse of them."

Progressing cautiously, they came upon an entrance to Chief Plenty Coups National Park. Manuel drove past it hoping the van occupants did not see them, then pulled off the shoulder as far as he could and turned off the lights. There were very few trees or other obstacles hindering anyone's vision of the open landscape.

There was nowhere to disguise a pickup truck. The van apparently drove around a metal bar gate and into the park. They decided to go on foot to investigate. They brought an infrared camera and low-density flashlights.

"What are they doing out here at this time of night?" Asked Manuel.

"Don't know."

"We haven't seen any other cars, right?"

"Nope."

They walked quietly on dried-out sage brush toward a few ash trees clustered together until they could see what looked like a road and a cul-de-sac. Burch looked through the camera lens. The only vehicle he could see was the van but he could see the silhouette of a few people.

"Let's use the cover of those two trees to close in and take some photos." Burch put his finger to his lips, and motioned for Manuel to move forward.

They walked more softly as they got closer. Manuel stepped on a stick that cracked the night sky like a bullet.

"Will you be quiet?!" Burch yelled in a whisper.

Before either could take another step, two headlights near the van lit up the landscape. They dove into the dirt behind the trees.

Lisa and Nick left Kale at the restaurant to ponder his future with Ava. Nick drove just up the road from Manhattan to the Land of Magic steakhouse in Logan. He had promised to meet Kale for breakfast the next morning to hear how things turned out. Lisa asked for a somewhat secluded table in the dining room and they ordered dinner.

"So, Nick, I guess we've crossed a few boundaries here."

"Yes. Yes, we have."

"I'm okay with it though. You?"

"Okay with what?" Nick asked.

Her head cautioned her heart, "You and me being together."

"What about Burch?"

"Hmmm…I'll have to figure that out."

"Figure what out?"

"How to amicably end that relationship."

"And tell him about us? Lisa, Burch is my client, and doing very important work. He cannot know about today."

"I have no intention of telling him, Nick! But, considering how quickly I've fallen back in with you, I shouldn't be with him. That's all I'm saying. I'm frankly a little shocked."

"At yourself?" Nick had not considered that Burch would be so disposable.

"At *our* circumstances, Nick."

Their entrées arrived. They ate in silence and drove back to their hotel. Lisa came to Nick's room. "Can we watch TV? My flight's pretty early tomorrow morning. I'm catching the hotel shuttle. Maybe we can just hang out."

Lisa stayed in Nick's room lying on the bed with her head on his chest until he fell asleep. Then she quietly went down the hall to her room.

Burch and Manuel stayed as still as possible while the headlights beamed toward them in the darkness.

"Probably a fuckin' bear," said one man with a Midwest accent. He threw a beer bottle in Burch's direction. It hit a tree next to Manuel and shattered. Then the headlights were turned off.

Manuel, in a whisper, "I thought you said there was just the van? Those lights came from a car."

"I didn't see the car."

"How many guys we think are here?"

"I don't know."

"What do you want to do?"

"Let's watch a minute and see if we can shoot some photos of that other car's license plate and any faces in the open. Then get back to our truck."

Manuel began to photograph with the infrared camera. Before he got many shots, both the sedan and the van turned on their headlights and drove right past them. They had a direct view of the car's plates from behind the trees as it drove by and Manuel shot several frames.

Kale, from his hotel room in Montana, called Nick early the next morning. "Nick, the media is about to destroy our old friend."

"Yeah, I've been watching." Nick replied from his hotel room. Lisa's plane had just departed an hour earlier.

All one needs to see good theater in motion is to watch a political scandal unfold. The opening act often involves a blatantly corrupt group of individuals and a corruptible elected official. The Dick Hanov story provided the perfect script, a meritless lobbyist ripping off his clients and flaunting his ill-gotten wealth on unsuspecting politicians. The Hanov scandal standing on its own in 2006 didn't offer much of a destructive force, but when attached to select candidates to whom Hanov had made contributions, it became a blunt instrument.

"Those campaign contributions were perfectly legal, Nick, and in accordance with federal election law."

"I know, and Hanov gave dozens of similar contributions to Democratic candidates too, but those facts don't seem to be helpful to this scripted story. Looks like the teacher just discovered the chipmunk, Kale."

Clarence Waters was the ideal target, a three-term Republican Senator standing for reelection who had a couple staffers with a penchant for bad judgment. Whether or not Clarence ever met Dick Hanov was irrelevant to the storyline. The fact that his reelection campaign had accepted contributions from Hanov and his Native American clients was enough fodder to convict him in the court of public opinion.

"Well, keep watching Nick. I have to go meet Ava for breakfast. We never really got to have out big talk last night."

Once the Hanov-Waters plot was cemented, it became acceptable to refer to Waters as if he and Hanov were long-involved in a criminal conspiracy. Classic guilt-by-association ads were pushed into the airwaves showing Clarence and Hanov in side-by-side mugshot-like photos. Journalistic sleight-of-hand imputed Hanov's illegalities upon Clarence by showing those photos during their hard news coverage. The cascading echoes claimed Waters was a key suspect in the Justice Department's corruption investigation.

Any inquiries to the department regarding that allegation were met with a polite, "The Justice Department does not comment on pending investigations."

Nick thought the local media would give a three-term U.S. Senator, and former U.S. Marine with a long record of public service, a stay of execution until some kind of actual proof emerged. But the Justice Department's non-denial was enough for reporters to accept the allegations of the Washington scandal on their face, and a newfound contempt against Clarence scurried rampant within media circles.

Manuel and Burch waited behind the trees for the van and car to leave. They believed from the direction of their headlights that they'd headed west again. They walked quickly through the dark to their truck. The driver's side window had been shattered. Glass was everywhere. Burch and Manuel's cell phones and wallets were missing. It was obvious who had taken them.

They cleaned the broken glass from the seat and started west down the road. They figured they were less than ten minutes behind the van. Burch turned on the bright lights and was driving about 50 miles per hour until the road suddenly turned to gravel. Dust poured in on them due to the missing window but assured they were on the trail of the van ahead. They continued at a good pace under a star-filled-sky until they crossed a single-lane bridge several miles further where Manuel saw a moonlit clearing on their right.

"Slow down, Burch. What was that?"

Slowing the truck, they drove quietly, headlights off. Once again they parked far off the side of the road, well past the entrance to the clearing. A structure appeared to be surrounded by a shiny tall fence. The vast darkness kept them from seeing exactly what the fence enclosed. What they could barely see was the front half of the van with its lights on. Burch got a pair of cutters from the truck. They climbed the fence, cut some razor wire strewn across its top and jumped over. Walking quietly, they moved through the blackness toward what appeared to be a large, concrete building.

As they came closer, they could see the van in a bay door with its rear end backed into the building. Light from inside the bay door illuminated the van's back end. They could hear muffled voices. Suddenly they heard footsteps and the lights went dark and an interior door slammed shut. They waited in silence.

Within a minute two pistols were at their heads, "Move one muscle, mister. Face down on the ground, hands to your sides."

Burch and Manuel did as they were told. They couldn't see who was behind them. They were both handcuffed and stood up, then prodded toward the building. They came to a sidewall where someone banged on a metal door. The door opened.

"We found these two hiding inside the fence. They had this fancy camera."

"What have we got here?" It was the man they'd seen in the van that evening. "Where the hell did you two come from? And what the hell are you doing?"

The man who handcuffed them spoke up. "We saw their pickup truck parked down from the entrance."

"Oh. Are you the guys who own the truck that has the busted window?"

Neither Burch nor Manuel responded.

The apparent head drug thug, a swarthy looking Latino with hooded eyes, looked at Manuel, "I asked you a fuckin' question, Injun."

Burch responded, "Yeah, that's our truck."

"What the hell are you doing following us around?"

"Just looking for some meth," Manuel said with a weak smile.

Much laughter from the group followed. "You sure came to the right place, boys." More laughter from around the room.

"Where the hell are we?" Burch asked.

The head thug pushed a button on the wall and large panels of lights across the ceiling lit up. He pushed another button, a loud buzzer sounded, and two large metal gates opened disclosing two long walls of bars enclosing a lengthy corridor. "Look familiar?"

"No," Burch said.

"How about you, Injun? Ever been in prison before?"

"No."

"Get used to it. You're going to tell us who you are and what the hell you're doing here."

He pulled Burch's wallet out which they'd stolen from the truck. "Well, let's see. Mr. Maloney. A member of the Texas Bar Association. We got us a lawyer here – very impressive. What's your story? And Mr. Sandoval, not much in your wallet except an old Arizona driver's license, a current Texas driver's license, a very faded photo of an elderly gentleman, maybe an elder Mr. Sandoval? And only forty bucks cash. What exactly is your story, gentlemen?"

Burch and Manuel stood silent.

Washington, DC

Spring 1997 The Lobbying World

There are lots of receptions every night on Capitol Hill celebrating one cause or another. In addition to the usual holiday parties, there are also receptions for retiring Members and those for Members who've been appointed to ambassadorships, governors' offices, or cabinet posts. They are all fairly routine.

On this balmy spring evening in 1997, young lobbyist Nick Taft was attending a reception in the House Energy & Commerce Committee Room to celebrate the unveiling of the portrait of a former chairman. Hanging on the walls of any large committee room in the U.S. House are regally-framed portraits of former committee chairs – most staring sternly, some slightly smiling.

At five o'clock, Nick walked into the committee room in the Rayburn Building. All the seats usually reserved for the public had been removed. A long white-tableclothed-buffet with lots of enticing food divided the space. There was a bar in each corner with colleagues from different industry segments drinking and conversing. Nick got a drink and said hello to a few familiar faces. Most lobbyists were waiting for the opportunity to bend the current chairman's ear or hit up his staff for intel on upcoming committee business. Nick was waiting for an opportunity to question the right lobbyist for information on Hally's alleged extracurricular activities.

No one in the room cared a whit about the portrait except the former chairman whose likeness it was supposed to reflect. After a few minutes, the current committee chairman, standing next to an easel covered with a white sheet, dinged his drink glass with a fork and asked for everyone's attention. Most people paused and turned toward him, except those wolfing down hors d'oeuvres in order to get something in their stomachs before the next reception on their schedules.

The current chairman offered kind words about the former, though they were fierce opponents. The reason the former was a former was the current chairman's party defeated the previous one's in a bitter election. Once the salutary remarks were finished, lobbyists went back to digging for information. Nick especially liked watching the freelance lobbyists work the room. They weren't employed directly by corporations but were hired as outside consultants by in-house lobbyists to help them cover the Hill. One freelancer in attendance who consulted for the ACC had befriended Nick during his first week at the coalition.

Though reluctant to expose his hand, Nick needed to see what the consultant might offer on the destructive gossip. While waiting for an opportunity, Nick watched him work. He and his kind were interesting because they had something at stake at every event in Washington. They would usually have several clients, each of whom needed something from somebody. So, unlike the corporate flacks who only needed to be seen and shake hands while picking up some general info, these lobbyists worked the room like cerebral pickpockets. After talking with each Member or staffer, Nick would observe the consultant take out a card and write a few notes.

He finally isolated the consultant at a corner bar. "Hey, Nick. What's up?"

"Oh, the usual. Nice event."

"Please. These things are so boring."

"Yeah, part of the job – right? Hey, I was wondering if I could ask you something."

"Okay."

"There've been some weird rumors swirling at the ACC, you know?" Nick looked around to see if anyone else could hear him, which didn't go unnoticed.

"And…?"

"I was wondering if you knew anything that might shed some light on them."

"What the fuck do you care?"

"What?"

"Look, Nick, one thing you don't do in this town is shit where you eat."

"What's that?"

"As you know, I do consulting work for the ACC. Hally pays my retainer."

"Right."

"So, I don't know anything about any rumors around the ACC. Know what I mean?"

"Sure."

"And, Nick, it might be a good time to keep your own head

down over there and not do anything stupid. I hear your close to the chopping block yourself."

"I thought you didn't know anything about any rumors around the ACC?"

"In Washington, Nick, you've got to pick sides. Step back and look at the bigger picture."

The consultant put a hand on the shoulder of a reluctant looking Congressman who walked by and was gone.

Bozeman, Montana

Fall 2006 The Campaign Trail

Before departing for Texas, Lisa had left a gift along with a note in Nick's Bozeman hotel room expressing her mixed feelings about their last twenty-four hours together. She wrote that she realized the gift, a thick wool scarf, was a little warm yet for the season but bought it as a security blanket for him – she thought he might need one. She signed the note, "Love you forever, Lisa."

His hotel phone rang. It was Kale again, "Nick, you need to come meet me for lunch."

"What now?"

"That woman has really fucked with my head."

"Kale, where are you?"

"At the Western Cafe having coffee. But I'll meet you at your hotel in a few."

"All right. But give me an hour, I need to take a shower and make some calls."

On a hunch, Nick had e-mailed the info on the Billings lawyer, Ace Hargrove, which he'd garnered from the construction worker to his firm colleague, Luke Lessman, to see what he could dig up.

He telephoned Luke in DC. "Nick, you picked an interesting lawyer out there."

"Actually, I didn't pick him, just curious about his connections."

"He's a decent criminal lawyer by reputation but has his own share of legal problems."

"Like?"

"He lied to the FBI about a client and got sued for legal malpractice in a related case which he must have settled because I can't find any further filings or a judgment on it anywhere."

"No judgment, huh? Could you tell who represented him in the malpractice case?"

"Yeah. A New York lawyer by the name of Hugh Haddad."

"Really? Thanks, Luke."

Nick feared if Haddad was involved in Montana there was likely much more to the Crow Reservation introductions than Ava's steakhouse bar fly, Benny Candler, could have imagined. He decided to make one more call – to John Lowman, the prosecutor he'd last unexpectedly met up with in The SeLaSsh Club in West Palm Beach years before.

"John, it's been a while. Thanks for all your info on The SeLaSsh Club gang over the last few years. You still dealing with drug dealers and money launderers?"

"All day every day. Your friend, Thurlow, ever get that woman's hooks out of him?"

"Good question. Not sure. Hey, John, this may be a little out of your area, but I wanted to talk with you about some things I've learned and some dots I've been struggling to connect."

"Okay."

"You ever hear of a New York criminal defense lawyer by the name of Hugh Haddad? "

"Nick, everyone who's involved in the drug wars has heard of Hugh Haddad. He's one of the more notorious if not colorful ones who represent scum of the earth drug dealers. Unfortunately for us, he represents them very successfully. But his practice is mostly in the New York area."

"John, what if I told you I could make a connection between Hugh Haddad, a Mexican drug cartel and a powerful U.S. Senator?"

"I'm listening."

Kale waited anxiously for Nick in the hotel lobby. He needed his friend's advice.

Once seated in the dining room, Kale started up, "Well, your ex-girlfriend's advice sucked."

"Why?"

"She told me to just ask Ava if she loved me, and…"

"That's *not* what she told you."

"Or where our relationship stood or whatever."

"And?"

"She threw me over, Nick. I knew she would."

"Maybe it wasn't meant to be. Rejection is a part of life, Kale. Nobody can avoid it."

"No, it was meant to be. The only woman I've cared for since my divorce – kept my heart from growing cold, Nick. She was my future."

"So, you're sorry you asked?"

"No. But, I guess it's true – it's not really a question if you know the answer too."

"Actually, sometimes the questions are more important than the answers, Kale."

"And why the hell is that?"

"Because they create space in your head to help you find the answers."

"Maybe the stupidest thing you've ever said, Nick."

"So, what now?"

"Oh, I bow out. I'm done." Kale conceded.

Seeing his friend's discouragement, "Sorry, old friend. I know how much you liked her. Maybe she just doesn't appreciate you."

"No, it was me. I attach too much meaning to things. But never show it. It's what I do."

"Well, too bad it didn't work out."

"Yeah, it's a real fuckin' tragedy. Looney bitch – to hell with her."

Nick smiled. "Now, there's the old Kale we all know and love."

Kale looked blankly around the hotel restaurant. "You know, Nick, when I was young, all I really knew about anything was that I had a future. I didn't know what it was but it was out there – somewhere. Then I reached an age, maybe in my thirties, when I realized I had a past."

"You definitely have a past, Kale."

"But, then you get to be my age, and you begin to wonder if you *have* a future. I'm so old I can remember when TV used to go off the air at night. There'd be the national anthem playing and then poof – just a bar code."

"Wow, you are old. You know what, though, Kale? Your life's like a movie – a continual loop. I can remember when a woman leaving you of her own free will was the *good* news."

"Like a movie, huh? Well, here's to a good ending." They clinked their coffee mugs together.

"Kale, don't let Ava be your one hope for a better life. Just stay with it. You're going to find what you're looking for." Nick then changed the subject. "Now, what have you heard from Congressman Parker's office lately?"

"Not too much, actually. Maybe your conversation with Sheila had an impact." Kale said.

"But Sheila didn't acknowledge that she was behind the letter, more like somebody else was. I told her that helping you might indirectly help Clarence get reelected which would directly hurt Mo Kauffman." Nick refreshed Kale's memory on Sheila's college roommate being found dead years ago while working for then-freshman Congressman Kauffman. "Thought it might add a little motivation to her task. I haven't heard back from her yet, but she said she'd help."

"Did you believe her?" Kale asked.

"She didn't take a blood oath on it, but said she would."

"Good. I don't want to hear any more promises from any more women. But, Nick, I may have a new job opportunity that could save me from all this bullshit anyway. Can't tell you much about it because I signed a non-disclosure agreement. But it's to head up a new DC office of a very big company with one of the biggest PACs in DC."

"That's great, Kale! You've been interviewing for it for a while?"

"Yeah. Should hear something fairly soon."

———————

Leaving Kale to ponder his next moves, Nick called Burch's cell phone for the third time that day. He'd received no response and was beginning to worry. He figured that cell reception on the Crow Reservation might be spotty but hoped they would check in soon. He decided to touch base again with Thurlow Carmine to see if he'd come up with any money to pay Burch. Considering the risky situation Nick may have put his investigators in, he certainly wanted to be able to pay them.

Burch and Manuel had spent the night in separate cells down the hall from each other in the newly constructed prison. Their interrogation from the night before was interrupted by a landline phone call which distracted their captors. They were each given a thin blanket and a bottle of water. Fortunately, due to the cold fall weather, they both were wearing thick shirts and jackets, wool-lined jeans and boots. The next morning they heard a loud buzzing noise and familiar voices down the corridor. They were marched to the front office and sat down in front of the head drug dealer.

"So, my Texas friends, what are we to do with you? You say

you're looking for meth, but instead of contacting us, you shadow us at Chief Plenty Coups and then again here last night."

They both looked at the floor. They had been situated too far apart during the night to get a story straight between them and weren't sure if any new state-of-the-art prison might have listening capability. Burch could sense that Manuel was scared and losing hope – he could see it in his eyes.

"So, the question is, what are you doing? Who are you working for and why?"

Burch quickly responded, "Okay. I'll tell you straight up. We get hired to track drug usage in rural parts of the country. We're not cops and don't deal with law enforcement at all." Burch casually crossed his legs and folded his hands as if he had these conversations all the time. "We get hired by private organizations with an interest in the patterns and usage of illegal narcotics. We've been asked to help figure out why meth use on the reservations has increased so substantially in the past year."

The dealer spoke up. "Wow. You know what? That actually sounds legit. But why the fuck here and now?"

"The Way of The Light Foundation hired us," Burch just picked a name. "It's headquartered in Montana. We heard some dealers were working the Southwest part of the reservation. So we started out and after connecting a few dots, ended up here."

"Huh. And now what?"

"We understand that most Crow youth don't have a lot of extra spending money. We're really just trying to figure out what price they're paying and how much the meth being distributed here costs. That would all be put in our report back to the foundation. Then they do what they choose with the information."

"I see."

Manuel caught on and spoke up, "We...we've got n-no beef with you guys. We're not about identifying people, users or sellers, just about determining p-patterns of usage and costs across certain states."

"And so your question to us would be?"

"How much does meth cost on the Crow Reservation? How much for how much?"

"And that's it?"

Mexican drug cartels knew better than anyone the high addiction rates on the reservations as well as the going rate for any drug on any given day – it was a critical part of their business. But the meth they'd been giving out on that reservation for free was being paid for by someone in New York. It was not the usual money-for-product exchange nor one they planned to divulge to anyone.

"That's pretty much it, yeah." Burch concluded.

"Well, Mr. Burch and Mr. Sandoval, that certainly is an interesting story. But frankly, you're starting to make my coffee taste *real* bad." He turned to one of his minions, "Get 'em outta here. Unfortunately, I now have to make some awkward phone calls. We'll have to figure out how to dispense with them later. May have to deep freeze 'em."

Washington, DC

Spring 1997 The Lobbying World

Of the more interesting political fundraisers in Washington, are those hosted at lobbyists' private homes. These are social and political outings combined and either theme may rule the night. On this spring evening in 1997, Nick drove to a stately home in Northwest DC. The husband lobbied for some big tech companies and though uncertain what his socialite wife did all day, she threw great parties. The guest list included about fifteen corporate flaks from Fortune 500 companies who stood around the living room awaiting the Congressman's arrival.

Conversation meandered from the latest showdown between Congress and the White House over budget issues, to Tony Blair's May 2nd election to Prime Minister of England, to the new Austin Powers movie recently released starring Mike Myers and Elizabeth Hurley. The honored guest arrived and everyone sharpened their elbows to get a chance for a quick semi-private conversation before dinner. The Congressman was a Republican chairman of a key subcommittee. All of the guests were Republicans as well.

As the lobbyists maneuvered close to the politician, Nick stepped back into the bar. His goal for the night had nothing to do with lobbying. He knew one Big Telco lawyer would be attending, and hoped he might level with Nick as to where on the political Richter scale the Hally rumors were registering. He believed her problems were becoming his problems. The Big Telco guy was at the bar waving irritably at the bartender about just how he wanted his gin martini prepared which was unhelpful to the young server who spoke no English.

"Wen, how are you? Good to see you, sir."

"Hello, Nick. How are things at the ACC these days?"

"I was about to ask you the same thing?"

"How's that again?"

"Wen, I know that if anyone has, you've heard the gossip. I'd appreciate your advice on it."

"My advice?"

"One, do you think Hally's maybe a little over-involved with these outside fundraising groups? I know you support her, but her priority is supposed to be our industry. There's a lot of talk going around. And, two, do you think the rumors about her and Raines have any credibility? For the record, I don't."

"At this point in time, Nick, in this town, it doesn't really matter if the Raines rumor is true. The damage is done. I couldn't care less about her level of involvement with her fundraising network. With the kind of dark money the Dems are funneling against our candidates today, I wish her all the success in the world – within the law, of course. And you might want to wake up, my friend, the conservatives are making a comeback. By the way, are you the least bit aware that your shirt sleeves are way too long for that jacket?"

"Yeah, I keep meaning to get some tailored shirts." He understood Wen's take on Hally, but had remaining doubts about the veracity of the gossip. Nick despised gossip and tried not to partake in it, but that was an impossible challenge in his line of work.

"Wen, do you think this talk about Hally is hurting the credibility of the ACC?"

Wen looked toward the high-ceilinged living room under which the lobbyists were herding around the Congressman. "Not yet, Nick. Not yet." He walked back in to join the rest.

Western Montana

Fall 2006 The Campaign Trail

By the time Nick got in touch with Thurlow in Montana, his priorities had changed from whether or not he'd identified a good source of funding to pay Burch and Manuel to whether Thurlow might help Nick find them. As the 2006 fall season progressed, the temperature had dropped below freezing more than once. Nick was worried about the wellbeing of his investigators in the vast wilderness of the Crow Reservation. Nick explained to Thurlow that when he'd last heard from them they were *somewhere* in the middle of the reservation.

Thurlow responded. "For crying out loud, Taft. Those guys can find themselves in a world of hurt on your so-called mission. How long have you been trying to get a hold of 'em?"

"All day."

"When did you last hear from them?"

"Last night. They thought they were on the trail of a dealer, and were headed southwest of Crow Agency. I think maybe near the town of Saint Xavier. Said they would stay the night out there if need be."

"Stay out there in the middle of nowhere? Determined sons-a-bitches, aren't they?"

"Yeah." Nick said with a discouraged tone.

"Don't panic just yet. Cell coverage can be sketchy out there. Near Saint Xavier, huh?"

"Yeah, I think that was the town."

"I know that area pretty well, Nick. If they were headed southwest of there that would likely be taking them out toward Pryor. Hmmm."

"Yeah?"

"Maybe we should take a drive out that way, snoop around a little."

"You could do that?"

"Not much I can do to help Waters' campaign from the outside where I've been relegated. Nick, pick me up at the Grantree Hotel in a half hour."

Burch and Manuel listened from their detention block to the muffled sound of people scurrying around, external doors slamming and truck engines starting. After a few minutes there was dead silence. They believed they were alone in the prison. They began to talk to each other from their cells on opposite ends of the long hallway.

"Well, boss, how the hell we going to get out of this one?" Manuel asked.

"Been thinking on that."

"And what have you concluded?"

"I'm hoping the cavalry is on the way."

"But, Burch, nobody knows we're here."

"Some people know generally where we *were* though – right?"

"You mean Nick?"

"Yeah, and the Billings police detective we talked to – maybe."

"And the staffer at the Crow headquarters!" Manuel added, enthusiastically.

Burch perked up. "Right. Right, he's the one who pointed us in this direction."

"But how the hell are they going to track us to this deserted fuckin' place?"

Having once been a key staffer to a U.S. Senator from Montana, Thurlow had good relationships with most law enforcement personnel. While Nick drove toward the Crow Reservation, Thurlow talked on Nick's cell to a Billings detective. The detective was aware that Burch and Manuel met with one of his officers about their investigation the day before. Thurlow asked if he had any idea where they might be headed. He also inquired about Jacey's big sister who worked with a Billings police-supported rehab center, and if there were any new developments in the case of the young Crow woman's demise. The officer acknowledged that the girl's sister had been pushing law enforcement but was unaware of any breaking news.

"I believe my officers encouraged your friends to check in with the tribal government on the res. Don't know who exactly. Crow Agency's probably the place to look though."

It was almost six o'clock by the time they arrived at the Crow Tribal headquarters. Nick had missed a few turns and had no idea where he was. The staffer that Burch and Manuel had previously met with was there.

"Yes, I spoke with your friend, Mr. Maloney," admitted the young staffer. "I directed them to the southwest sector of the reservation where meth activity has increased. Anything wrong?"

"Yeah, they're sort of missing," Nick said before Thurlow could respond.

"Sorry to hear that. We don't have much in resources, but I'll keep an eye out and see if I can pick up any information."

Confirming with the staffer that his boss was Big Jim, Thurlow gave him a piece of paper with his cell phone number on it. "Ask Jim to give me a call when you're able, will you? It's important. Big Jim and I are old friends."

Thurlow knew the roads on the reservation like he was born there. Since Nick was directionally challenged there and unfamiliar with the land, he decided to let Thurlow drive. They made it to Saint Xavier just after seven o'clock. Nick's cell phone had some limited service. Thurlow got out to ask people milling around the post office if any folks he knew were around.

While he was doing so, a man who seemed to come out of nowhere put his hand inside the passenger door of the Jeep and touched Nick's arm, "You got any fuckin' money?"

Nick was so startled he couldn't respond. He looked away to see if Thurlow was in sight.

"You hear me asshole?!" The large man had snow-gray hair and wore a floppy hat.

Nick reached under his seat and pulled out Cotter's Colt .45 revolver. He stuck it square in the man's face. "Step away or I'll blow your fuckin' brains out."

The man stared at the gun, wide eyed.

"Did you hear *me*, asshole?" The man quickly backed away.

Thurlow got back in the driver's side. "What the hell was that all about? Where'd you get the hand cannon?"

"Was under my seat. A forgetful friend left it there."

"Good, we might need it later."

The only roads out of town, other than the one they drove in on, went south further into the reservation or west toward its boundary. They headed west.

As they drove into the twilight of the evening across a lost frontier, Nick couldn't help but notice the discouraging poverty around them. It reminded him of the destitution of some inner cities back East, except those inhabitants hadn't been corralled there by the federal government. As far as Nick knew, the only thing those very different places had in common was the billions in federal dollars squandered to help them.

Thurlow's cell buzzed. It was Big Jim from the Crow Tribe. "Thurlow, you out here bothering my folks again?"

Thurlow laughed, "Your folks? These are *my* folks! How are you, Big Jim?"

"Just okay. Lost my election today to the gold miners' candidate."

"Sorry to hear that."

"No matter, I've done my best. They'll be booting out all my folks soon and replacing them with all their cronies. What are you looking for out there, Thurlow?"

Thurlow explained as much as he could without getting into too many details.

"Meth and its dealers are not hard to find, Thurlow. Just turn your head in any direction. And watch your step, old friend. My people think drug dealers murdered some men earlier this summer."

"Hmph. Thanks."

"I'll tell you one thing, whoever these people are, they're like magicians. We've had good people try to track them going off the reservation, but it seems we're always one step behind before they disappear into the wind."

"Into the wind, huh? Like ghosts?"

"Like bad spirits."

Unfortunately, the same law enforcement personnel in Billings that Thurlow knew were also acquainted with Waters' current deputy chief, Zach Gerkin. Timely political business prompted Zach to check in with the Billings chief of police that same day to pick up any intel regarding campaign-related activity.

"Zach, it must be your campaign's day to check in with law enforcement. You guys sure are diligent."

"How's that?" Zach asked.

"I just got off the phone with your colleague, Thurlow."

"What did he want?"

"Wanted to know about a couple of fellas one of my detectives talked to and where they were headed. Some political activity of some kind on the reservation, I guess."

"Is that so? Where were they headed, do you know?"

"I suggested they check in with the folks over in Crow Agency."

After a few follow-up questions, Zach quickly hung up the phone in bewilderment. He thought to himself, *What the hell was Thurlow up to?* Zach didn't like or trust Thurlow, and helped orchestrate his alienation from Waters. In fact, Thurlow had been asked to keep his distance in every manner. Zach considered the information he had stumbled upon to be potentially damning, especially regarding any political involvement on the reservation.

He did not waste any time, it was too good of an opportunity. Zach didn't like the friendship between Clarence and Thurlow, nor the recent tone the Senator had been taking with him. He wondered if Thurlow had been muddying his and the Senator's relationship. He decided to take this damning information straight to Waters.

Reaching the Senator by phone, Zach explained his discovery. "Clarence, I told you Thurlow was potential trouble. Now he's gone rogue and is working the Crow Reservation."

Clarence inquired, "And you say that trip to the reservation was made this very afternoon?"

"Yes, sir."

"You know what? That's odd to me, Zach. Because I spoke with Thurlow earlier today. He's still my friend you know?"

"Yeah. Yes, sir."

"And he told me today that he was about to take a drive to Billings with Nick Taft. They're old acquaintances. As you know, Nick and others have been out here doing some volunteer work."

"Yes. I know that."

"How do you know they were doing politically-related work on the reservation?"

"I assumed that Thurlow was…"

The Senator interrupted, "You assumed?"

"Yes…Yes, I did."

"I'll tell you what, Zach. I'll look into this myself. You just stay put and tend to your congressional work. All right with you?"

———

The last phone call a weary Nick Taft would receive while still barely in cell range on the reservation was from a number he did not recognize. But anxious to hear from anyone, he answered it.

"Hello. Oh, yes sir. Uhhh…yes, yes he is. Well…uh…yeah, sure." Nick put his hand over the phone and turned toward Thurlow with a pained look.

"Who the hell is it?" Thurlow asked.

"It's Senator Waters. And he wants to talk to you."

"Are you fucking kidding me?"

Nick shrugged his shoulders and scrunched up his face. "I have no idea. He's never called my cell before."

He pulled Nick's rental Jeep to the side of the road and took the phone. "Yeah?"

"Thurlow, what the hell are you up to? Are you on the Crow Reservation?" The Senator asked, abruptly.

"Yeah, sort of. Just heading out of it." He turned toward Nick with a tortured grimace.

"Can you please tell me why?"

"Clarence. Uh, Nick and I are doing a little reconnaissance for some friends who, uh, may have gotten lost out here."

"Keep talking."

"Senator, I don't think you need to know this whole story. But there are some guys who may have gotten themselves into a bit of a fix and we're trying to help them out."

"I see." After a pause. "You need help?"

"We might."

"Where exactly are you?"

"We're headed toward Pryor on the reservation. But I don't think that's where we'll end up. I've been to Pryor, and doubt the guys we're looking for are there. I'm guessing somewhere in the middle of nowhere is where we're headed. Frankly, as you know, there ain't a lot out here and I'm guessing we're about to travel out of cell range."

Clarence encouraged them. "You two be careful and check back in with me when you get in range again. Let me think on this a little."

In the dim stillness of the prison, Burch reluctantly spoke down the long corridor, "Manny, you still there?"

"No, I went out for a burger and fries."

Burch smiled, "You know, I haven't heard a sound around this place all day."

"Not a peep," Manuel replied.

"Where the hell'd they all go?"

"To sell meth? To Indians?"

"But what do you suppose all that scuffling around we heard this morning was about?"

"I don't know. Seemed like some frenzied activity."

"You think of any way to get out of here yet?" Burch asked.

"I have to say this appears to be one well-built facility. They didn't cut any corners. It also seems brand spanking new."

"We were a good ways past Pryor when we saw this place – right?"

"That sounds about right. On a narrow road."

After a few minutes of jailhouse chatter, they were surprised by one of the meth thugs who appeared on their corridor seemingly out of nowhere. "Okay boys, hands in front of your hips. We're moving you to a much cooler part of the prison. You're going to love it."

He cuffed Manuel first, and marched him down in front of Burch's cell. But as Burch's cell was being opened, the head thug interrupted. "No. Keep the Texan in his cell. I need to talk with him. Go ahead and put the Injun on ice."

Burch watched helplessly as the thug led Manny away down the corridor.

———————

Thurlow drove so fast it made Nick nervous. But it seemed he knew the roads so he had tried not to distract him.

"Hey, you know, we're not trying to break any land speed records here today," Nick pleaded.

"No. We are trying to stay ahead of the sun though. One thing I can tell you is when it gets dark out here, it gets seriously fuckin' dark."

They stopped briefly when they reached the intersection at Pryor. The self-serve gas station was closed. While driving on into the approaching dark, Nick took stock of their situation. As much as he had to acknowledge that the worst of fates may have befallen his investigators, he still believed they just might be somewhere safe and sound. Thurlow drove westward toward Edgar as the road turned from pavement to gravel and the sun disappeared over the horizon.

———————

Manuel was walked to a large metal door with a horizontal lever on it. His handcuffs were secured tight in front of him and he was shoved into a dark and cold room. The door was locked fast behind him. He yelled out but heard only the echo of his own voice. After struggling to secure his shirt and jacket sleeves and fasten the top shirt button of both, he began to feel his way along the perimeter of the pitch black room. Manuel couldn't cover much ground very quickly with his hands cuffed but continued on methodically. He was curious as to how much space he had around him, and if there was another door somewhere in his midst.

As he cautiously felt his way along the cold walls, he came across what he thought might be metal shelves or grates. As the minutes ticked by, he navigated his way around the entire room and was back at the large levered door. He then decided to attempt to walk diagonally across the center of what he presumed was the prison's rather large walk-in refrigerator. With his hands and arms stretched out as far in front as his handcuffs would allow in order to avoid running head first into any hard objects, he began his cautious step by step journey.

He counted the steps as he went in an attempt to determine the size of the area. About thirty steps across the room, he ran straight into a heavy object and instinctively yelled out. The object moved quickly away from him. Then it lurched back and struck him square in the chest throwing him to the floor. The impact momentarily knocked the wind out of him.

Manuel yelled out, "Who's' there? Who are you?"

He sat back for a moment trying to catch his breath. There was no reply. He listened carefully for any movement or footsteps. He managed to get off the floor and regain his footing. He began to move forward more slowly with his hands and arms reaching out blindly in front. He encountered the object again. This time it was perfectly still. Manuel began to inspect the heavy object inches at a time with his bound hands and cold fingers. First he felt an almost frozen cylinder-like appendage similar to a table leg, then worked his way to a thicker center of the glacial oddity.

To his frightened dismay, the more he inspected, the more he realized the frosty object could be a human being and that it appeared to be hanging from the ceiling. As his slowly numbing hands inspected further, he made the disturbing discovery that it was in fact a cold, naked, dead man hanging from his feet. Manuel moved away so abruptly that he backed hard into a solid wall.

He sank to the floor in despair. He pulled his shirt and jacket tighter around his neck. He'd been in dire situations before in his life. Over the years he'd purged most of those old memories, yet here he was again. In his past, Manuel had been able to escape such predicaments, but he could see no way out of this frigid hellhole. He began vigorously rubbing his arms and legs as if doing so might keep his rapidly cooling body somewhat warmer.

Washington, DC

Fall 2006 The Lobbying World

Kale awoke early back in his DC Capitol Hill townhouse. His bedroom was still and quiet around him. There was less traffic than usual on the street outside his windows, fewer horns and less general noise. Congress was in recess pending the outcome of the 2006 November elections. He moved slowly toward his kitchen. An empty bottle of scotch lay on its side on the dining table next to his open checkbook.

He'd spent much of the night figuring out how to pay his growing credit card debt and delinquent tax bills. There was also the letter from the D.C. U.S. Attorney's office which remained untouched. He refused to open it so he could deny knowledge of its contents. The evening's biggest challenge had been matching his high-end restaurant meals for the past month on his corporate expense account to any credible work-related causes. He'd become creative at that challenge over the years. There were after all 435 Members of the U.S. House and 100 Members of the Senate, and about 15,000 congressional staffers from which he could choose for a match.

Since his divorce, Kale ate most of his meals at trendy restaurants, all expensed to his company. His upscale golf club membership was also picked up by his company and he ate and drank a lot there too. The general attitude of his colleagues in the lobbying business was to get away with as much as possible until they tell you to stop. He even knew one lobbyist whose company paid for his kid's babysitters. Kale was also allowed a per diem reimbursement for each day he was on travel, usually on a PAC-related trip to a nice resort. That allowed him to occasionally have some extra cash.

Despite all those perks, the collective weight of his alimony payments and gambling debts left Kale broke. If it weren't for his liberal corporate expense account, he wasn't sure how he would even manage a decent meal. Consequently, he was more painfully aware every day of the risk involved for him in the potential success of the Democrats' "Culture of Corruption" campaign. Their promise to rein in lobbyists' spending if they took control of Congress hit very close to home. After worrying most of his morning away, he called his friend, Nick, in Montana to discuss his latest paranoia.

Nick was driving through one of the areas of the Crow Reservation that had cell reception. "Kale, you better have a good reason to call. I've got a lot of shit going on right now."

"I do. We've got to talk about what the hell's going on with this election."

"What now?" Nick asked.

"Well…the *Washington Herald* seems to think the Dems have a chance to take control of the House. What do you think about that?"

"Kale, the *Washington Herald* always predicts the Democrats are going to win – every two and four years like clockwork. You know that! What's wrong with you?"

"Listen Nick, if the Democrats take the House and Senate, I'm screwed thanks to who will be the new Ethics Committee Chairman – Judd Parker. But I'm also screwed if they come in and pass some newfangled anti-lobbying law that shuts down my expense account."

"For the hundredth time, Kale, the Democrats are not going to win. Maybe they take the Senate, due to some bad judgments and campaign mistakes, but not the House. It's just too big a lift. Now Relaaax! You're driving me crazy."

Bozeman, Montana

Fall <u>2006</u> The Campaign Trail

The last debate to be held in the Waters/Sutter 2006 campaign was hosted by Montana State University in Bozeman on a fall evening. Everybody who was anybody in Montana's political world attended. Even Clarence's grown children attended. Though they'd witnessed most of his campaigns growing up in Montana, they'd never seen their father or family so personally degraded. The race was tightening. The pounding Clarence had taken from journalists, the National Democratic Party, and allegations from Washington around the Hanov investigation, had thrown him off his game. The debate might give him a chance to regain his footing.

Clarence knew he needed to stop responding to the slander thrown at him and get back to talking about his core beliefs. Those were the principles upon which Montanans had previously voted him into office. He needed to articulate that vision and not be diverted by the conspiracy theories his opponents promoted or the press constantly repeated. Whether or not he was up to the task was the question on the minds of his supporters that evening.

Sutter's balancing act to camouflage his liberalism while remaining loyal to his Western Democratic base was just as tricky. Once in office, his contrary votes could be obscured by the Senate process well enough to betray even the most basic common sense. In prior years Montana Democrats were pragmatic moderates whose down to earth instincts allowed them to work in bipartisan ways with people of all parties. But those days were quickly waning. Sutter threw out numbers in the debate and quoted CliffsNotes-like summaries of federal policy as if second nature to him. The softball questions allowed him a moderate's varnish, but it would be no match for his party's liberal leadership should he make it to DC.

Clarence Waters, despite his eighteen years' experience in federal policy and law, abided Sutter's well-rehearsed performance. Sutter promised, if elected, not to seek federal spending earmarks for which the media had bludgeoned Waters, and to not travel on private jets – always to fly commercial. Clarence started out on-message and offered his conservative take on the direction the country should go. One of the moderators, a local reporter, asked two awkward questions. One was why he was trying to fill a prison that wasn't even authorized by the government; the other was why the Justice Department was investigating him if he hadn't done anything wrong.

His newfound discipline allowed Clarence to ignore the bait. Instead, he gave vague policy- and process-based answers to both questions. That control, and the fact that his supporters had packed the room, enabled him to offer his strongest debate performance of the entire campaign. If Waters had made one factual error during any of his answers, it would have been huge news. Since he hadn't, the debate was not much of a story the next day. The media quietly characterized the debate as a draw which everyone knew meant Clarence had won.

Washington, DC

Spring 1997 The Lobbying World

Creative companies find unique ways to entertain politicians and their staff in DC. On this wet Thursday evening, the East Coast Telco was hosting a competition at the Corcoran Gallery of Art near the White House. The art world had been abuzz with the recent theft of Pablo Picasso's painting, "Tete de Femme," from a gallery in London in March, 1997. For this timely event, staff and Members of Congress would enter their artwork to be judged by the prestigious museum. Nick arrived late, snatched a glass of wine off the tray a waiter was carrying and headed in to mingle with the amateur artists.

Guests had an opportunity to comment on the exhibits of the participants. Most of the guests were lobbyists. Most of the artists were congressional staff. Most of the observations were very complimentary. As Nick was perusing the halls and visiting with others, he came upon Tad Larson. Tad anxiously guided Nick down a less crowded corridor.

"Nick, do you know how explosive this info on Hally is getting? My friend, you've got to strike while the iron's hot."

"Honestly, Tad, I'm not inclined to do that. And, frankly, I don't believe the rumors."

"You've got to be kidding. You know what, Nick? At this point it doesn't matter what you believe. The story is having a destructive impact on the ACC and frankly, upon you as well."

"Me?"

"You are her closest confidant. I wouldn't be surprised at this point if people weren't suspecting you of helping cover for her."

"That's absurd." But Nick was mindful of an unnerving e-mail he'd recently received from an FEC investigator to which he had yet to respond.

"All I'm saying, Nick, is people in this town talk. You try not to be in the loop so you don't always know what's being said. If you're not a part of it, you don't get to affect it. By the way, I hear the FEC has begun an investigation into Hally and her conservative cohorts' fundraising methods. Maybe she thinks her lover, Senator Raines will protect her."

Nick looked at Tad and shook his head. Rather than relenting, he considered going public to let people know he believed most of the rumors were false.

Tad continued, "You know she has no life here, Nick. Even at her age, she still goes back to Boston like every other weekend to hang out with her parents. Raines and her conservative wingnut friends are all she has – what a loser."

Weighing the political risks of going public, Nick reacted, "You know, Tad, I understand you've got some political campaign activities of your own involving contributions that may not exactly be in sync with FEC rules and if I were you…"

He was interrupted by the unexpected appearance of Hally in the long corridor. She was looking toward the paintings on the wall but Nick suspected she'd heard a few words.

Nick spoke up, "Hey, Hally…what do you think of our congressional artists?"

"I'm pleasantly surprised at the honesty of their work. What do you think, Tad?"

"Oh, yeah, they're pretty good. This was a hell of an idea." He looked at Nick with a worried expression.

Hally continued, "I was just thinking, I hope someone has sufficiently persuaded the judges to take care of the artists regardless of their work product. You know how sometimes people need a little bit of nudge?"

What Tad had underestimated was Hally's network of political friends in DC who'd been monitoring Tad's activities. He was also unaware that she'd recently convinced one of them to file a civil complaint at the FEC regarding Tad's work for a Democratic Presidential Exploratory Committee.

"Uh, yeah. Might be personally insulting otherwise," Tad offered.

"Yeah. Everybody who's on equal footing should be given the same consideration. Shouldn't they, Tad?" Hally smiled and moved on down the hallway.

Tad gave Nick a raised eyebrow and moved nervously down the hall by himself.

An hour later, Nick was waiting for his car at the valet in front of the gallery. He observed Hally in a drizzling cold rain wrestling with her collapsible umbrella as she stepped toward her high-end

Mercedes to drive to her secluded house in her posh Maryland neighborhood. He couldn't help but think of Hally as another lonely DC workaholic caught up in the rat race of Washington just trying to figure out what she was doing there.

As she fumbled with some cash to tip the valet, she looked up from her focused world for a moment toward Nick waiting on the steps, "Oh, hey. Have a good weekend, Nick."

"You too, Hally."

Western Montana

Fall 2006 The Campaign Trail

No windows adorned Burch's cell, but he could tell it was night. The modest sun rays that sometimes bent through a slim opening near the ceiling were gone. There were no lights turned on in the building. He had not heard a sound all day – no trucks, no doors, no voices. He had no food or drinking water but the miniature sink in his small bar-enclosed space had running water.

He wanted to yell down the corridor to talk with Manuel, but knew he was gone. He feared what the meth thugs had done to him. He almost wished his captors would return just to break his increasing anxiety. He regretted getting Manny involved in this adventure and realized he might be responsible for his death.

Wondering if their captors planned to kill them both, he tried to convince himself there was no way to really know. But he did.

Thurlow and Nick flew down the gravel road on the edge of the reservation. The landscape was black and still, and darkened more so by invisible enemies. Thurlow did not like their odds against meth dealers. He drove so fast they blew right past the new prison and saw neither a glimpse nor glimmer of Burch's dust-covered pickup parked well off the side of the road.

As they drove on, Nick inquired, "Thurlow, can I ask you a hypothetical question?"

Thurlow stayed focused on the road. "Shoot."

"What if you were interested in a colleague's girlfriend and..."

"Oh, this should be good." Thurlow said, smiling. "Go on."

"And, okay. Let's just say, you actually slept with her."

"Uh huh."

"But, you felt bad about it. Would you tell him?"

"Tell him what?"

"That you slept with her."

"Are you crazy? No!"

"Well, let's just say you've also put that colleague in a tough situation, which you also regret."

"Are you kiddin' me? What'd you do, sleep with Burch's wife?"

250

"No, not his wife. She's his girlfriend, who used to be my girlfriend."

"Oh, shit." Thurlow paused as he digested that news. "Well, that's a little different. She's just his girlfriend? No ring? And you two used to date?"

"Yeah."

"Then, hell no!" Nick considered that a generous take on his betrayal of Burch.

Thurlow continued. "Though, I'd say you're dealing with a bit of a moral ambiguity. And probably sort of a conflict of interest regarding your client. Wouldn't you?"

"Yeah, yeah, I would." Nick said in a tired, hoarse voice. Deep inside Nick believed his reunion with Lisa was the best thing that had happened to him in years but under the circumstances was struggling with his judgment. It was not something he would want on his soul's resume.

"Nick, I'm afraid I've got worse news than that."

"What?"

"We're in the middle of fucking nowhere and very close to being out of gas."

"Shit!" Nick looked over at the instrument panel. "When did the fuel light come on?"

"About a half hour ago."

"Damn, Thurlow! Where the hell are we?"

"I thought we'd be in the town of Edgar by now. It's got to be up here somewhere."

"Maybe you should slow down, try to conserve fuel. I'll be honest, I have no idea where we are," Nick admitted. "We could be in Wyoming for all I know."

"Yeah, maybe slowing down makes sense." Thurlow nodded as he eased off the accelerator. "Don't worry, we're still in Montana." Thurlow had an easy confidence about him that gave Nick a sense of security.

"Okay, let's just cruise at a slower clip like this and hope for the best." Nick said.

"Good by me. By the way, Nick, did you hear that cool old bar on Bimini Island in the Bahamas, the Compleat Angler, recently burned down?"

"What? No, I hadn't." Nick said. "That's too bad. It was a really great place. I had a few beers there in my younger days."

"Too bad?! It totally sucks! I loved that old joint. Geneveve and I have had a lot of fun there over the years. Wonder what happened?"

"Maybe they couldn't get the island fire truck there in time to save it because some idiots a few years back submerged its engine in saltwater – and it hasn't run quite the same since."

"Very funny." Thurlow responded.

After another few minutes, they rolled into the one-bar town of Edgar. Just past it was the only working gas pump within about 50 miles of the middle of the reservation. While Nick was filling up the Jeep's tank, Thurlow came out of the station with two beers.

"Thurlow, we're looking for a needle in a haystack out here."

"Yep, 'bout sums it up."

"I just got cell service for the first time in a while." Nick said.

Thurlow checked his voicemails. "Let's see if I can get any news on Clarence's debate tonight."

"I'll check mine too."

Thurlow smiled, "Ha, Waters kicked ass. Sutter was off his game. Great timing!"

Nick listened anxiously to his voicemails. None were from Burch.

"That's great news, Thurlow. What do you think our next move ought to be to find Burch and Manuel?"

"Yeah." Thurlow looked back, "No sense in sugarcoating this anymore, Nick. We're a little short on options," he said gravely. "And, your friends are probably toast."

Nick looked down. He finished topping off the tank and slowly replaced the pump handle. They both stood at a loss for a moment.

"Hey, Nick, since we've got service again, why don't you at least try Burch's cell one more time?"

Nick hopelessly dialed the number again. There was no answer. Nick did not bother leaving another voicemail. He shook his head at Thurlow.

But Thurlow was preoccupied searching for his own cell phone that he thought he had just put in his pocket. He found it and looked at the screen. "Nick, did you call his cell?"

"Yeah."

Thurlow gave a curious look, "No answer?"

Nick shook his head.

"Do it again." Responding to an annoyed glance from Nick,

Thurlow waived his hand in the air in a circular motion, "Just do it."

Nick dialed the number. Thurlow tilted his head and walked from one gas pump to another and back again.

"Nick, come over here. Dial it again."

Nick shook his head and rolled his eyes. "What the hell for?"

"Just dial it!"

Nick hit the redial button. Thurlow honed in on a garbage can and started rummaging through discarded plastic oil bottles and greasy, wet paper towels. "Shit! One more time."

Nick did as he was told.

Thurlow pulled a cell phone from the bottom of the can. He held it up. "Do it again!"

Nick did. The phone lit up. It was Burch's cell.

"What the fuck?"

"I don't know." Thurlow kept pulling waste out the can. "Let's see what else is in here."

To the dissatisfaction of the station attendant, they continued to riffle through the contents of the overstuffed trash barrel and dumped much of it onto the weathered cement between the gas tanks. "Hey, what the hell are you two doing?"

Nick, with his hands up. "We'll clean it up. We're looking for something important."

"In *there?*"

Thurlow held up Burch's wallet. "Look here."

Nick thumbed through Burch's license and credit cards. "This is not good news."

———————

Clarence Waters, still glowing in the aftermath of his debate performance, was at dinner with supporters who were relieved as much as they were celebrating. They repeated with glee the zingers Clarence had deflected and some he'd landed. He was back in his 20 year-old pickup, about to head to his hotel for the night when his cell phone buzzed.

"Thurlow? Did you see the debate?"

"Sorry to say I didn't. Heard it went well."

"Where the hell are you?"

"Got some disconcerting news, I'm afraid."

"Go on."

Thurlow told the Senator the basics of their evening without getting into too much minutia. "Clarence, the situation is looking to be more serious than I suspected. We could use some help."

"What kind of help?"

"I was thinking the State Police."

"Why?"

"The guys we're looking for may be somewhere in, near or around the reservation. I don't know who or what we're dealing with. I'm guessing probably somewhere off the reservation, though."

"Thurlow, you've got confusing jurisdictions around there. The FBI's the only ones with any real authority inside and out of the Crow Nation."

"Yeah...yeah, I know. But frankly, Clarence, I don't know if the guys we're looking for are dead or alive."

"Damnation, Thurlow. Sounds like you guys have a few tough conflicts goin' on out there. Is Nick still with you?"

"Yeah. And, for the record, we've got more conflicts than you might imagine." He looked at Nick with a raised eyebrow and a wary smile.

Nick regretfully shook his head looking out the front window. They rolled up the windows of the Jeep and clicked on the speaker phone.

"Hey, Senator. It's Nick."

"Well, hey, Nick. How you doin'?"

"I've been better."

"So, you guys have been looking for some underhanded activity out there?"

"Yeah."

"Hmmm..."

"Senator, I don't want to drag you into this mess. I'm sorry I created it."

"Oh well, just hang on, Nick. Nobody's pointing any fingers here. Whereabouts are you guys now?"

"We just crisscrossed the reservation between Crow Agency and Edgar and everywhere in between," Thurlow said.

"And that's where the trail led you while tracking these fellas?"

"This is where they were last headed. Not much out here though," Nick said.

"That's for sure," Thurlow chimed in. "I can't even think of a place out here they could hide if they wanted to. Everyone out here kind of knows everyone else. And there hasn't been anything new out here in years."

"You got that about right. But, you know what, Nick…"

The Senator went silent. There was static on the line.

Nick looked at the phone with his brows furled, "What's that, Senator?"

"The prison you've been talking to my office about. I thought Cody told me it was out there somewhere? He visited it once. That's something new."

"That's out *here*? I was there once, but this doesn't look at all familiar to me." Nick said.

"I'm pretty sure it was out that way."

"I'll be damned. A secure remote place within proximity of the reservation to put the ingredients together," Nick said as if in a weary trance.

"What's that?" Thurlow asked.

Nick sat back in his seat. "That could be where they're making the meth to distribute on the reservation."

"In a prison?"

"Yeah. A deserted prison, with all the necessary facilities but no one around," Nick said.

"Where exactly is it, Clarence?" Thurlow asked.

Waters replied, "I don't know precisely, but Cody does. I just left him at the restaurant here. I'll go back inside and have him call you right now. Good luck, you two."

"Thank you, sir." Nick said.

"We may still need some law enforcement help, Clarence." Thurlow reminded him. He was interrupted by static on the line. "Maybe you could call the State Police for us."

"I'll see if I can get ahold of my old friend, FBI Agent Braggs, and have him call you."

Thurlow responded, "No, uh, no…don't do that. We'll figure it out."

But the phone went dead.

"Thanks anyway, Senator. Senator?"

Looking dubiously at Thurlow, Nick asked, "What's the matter with you? Why not the FBI? With all the bullshit we may be facing, I hope the whole fucking bureau's on the way."

Texas/Montana

Fall 2006 The Wires In-Between

Lisa Castile called the cell number for the fifth time in a row.

It was a bad connection. "Nick, where the hell have you been? I've been trying you forever."

"Lisa, I've been driving through remote areas of the state. There's very little cell coverage out here. Can I call you back in a while…"

Lisa talked over him, "Don't you dare hang up on me. Nick, I haven't heard from Burch in two days. He usually checks in with me every day. I've tried his cell a hundred times. Is everything all right?!"

"Actually…" Static interrupted their call. "Everything is not all right."

Nick took several steps away from the Jeep and gas pumps out of ear shot from Thurlow. "Lisa, I've been struggling with whether or not to call you. The fact is, I don't know exactly what's going on and was waiting to call until I knew more."

"Nick, what the fuck does that mean?" More static interrupted their connection.

"I'm sorry, what'd you say?"

"Go ahead."

"No, you go ahead."

"I haven't heard back from Burch or Manuel in…uh…two days either. I've tried to contact them but no luck."

"And?"

"I'm out here near the reservation looking for them."

"Nick, are you crazy? If Burch and Manuel are in trouble then you shouldn't be out there too. Why don't you call the police?"

"First, I'm not alone. An old Montana friend who knows this area pretty well is with me and we've been in touch with the police and the tribal authorities."

"So, what do they think?"

Nick didn't want to divulge much to Lisa, "They're trying to help us locate them. Look, Lisa, there's very little cell service out here and they could be anywhere and they could be fine."

"Wonderful."

"Their last report mentioned they were on the trail of some dealers on the reservation so that's probably where they still are."

"Shit, Nick. You could be putting yourself in danger, too. Drug dealers are not ones to mess with. Do you even know where the hell you are?"

"Look, I may have gotten in a little over my head here, Lisa." Nick said trying to downplay his own discouragement. "But I think we're going to be okay and…"

"Nick, a few weeks ago you said to me, 'All this politics, it's not who I really am.' But that's bullshit. It's all you really are. Look at you, endangering the lives of others and your own just to help some politician stay in office."

"I think maybe you're overstating the case, Lisa." Her observation was from the present but her sober assessment was from their disquieted past. "Perhaps, Lisa, it just looks that way from where you are."

"Wow, Nick. Now there's an unmoored illusion where a glimpse of the real world belongs. Why don't you just walk away from DC? Remember years ago when our very lives depended on Congressman Staunton losing his election? Here you are again twenty years later desperate to see a politician reelected for your own survival. For crying out loud, just get out of that unblessed world."

"That's probably good advice, Lisa. I'll think on it."

"And while you're thinking, why don't you think about moving to Texas. Trust me it's a lot safer and more real down here than in our nation's capital."

"Hmmm," Nick responded absently.

"Honestly, Nick. For your sake, I hope Senator Waters loses."

Western Montana

Fall 2006 The Campaign Trail

While waiting for Cody and some law enforcement to call, Nick and Thurlow rummaged through the rest of the garbage cans at the gas station. They found nothing else and cleaned up the mess they'd made. They asked the attendant if the station had security cameras and any footage they might look at. It did not.

"Why would someone dump Burch and Manuel's wallets and cells in a garbage can?"

"Lots of reasons." Thurlow said. "Maybe they broke into their truck and stole these things."

"But there's nothing missing from either wallet. Drivers licenses, credit cards, everything is still here. There's even forty dollars cash in Manuel's wallet. Wouldn't a thief take those?"

"They would." Thurlow said rubbing his chin between his thumb and index finger.

"My other question is, why here? Why would they dump them here?" Nick asked.

"Well, it is at the moment anyway, the first functioning gas station within miles of the middle of the reservation."

"So?"

"So, if they were coming from there, this would be the first place to stop for gas, and those would be the first garbage cans they'd come across."

As if on cue, Thurlow's phone rang. He put it on speaker.

"Cody?"

Cody informed them that the unopened prison was about fifteen miles east of Edgar on the road toward Saint Xavier.

Thurlow spoke up. "But, Cody, we just drove that stretch you're describing and a lot more. We saw nothing resembling a prison."

"What? It's huge. You can't miss it."

"Well, we did."

"Did you drive it today?"

"Actually tonight."

"In the dark?"

"Yeah."

"Should be about forty yards off the road on your north side.

There's not a lot of foliage out there. But, then again, it's not likely to be lit up either since it's closed. Has a large hurricane fence enclosing it."

"Hmmm. Okay. I guess we could've missed it, but frankly I don't think so. And I don't like our odds out here in this dark night with just us against however many of them there may be. First thing in the morning might be our best shot."

"Clarence indicated you might need some help. I already got in touch with FBI Agent Braggs. He says they'd like to help and thinks you guys might be onto the trail of some dealers they've been looking for. Said he'd dispatch some field agents to Red Lodge right away. Can't see how they'd have probable cause to enter the prison though – based just upon a hunch by you two."

"You're probably right. Thanks for your help, Cody." Thurlow gave Nick a look of resignation. "Yeah, have Agent Braggs give us a call."

Agent Braggs from Billings assured Cody he would meet Thurlow and Nick in the town of Red Lodge early the next morning. They would determine from there what authority they had and how they might approach the dormant prison. Nick drove south. They booked rooms at the Pollard Hotel in Red Lodge and ate whatever the cook from the diner next door had left over from the menu that night. Thurlow told Nick his cell phone was dead and asked to borrow Nick's. He walked from the table toward the front of the restaurant to make a lengthy call. After dinner they went to their separate rooms and crashed.

The next morning Nick was awake before sunup. He dressed and went down to knock on Thurlow's door. But the door was open and there was no sign of him. Nick went to the front desk and was told he had checked out twenty minutes earlier. Nick was dumfounded. He didn't believe Thurlow would bail on him. As reluctant as he was to do so, there was only one person he could call, Waters' state director, Cody.

As political work would have it, Cody had been up and working before 6:00 a.m. Nick explained his situation. "Damn, Nick you two were supposed to meet Agent Braggs and others for breakfast at 6:30 next door to your hotel. Look, Nick, Braggs knows Thurlow and there's a comfort level between the two of them. But with all due respect, he doesn't know you from Adam. You know what, as much as I hate to, I need to call Clarence on this."

"Why, Cody? He shouldn't be any more involved than he already is. I can meet with the FBI. I'm the one who got Thurlow involved with this whole fucked-up mess to begin with."

"Yeah, but Clarence is already involved, and I think he's been suspecting something's sideways with Thurlow these days. I'm sure Clarence is well over halfway from Bozeman to Billings – shouldn't be that far from Red Lodge about now. I'll give him a call. By the way, did you hear? The gold mine-backed candidate won the tribal election yesterday. Might make for some unexpected consequences."

––––––––––––

At 6:30 sharp Nick met Agent Braggs and three FBI field agents for breakfast. Nick informed them of Thurlow's odd disappearance and then unloaded his and Kale's and the missing Thurlow's entire story and theory about the meth dealers and the prison.

The agents were familiar with the activities of the characters described. "We've been trying to pin down these dealers for months. If your friends came across them, they are likely in grave danger."

Another agent spoke. "Those guys are a vicious lot and have managed to stay one step ahead of us for a long time."

"It kind of makes sense to me," Braggs admitted. "If they've been holed up at that prison all this time, using it as a base of operations, it's no wonder we kept losing their trail. Who the hell would have thought to look for drug dealers in a prison?"

"So," Nick said, "how do you think we should approach 'em?" Eager to show Braggs that he knew something about criminal law, Nick asked, "Sir, do you think we have sufficient probable cause to enter that facility?"

Agent Braggs smiled. "Well, based upon your and Thurlow's observations, coupled with an unexpected but very credible tip we received late last night, I think we might have just the bare minimum. So, I think we'll proceed this morning."

Braggs looked sympathetically at his men, then back at Nick. "Some of my men went by the prison late last night and surreptitiously locked a solid metal bar wired with some loud but non-lethal explosives across the front entrance. It was dark and quiet when they observed it. If any dealers are there, and want to enter or leave through the front door, they'll experience a deafening blast."

Braggs took a sip of coffee. "But we'll take a pass by it on the roadway this morning and have a look-see. We'll drop one car down the road a ways and double up. What are you driving?"

"A Jeep Grand Cherokee."

"Perfect. You'll look just like a tourist. I understand there's no cell service out there so we'll give you one of our radios. Depending upon what we see at first glance, we'll either pull over and regroup or go back to the entrance and bust our way in."

"I'll be accompanying you and your team – right?!" Nick almost demanded.

Exhaling loudly Agent Braggs paused and put a pinch of tobacco inside his lip, then glanced toward his men searching for a reason to break protocol. "You're the only one who can identify the missing men – right?"

"Yes, sir." Nick said.

"Okay then. Just stay well behind us and far out of our way. Understood?"

Nick gave a thumbs-up.

The first shaft of sunlight filtered through the vent near the prison's ceiling. Burch had been awake for hours as he worried about Manuel's fate. He heard no sounds from the front office and didn't bother calling out as he figured Manny was either dead or secluded in some other part of the prison. He'd had no food in the past two days, but made himself drink the metallic tasting water from the tiny sink in his cell every few hours. Suddenly a loud noise like an explosion echoed through the prison corridor.

Burch was listening as best he could, but the loud blast after so long a silence dulled his hearing. He yelled out, "Manny, can you hear me? You around?"

There was silence.

As his hearing began to come back, Burch thought he could make out the familiar voices of the meth dealers.

The big doors by the front office slid open, but he couldn't hear anybody coming down the corridor.

From out of nowhere, a tall man appeared and pointed a gun at Burch's head, "Hands up! Where I can see them. Now!"

When Cody got in touch with Senator Waters he was driving East on I-90 to a meeting in Billings and was about forty-five minutes north of Red Lodge. Clarence listened as Cody relayed the story of Thurlow's disappearance while someone kept trying to call his phone. He had to ask Cody to repeat his story every few sentences while avoiding the beeps of the call-waiting function.

Once Cody was done, Clarence reacted. "That dumb son of a bitch. I know where he is. He has some old friends down there."

Clarence, who was approaching the exit for Columbus, instinctively swung a hard right, took the next exit onto Highway 78 and flew down the road toward Red Lodge. Clarence knew those roads; he'd been driving them since he was a teenager. Within forty minutes, he pulled his truck up to the front of an establishment on the northern outskirts of the town. Thurlow was a few beers into his morning.

Clarence sat down right next to him at the almost vacant counter. "What is it you're afraid of Thurlow? Facing the FBI or facing your future?"

"How the hell did you get here?" Thurlow asked, stunned.

"So, you skipped out on the FBI meeting and left our DC volunteer to face the music alone? Pretty shitty thing to do, don't you think? That guy doesn't even know where the hell he is much less what he's dealing with out here."

"Yeah, I guess you're right."

"What are you running from, son?"

"Well, it's kind of a long and sordid tale, but…"

"Oh, shut up, Thurlow. I know the whole damn story and have for months. What do you think I am, stupid? You think I don't have friends at the U.S. Attorney's office?"

"No sir, I didn't mean…"

"Now if you want we can sit here for a spell and rehash your haphazard life, or we can go help these guys." Clarence ordered two strong cups of coffee to go. "Let me tell you what we're going to do. You and I are going to meet up with Agent Braggs and Nick, and join them in whatever trouble they're about to face. And then, you are going to do what's right by the law. Thurlow, you're like family to me, but I obey the law, and you're going to obey it too. We all have to live within some boundaries in this world. And that's how it's going to be. You with me?"

Having held his Florida connections too close for too long, Thurlow realized it was time to put his cards on the table. "Yeah. Yes sir."

Clarence called Agent Braggs. He tried to explain Thurlow's tardiness. He arranged to meet up with Braggs, his men and Nick on Highway 212 near Rockvale. Once there, Thurlow would join back up with Nick, and Clarence would get back on the road to an important campaign meeting in Billings.

They all met up and Thurlow rejoined Nick in his Jeep. Before the FBI posse could take off east toward the prison, Senator Waters pulled his friend, Agent Braggs, aside and had some words with him. Whatever they discussed, they each offered a hearty hand shake on it. Thurlow watched this interaction with an uneasy curiosity from Nick's car.

"Good to have you back, Thurlow," Nick said. "I'm not even going to ask what the hell that was all about. Because we're getting ready to make a prison break – sort of. You with us?"

What Nick didn't say was that he'd checked the number Thurlow called from Nick's cell phone the night before during dinner. It was a Montana area code and the exchange looked similar to a number dialed the day before as they drove to Billings when Thurlow talked with a police detective. On a hunch Nick called the number.

An officious woman with a Native American accent answered, and Nick had asked if this was the Billings' rehab program. The woman said no, but that she worked there, and Nick hung up. He spent the next half hour connecting the dots between Thurlow's phone call, the FBI's probable cause-related anonymous tip, and the older sister of the deceased girl, Jacey.

"Yeah, I'm with you, Nick. Let's get 'er done."

———————

While Nick and Thurlow held back several hundred feet behind, the FBI agents observed the prison and having seen no sign of life, cut the lock on the gate and blew the steel-encased front door off its hinges. A shattering noise ripped through the dead quiet building. They quickly searched the front office but found no one. They scoured the equipment rooms, all were clean. No one saw any signs of life.

When they couldn't find any jail cells, Thurlow, who'd had some experience with prisons, stepped from behind the men and found a button to the metal doors opening the entryway to the corridors. The agents cautiously walked into the corridor with guns drawn. They cleared each cell as they moved. Nick and Thurlow stayed 50 feet behind. When they came upon Burch's cell, the lead agent trained his gun directly on him.

"Hands up! Where I can see them. Now!"

Burch did as he was told. Nick looked from behind the agents.

"Burch Maloney!" Nick yelled. "Man, we've been looking all over for you guys. How'd you wind up in here?"

"It's a long story, Nick, but we found your meth dealers. Manny was down the hall in another cell but last night they took him away."

Agent Braggs brusquely ordered his men to continue searching every other area and room of the prison.

From the refrigerator, Manuel, who had heard the loud blast, cried out, "Anyone there? Can you hear me?" But the big fridge was practically soundproof.

Agent Braggs ordered Thurlow and an agent back to the office to figure out how to open the cell doors. Within minutes the doors slid open.

"Oh, man, it's good to see you, Nick" Burch said, his voice slightly shaking.

"You okay?" Nick asked.

"Just hungry and thirsty. We've been here for two days and nights. We've got to find Manny."

Manuel worked his way in the dark back toward where he thought he'd previously come across some metal shelves. He found them, and pulled and tugged and kicked until a piece of thick molding fell onto the floor. He dropped to his knees and felt around. He clenched it in his cold cuffed hands and worked his way toward the door. He cried out from the impenetrable room and began to bang the heavy molding against the door. But after his third swing, the pain of the vibration on his numb fingers caused him to drop the molding which hit the floor with a loud clang.

Two field agents searching the prison thought they heard a faint noise from down a hallway and followed it toward a walk-in refrigerator. They cautiously opened the door with their guns drawn. Manuel stood silent squinting into their flashlights.

"Are you Manuel?" One agent asked.

A bluish gray, barely audible Manuel stuttered, "Boy am I glad to see you guys."

The agents grabbed some blankets from a nearby room and wrapped them around Manuel. They gave him some bottled water. Manuel's eyes struggled to adjust to the interior lights of the prison while he labored down the corridor. An agent on each side was supporting him as he walked forward.

Burch saw Manuel being escorted down the long hall. "You're alive!" He ran up and gave him a bear hug.

"Yes, my friend." Manuel rasped. "A little cold but still standing." Manuel looked to the other agents, "Did you get the dealers?"

"Dealers?"

"The ones who have control of this place." Burch explained. "They got all their meth-making crap in that second delivery bay."

"No, we haven't seen anyone."

"Well, they've been here and they'll be back. Cagey bastards, making and selling meth out of a prison," Manuel said with a hoarse voice.

"But there's nobody here. We've searched the whole place." Braggs responded.

"We know." Burch explained. "They've been gone for about the past 10 hours. They questioned us the first night and again yesterday. They've gone to distribute more meth."

"All their stuff is in that staging room at the end of the next corridor." Manuel croaked.

Agent Braggs spoke up. "Show us."

Manuel and Burch stiffly walked the long corridor. An agent handed each of them another bottle of water. When they reached the staging room, Burch and Manuel pushed the wide doors open.

They stepped in. "It's all right here."

They looked around the room and then back at each other.

"It *was* all right here. And set up over there in that loading bay." Manuel pointed.

"There were two 50 gallon drums here and what looked like a mixer over there." Burch explained as he walked through the area.

"There were bundles of meth lined up all along this wall," Burch continued.

"Just yesterday, or I mean, uh, the day before yesterday, in the morning, it was all here," Manuel repeated.

"And just the night before that when we were caught snooping around out front, all those drugs and chemicals were here!" Burch added, somewhat defensively.

Burch shook his head and threw his hands up in disbelief. They paced the length of the room looking for any remnants of their captors.

"Get a forensics team down here, ASAP," Agent Braggs snapped to one of his men. He looked at Burch and Manuel dubiously, "Who the hell owns this prison?"

"Hell if I know," Burch replied.

Nick responded, "It's a little complicated. It wasn't authorized by either the state or federal government."

"Then who the hell built it? Someone's got to have title to this place." Agent Braggs complained. "We'll get to the bottom of that."

An agent put another wool blanket over Manuel's shoulders. Braggs then looked at Burch and Manuel, "You guys eaten anything in a while?"

"No, sir." They both replied.

"Gotten any sleep?"

"No."

"Well, something's not right here."

Nick cut in, "Mr. Braggs, these guys have been tracking those dealers for weeks. They've been keeping me informed of their observations and movements. If they say there were dealers and meth here, I believe them."

"Let's see what our forensics guys come up with. Who's the dead guy in the fridge?"

Manuel shook his head. "Never seen him before. He was long dead before I got there."

"Okay. Listen, you boys get somethin' to eat, but don't leave Montana until I tell you. We'll get a sworn statement from you tomorrow."

"We'll get that done, Agent Braggs," Thurlow promised.

As they walked into the sunlight past the remnants of the mangled front door, they paused to look back at the prison. All seemed to breathe a sigh of relief. Agent Braggs looked at Nick and Thurlow and shook his head slowly. "Who the hell would have ever thought?"

"Pretty clever sons a bitches, huh?" Thurlow said.

Braggs responded, "Yep. For sure. And, Thurlow G. Carmine, while I appreciate all your help with this discovery today, I'm afraid I have a document here for you." He handed a U.S. government envelope to Thurlow. "Consider yourself served."

The solemn field agents waited for Thurlow to respond.

"Well, shit." Thurlow hung his head. "Those fuckers."

Agent Braggs responded, "Thurlow, it's not really any of my business. But that's a subpoena to testify to a federal grand jury in Palm Beach and I happen to know a little bit about the case – drug running and money laundering by the owners of the yacht, the H.H.S. ALES. I will put it in the computer later today that you've been personally served."

Braggs pulled Thurlow aside, "Look, Clarence Waters and I go back many years, and I know he's your friend. And, out of respect for him, I'm not saying a word about this to anybody. And I can tell you that each one of my agents is sworn to secrecy. But, I hope you'll get down to Florida, get on the stand and tell the truth of what you know."

Nick shook his head and only half under his breath said, "You moron. I told you…" But before he could finish, Agent Braggs interrupted.

"And, Nicholas H. Taft, I have a document here for you as well.

Consider yourself served to appear before a federal grand jury in Washington, DC."

"What?!" Nick blurted out. "What the hell for?" But Nick knew it must have involved his friend, Kale. He shook his head in disappointment at himself as he stared at the sealed envelope.

"Son, it's really not my place. You're a lawyer and can read it for yourself. But I can tell you it involves your potential testimony in a case regarding loan sharking, book making and money laundering on the U.S. - Mexico border near and around Nogales, Arizona."

There was a long silence in the car as Nick drove Thurlow, Burch and Manuel to a diner so the ex-prisoners could have a nourishing breakfast. After they ordered, Nick and Thurlow walked outside.

Nick started in, "You dumb son of a bitch. I told you to stay away from that woman. That's why you didn't want the FBI to come help us. You knew they were looking for you. What the hell did you do?"

"Nick, I have nothing to do with those folks or their operation. But I'm in love with Geneveve, and I have been visiting her there over the past few years."

"Great."

"Now I'm going to have to testify on matters that might get her in serious trouble."

"Yeah, Thurlow, I can tell you a thing or two about how all that works. If you truly care for her, you best not provide any testimony that helps indict her. You'll regret it."

"This is a raw deal, Nick."

"If you love her, Thurlow, why don't you just marry her?"

"I can't, Nick."

"Why not?"

"She's married, but separated from her husband. He's one of the major players in the whole former SeLaSsh gang. If she remains married to him though, they won't have to testify against each other – some kind of spousal immunity thing."

"So, you're going to testify to a grand jury to help indict a guy whose wife you're having an affair with. And I'm seeking ethical advice from *you*?"

"Whatever, Mr. Perfect. Have fun testifying about Kale's activities. Or is that *your* and Kale's activities?" There was a long pause. "Look, you know I wish you both well, Nick. Kale's a good guy who would help anybody anywhere. I hope you'll do the same for him."

They returned from the parking lot to the booth inside the diner. Thurlow warned Burch and Manuel, "You guys need to get your stories straight and down pat before you meet with the FBI tomorrow. Understand?"

"By the way, here's my cell if either of you need to call your wives or *girlfriends*," Thurlow offered, "maybe let them know you're all right."

Burch took the phone. "Oh yeah, thanks. I completely forgot about Lisa."

Thurlow looked at Nick with one brow raised.

After breakfast, they all headed back to Bozeman. Nick dropped Thurlow at his hotel and thanked him for all his help. "I would never have found these guys without your help, Thurlow. You probably saved their lives."

He wished him luck in Florida and encouraged him to call if he wanted to talk. "There just may be a way for you to tell the truth without incriminating her. I could give you some tips."

Once showered and changed back at the hotel, Manuel, Burch and Nick met for a late lunch in the hotel dining room to go over their observations again in greater detail.

"Nick, does the FBI think we're lying?"

"They didn't seem too convinced of your story, did they?"

Manuel spoke up, "Look, we heard a lot of movement and activity yesterday morning, but I swear they couldn't have moved all that equipment and all that meth in that short of time without leaving a single trace. No way!"

"Or could they have?" Burch questioned.

"Look, you guys were pretty far down a fairly soundproof corridor. Maybe you didn't hear how long they were working on that move. That's possible – right?" Nick asked.

"I guess, Nick. But, there's got to be some clue of their activities there."

"I had photos of them and their license plates, but they took my camera." Manuel lamented.

"Okay guys. Let's just see what the FBI comes up with. Get a good dinner and some sleep tonight."

The next morning, their stories to the FBI were consistent. After signing their statements, the FBI said they could travel home. The forensics team had swept the dormant prison and were able to lift a few clean thumb prints, and traces of several chemicals. They believed Burch and Manuel's version of events. They were still trying to discover the identity of the cold man hanging in the refrigerator. The agents reported they had discovered who owned the facility, and described their interaction with the Polaski Construction Company and how its owner had clammed up when questioned about it.

Burch, Manuel and Nick had a final dinner that evening. Nick announced that the meth investigation was over. He emphasized that he was grateful that nobody was seriously hurt and acknowledged they had likely caused the shuttering of a key cartel meth operation.

Manuel chimed in, "That's worth a lot, Nick. I've been battling those cartel bastards a long time. Just because they're hard to stop doesn't mean we shouldn't keep trying. One of the most violent fights of my life was against them in Arizona a long time ago. They're the scum of the earth. I'm sorry we failed you. I know how important it is."

"Well, Manuel," Nick said, "one of the more unfortunate fights in my life was about those cartel thugs and their money. So, we have that in common. But mine was in a bar just a few months ago."

Nick paid his investigators what he could. It was short of the $50,000 he'd promised if they nailed down the meth-for-votes scheme, but more than the $25,000 minimum payment initially discussed. No one complained. The next morning, Nick drove them to the airport where Burch coldly shook Nick's hand and was short on words. Nick reiterated that he'd really enjoyed having met Burch *and his girlfriend*. Few words had fallen so fast from his mouth before he regretted them.

Nick's last comments to Manuel were, "Hey, Manuel, or is it Manny?"

"Some of my close friends call me Manny."

"So, Manny Sandoval, you're from Texas – right?"

"That's right."

"But you grew up in Arizona near the border?"

"That's right. Why?"

"Just a crazy thought. One last question though. How old are you, Manny?"

"I'm 46. But I'll be 47 in February."

Before Burch and Manuel walked to the security area of the terminal, Nick asked one of the gate agent assistants if she'd take their photo.

"You guys don't mind, do you? Thought I'd get a picture for some kind of record of our adventure." Nick handed a small disposable camera to the woman and asked her to snap a couple photos.

Burch and Manny's plane departed Gallatin Field on its way to Texas. During his distracted drive back to the hotel, Nick checked his voice mails. There was one from Palm Beach prosecutor John Lowman. "Nick I've done some digging for you. Mo Kauffman has paid Hugh Haddad a fair amount of money. But not the kind that purchases large amounts of drugs. Looks to be in amounts more in line with legal representation. While that ought to concern the voters of New Jersey, there's insufficient evidence there to link him to Haddad's drug cartel activity. Just thought you should know."

Nick turned off his phone, and clasped the disposable camera tight in his hand as he drove down frontage road back into Bozeman.

Washington, DC

Spring 1997 The Lobbying World

The implicit assumption from the surprisingly limited scandal-mongering was that Hally was involved in a legally-questionable fundraising cabal in DC, and was having a secretive affair with Senator Jon Raines. Unfortunately for Hally, the secretive part was losing its conservative cloak. Raines had recently announced his Senate retirement to take over as Chairman of the *Greater America Foundation*. While Nick believed Hally may have been involved with some borderline fundraising, he remained unconvinced about the romance.

Nick had observed Hally for months and though was convinced she was one of many lonely DC workaholics, was certain she did not want to be perceived as such. Many single people in Washington who work long hours have few friends and their work-related identity sometimes becomes all they have. Nick noted Hally's impulse-like enthusiasm at the slightest hint of office-related social opportunities, as well as her lack of zeal whenever asked about her own weekend plans. Yet he found it hard to believe she would allow rumors to persist simply to cover an isolated existence.

Most telling to Nick was the one person most ignoring the rumors was the only one who could act on them, the head of the ACC, Mike McDuffie. Tad's wearisome prodding that it was Nick's duty to confront Mike had lost its effectiveness. While he advocated persistently that Hally's demise would benefit Nick's career, it seemed a tenuous basis upon which to snake his way to success. The clincher for Nick was the lingering doubt in his own mind about the veracity of the gossip. If true, then it was the coalition's CEO's obligation to deal with it. If it wasn't true, then it was just another of the hundreds of DC rumors, ninety percent of which turn out to be false.

After considering the ramifications, and consulting with his closest friends, Nick took a pass. Despite the potential promotion, it was not a good time for him to go against the grain of his Big Telco colleagues. He never once specifically repeated the rumor and he never confronted the head of the ACC with the story. Much to the disappointment of Tad, Nick refused to take the bait, and Hally would remain head of Congressional Affairs for the foreseeable future.

Bozeman, Montana

Fall 2006 The Campaign Trail

Nick awoke to his phone buzzing on the bureau in his hotel room. It was seven o'clock in the morning in Montana, nine o'clock on the East coast.

Paul from his DC firm was on the line. "Hey Nick, how you doin'?"

"Oh, hey, Paul. I'm alright. How are you?"

"Didn't wake you, did I? Just remembered it's two hours earlier out there."

"That's okay. What's up?"

"We're pulling the plug on this Montana client. You can come home now."

"*We're* pulling the plug? Why?"

"Ahhh...they got tired of paying us. Can you believe it?"

"Yeah. I can."

"We were doing good work for them though, Nick. They just couldn't see it."

"Neither could I, Paul. They hire another firm?"

"No. They're done."

"Okay." Nick suspected the timing of his firm's firing was directly related to the results of the Crow Tribal election.

"So, pack up and get back to DC. For crying out loud, there's work to do here."

"Paul, with all due respect, Congress is in recess. Everybody who's anybody's out campaigning for somebody somewhere. What do you say I stay out here and help Senator Waters with his campaign through Election Day?"

"You've been out there forever."

"Yeah, at your behest! It's only two weeks until Election Day. And Waters needs all the help he can get."

"Will the campaign cover your hotel, car and expenses?"

"I doubt it. And I'm not going to ask. This guy's on the ropes out here, Paul. If he loses, and a couple more seats go down, Republicans could lose the Senate."

"I'll take it up with the partners. Do me a favor though, check around and see if there's someone's house or somewhere you can move into for the duration. Maybe I can carry your rental car but probably not your hotel. Just make damn sure Waters wins."

———————

Recognizing that much of Waters' campaign, along with its candidate, had been discouraged by the barrage of negative press into partially withdrawing from public outreach, Nick took it upon himself to drive around the southwest part of the state to distribute flyers. He was not on the campaign staff so had no politically-ordained role. Nick would stop by one of the campaign offices each morning in his Jeep filled with signs, and have the same conversation with some self-exiled staffer in charge.

"The public side of this campaign has disappeared. You think holing-up volunteers inside offices calling the same phone numbers of potential Republican voters over and over is actually going to help at this point?" Nick would ask incredulously.

"Yes, we do," was the usual response. Most campaigns under siege turn to election playbooks to close out. It wasn't a lack of initiative holding them back, but rather the fatigue of being pummeled at every turn by negative print, radio, internet and broadcast media.

Nick would look across the room to untouched *Waters For Senate* signs. He could almost smell the boredom in the makeshift offices. Aware that one of the best tricks a campaign can pull off is to convince their opponent they cannot possibly win, he would speak up. "Well, I just need two or three volunteers to help distribute get-out-the-vote signs and flyers. We'll be covering some small towns west of here. Do you have anybody available?"

Some supporters would always jump to their feet to volunteer – anything to get out of phone-calling duty. They would drive the back roads to towns like Norris with its popular hot springs, Ennis that bordered the Madison Range, Alder where the Alder Gulch gold rush began and Twin Bridges where the Wagon Wheel restaurant served the best cheeseburgers.

Once parked in the middle of town, the volunteers would fan out putting flyers on every car or truck. They'd also speak with every person they came across and hand them a Waters campaign flyer. If the campaigners found someone at home or at their business, they were asked to put a *Waters For Senate* sign on the property.

One day, the carload of volunteers made it up to Butte, the mining history of which made it once the richest, if not most violent, city in America. From there, they drove on to the state capital, Helena, to check in with the campaign's legal team. Local Montana lawyers worked alongside attorneys from the Republican National Committee who had flown in from DC.

"So, how are things looking?" Nick asked.

Unlike most of the rest of the campaign, these guys were feeling fairly upbeat. One Montana paper had run a story that morning *actually* highlighting some of the good things Waters had done for the state during the past eighteen years – especially for the universities. "We're ready to defend and bring legal challenges all day long against any voting irregularities."

"Good. You expect any dirty tricks?"

"What do you think?" One volunteer offered. "This place is notorious for finding late counted votes from some obscure town – and coincidentally just enough to win a close election."

Nick nodded. "Well, we've been talking to people in small towns throughout the southwest part of the state. Waters has a lot of support out there and they're going to vote."

"You bet he does. But it's gonna be razor close."

A local lawyer chimed in, "Senator McMahon's flying in Sunday before Election Day for a 'get out the vote' rally in Billings. I'm telling you that's going to put us over the top. He's a veteran, a war hero and people out here really like him."

Nick nodded, "Yeah, that'll be big, and great timing."

Unknown to most, Clarence was so occupied with pressing congressional business, he'd missed several calls scheduled to finalize the details of McMahon's fly-in. The last call between them was scheduled to take place the morning after the last debate where Clarence had done well and momentum had swung back in his favor. Waters was supposed to be in his Billings' campaign office the next morning to do call with McMahon and his staff. But Clarence had taken a detour toward Red Lodge to help his old friend, Thurlow, get his life back on track. By the time he'd finished with Thurlow and the FBI, he was late to his Billings office and missed the call.

Senator McMahon, though initially encouraged by the Republican Party to do the rally, was losing interest each time a simple call on details couldn't get done. He'd even tried to call Clarence on his personal cell to no avail. Clarence would attempt over the next days to smooth things over. After all, McMahon was an old friend and, having been in tough campaigns himself, would understand.

But, regrettably, Waters was much distracted again the very next morning by a story published in the Washington Herald that Dick Hanov had just pled guilty to several felony counts including some involving clients on Montana's reservations. It was as if a political bomb had gone off. The Herald referred to Waters as one of the most corrupt Members of the U.S. Senate.

Washington, DC/ Palm Springs

Spring 1997 The Lobbying World

If Vail, Colorado was the most popular winter destination for DC lobbyists in 1997, Palm Springs, California was one of the more popular spring destinations. A telecom association decided to host a congressional conference at a lush golf resort nestled up against the San Bernardino Mountains. Several lucky lobbyists from each Big Telco and related industry consultants, along with Members of Congress would eat, drink and play golf for three days. Nick, still the relatively new guy, was grateful to escape the machinations of DC for a few days.

Six Congressmen, eight congressional staff and a dozen lobbyists made their way to the bar at the resort on a Thursday afternoon for a welcome drink. Some then headed to the driving range to sharpen their golf skills for the following day's Member/Lobbyist Tournament. Others lounged by one of the many pools and jacuzzis and caught up on the latest industry gossip.

The golf tournament began early the next morning amid rumors of some lobbyists and congressional staff getting into trouble at a strip club the night before. Nick had gone to bed early and practiced on the driving range for an hour before the tournament began. He and a Congressman from Ohio rode in a cart together for the first nine holes, talking about anything other than politics. It was a great first several holes, and Nick ended up shooting a 41 on the front nine. Tournament rules required players to switch carts after the first nine to give lobbyists a chance to play some of the round with a Member.

The golfer Nick was paired with for the second nine was a staffer to a Louisiana Member who demanded they order another drink every time the drink cart came by. Nick's game began to falter by the 15th hole, and his second nine score came in at 55. Once back at the clubhouse, they recounted the day's best and worst play over drinks. But the best story of the day was that one inebriated foursome had gone missing during the round. It turned out they got confused coming off a green on the back nine and accidentally played the last four holes of an adjacent golf course. They'd had a cocktail at the outside grill of the other resort before realizing they were at the wrong club.

En route to dinner, Nick received an e-mail from DC that Hally had resigned from the ACC. She would begin as second in command in the DC office of the *Greater America Foundation* – right after her marriage in Boston in two weeks to Patrick Stark. Nick was surprised but happy for her. Within seconds, he received a second e-mail revealing that Tad would not be filling Hally's position.

Western Montana

Fall 2006 The Campaign Trail

Late October of 2006, one week before Election Day and there they were again: Kale, the cynical political veteran, and Nick, the Chauncey Gardner of campaigns, muttering inspiring platitudes about winning. Kale's hunch about a political payoff scheme on the reservation proved to be true, but not for currying votes for a U.S. Senate race. The outcome of Waters' election had become more critical to both of them. The landscape ahead did not look outrageously encouraging.

"You're simply not seeing what you don't want to see, Nick. Please explain to me how Clarence can win."

Nick began haltingly, "Kale, I've looked at the same poll numbers and media-permeation you have. I just see it differently. I think Montanans will look past all this orchestrated deceit. There may just be a reservoir of sanity left in this country – in rural America. I think they will turn out for Waters."

One detriment to the unprecedented money spent on negative ads that summer was the involuntary lobotomization of the average Montana voter. It wasn't accomplished through clever ideological saturation, but by the simplest of rote ad hominem attacks reduplicated until the outsiders' budgets ran out.

"It's called cognitive dissonance, Nick. Dismissing facts you see but don't want to accept. Clarence's name is mud. He's done."

As in many lines of work, campaign politics has it missionaries and mercenaries. Nick was clearly a missionary, convinced he was doing what was best for his country – and certain that Clarence Waters was a good man. Kale was a classic political mercenary – uninterested in Water's character and cared less what was good for the country. He was simply covering his political bases, and he liked spending time in Montana.

"So what's your advice, Kale? Give up on your old friend, Clarence? Just walk away?"

"I don't see much point in carrying on."

"Have a little faith, Kale. There are only seven days left. Isn't courageous stubbornness enough reason to carry on at this point? The poll numbers remain close."

"I don't know." Kale said, as if pondering it but his lack of commitment was palpable.

"Isn't loyalty to an old friend reason enough to stay in the fight? For crying out loud, I'm paying my own room and board for the duration. Why don't you just hang in here with us?"

"What is it you're trying to extract from all of this, Nick?"

"I'm trying to help Waters survive."

"Is that it? And if he wins, what then will you have?"

Kale had recently become even more cynical due to being rejected to head up the new DC office of a large company. He thought he'd get an offer, and the new job would solve a lot of his problems. But an industry colleague he hoped would give him a good recommendation knifed him in the back, and then told him so to his face. It was a brutal betrayal by DC standards, where people went out of their way to avoid being too upfront about anything.

"I simply think this is one campaign and one friend worth staying in the fight for, Kale."

"I appreciate your loyalty, Nick. And I'll admit you've almost convinced me to bet against my better instincts on this race. But I'm also a realist."

"I'm in it for the long haul, Kale. I'm betting Clarence can win this campaign."

"You mean the campaign to save your job, Nick? Everything's a campaign or a wager, my friend. Life's a campaign, Nick."

"I see. And then Election Day is?"

"The day you're born or the day you die – win some, lose some." He winked at Nick.

"Is it that simple, Kale? That's your take?"

"You and I are not so different, Nick, when it comes to wagering our financial future."

"I have to take issue with you on that one, Kale. I don't begrudge you for how you got into debt – especially knowing the backstory. But I couldn't live my life on the edge like you, always waiting for that ace in the hole to save me."

"Don't kid yourself, Nick. We're all waiting on that card. You and I both live and breathe probabilities. We just use different bookies."

"Kale, I'm not betting with bookies or with other peoples' money."

"You're not? How many of your firm's clients have given you *their* money for Clarence Waters' reelection? For fundraising events that you've hosted or co-hosted in the past several years, Nick? What are they into you for right about now – around $300,000?"

"But I don't owe them anything if Waters loses, Kale."

"No. You owe them if he wins. Because you represent them, and they expect you to help them with Waters if he stays in office. You're betting your professional future and their political well-being on Waters winning. Who's the bookie in that scenario, Nicky? You see, we're not so different. In fact, we're almost exactly the same."

Nick only looked down and shook his head.

"Don't get lost on the campaign highway, Nick. It can get confusing."

Kale caught a late flight back to DC, not to return to Montana again before Election Day.

Texas/Montana

Fall 2006 The Wires In-Between

Lisa Castile looked at the caller ID on her office phone and picked up on the first ring.

She was relieved to hear his voice though not as much as she expected to be, "Hey, I've been waiting for you to call."

"Sorry, I've been distracted," Nick said. "So, I assume you heard how it all turned out. Burch and Manny are okay. I'm sure Burch filled you in on the details."

"To the extent that we're still talking, Burch told me that he thinks they were set up by someone involved in the tribal campaign out there. He said it could have been one of the people working against the tribal leader's reelection."

"What do you mean, 'to the extent you're still talking'?"

"We sort of had a bad conversation when he returned."

"Lisa, did you have any of that *bad conversation* before Burch left Montana? He seemed more than a little cool to me when he departed."

"Well, we had kind of a harsh discussion while he was still there, but I don't think he suspected anything."

"Oh, yes he did! So, what was the upshot of your conversation when he got back to Texas?"

"He basically told me to fuck off," She said, a trace of sorrow in her voice.

"I see. So, how *are* you doing?"

"Well let's see. I've been given notice by my boss that I'm being reviewed for apparently violating some vague rule against involvement in political activities, which I haven't done. I've recently been asked to leave the home I've been living in which belongs to my apparently previous boyfriend, and my Visa card's been canceled. So...I don't know, Nick, how am I doing?"

"I'm...I'm really sorry I dragged you into all of this, Lisa."

"Really? I'm glad you did, Nick."

"You know I never intended any of that to happen, Lisa."

"Even the breaking up with my boyfriend part?"

"I'm not terribly saddened by that happenstance."

"Neither am I. I'm actually thinking of re-opening my grandparents' old ranch up near San Antonio and moving back in. I haven't visited it much since my grandmother died, but she left it to me. There's a foreman still working the cattle there, even though the old log cabin house has been closed-up for a couple of years."

"Great idea, Lisa. I loved that old place when we visited your grandparents there years ago."

"I recall that you liked it there. Maybe I'll rent you a room."

Washington, DC/Montana

Fall 2006 The Wires In-Between

Kale McDermott lifted a soggy Washington Herald off his door step on Capitol Hill on a slow evening in DC and saw the front page headline: "Republicans' Culture of Corruption Erupts Again." During the entire year of 2006, Republicans had been involved in numerous scandals independent of the all-encompassing Dick Hanov embarrassment. This time a House Member had been accused of sending sexually suggestive e-mails to congressional pages. The specific story included just enough salacious material to keep readers interested, but the recurring theme was that the entire Republican Party was corrupt. He picked up his phone.

Nick was driving in an area of Montana that had decent cell coverage. "Hey, Kale, I drove through Anaconda and Philipsburg today and made the trek all the way out to Hamilton. I crossed over Rock Creek earlier. Remember when we fished that together years ago? It's beautiful out here this time of year. What's up?"

"Taft, you said nobody was predicting Republicans could lose the House. But you forgot to tell CNN that."

"What are you talking about?" Nick could tell Kale had been drinking. He could hear the ice cubes sliding as he drained another glass of what was no doubt some expensive scotch.

"You haven't seen the news lately?"

"No. I've actually been out talking to real voters. You should try it sometime."

"Maybe you should try getting your head out of your ass and looking at the real world. Perhaps they don't buy into the constant media spinning out there, Nick, but the East Coast is eating up this latest soap opera like it was their last meal. And, the national media is tying every spurious allegation against any Republican to Hanov and his idiot cohorts. So now all our candidates running for reelection look like they're part of a Dick Hanov corruption special. It's like a Hollywood movie production, and a good one."

Kale went on to explain how the latest scandal the media had timely rolled out was about a Republican from Florida who had e-mailed some teenage boys with salacious suggestions.

"Hmmm." Nick pulled to the side of the road and parked.

"Were there allegations of actual sexual misconduct?"

"Let me stop you right there, Nick." The scotch was starting to take over. "You don't fuckin'get it. This is the National Democrats' fall campaign. It doesn't matter what actually happened! The media is painting the entire Republican Party as a bunch of irresponsible perves because of this nitwit and the other Republicans who with Hanov's help have screwed up royally over the past eighteen months..." Kale's words trailed off into a garbled mumble.

"Kale, Democrats would have to successfully defend every single one of their current seats and win every open seat available – and then pick off fifteen incumbent Republicans to take the House back. Not happening."

"Nick, please tell me you're not still clinging to your Peter Pan faith in the Republican Party. In fact, I'll bet you $1,000 right now, Nick – straight up, no odds – that Republicans lose the House."

"Kale, I think it's fair to say I'm still hopeful we can win."

"Your hope's just a tease, Nick, designed to keep you from accepting reality."

"Try to get a grip, Kale. That story about one pervert from Florida isn't going to take out fifteen respected Republican Congressmen scattered across the entire country."

Kale didn't need a grip, he needed to win a lottery. He'd actually just bet $50,000, his limit with his new bookie, that Republicans would lose the House. But in an out of character move, he'd also decided to bet $25,000 with his old bookmaker that Waters would win the Montana Senate race. His old bookie had been convicted of illegal betting months prior for which he paid a huge fine, but was already back in business under a new name. If Kale had predicted correctly, he would be completely out of debt by Election Day.

His old bookmaker was a sports guy only and never bet on political races. But Kale had practically begged him, so he made some calls to Vegas. He was told that the Montana race had been up and down but the latest odds were on Waters to win. So, the only way he would lay off a bet like that was if Kale would take 2 to 1 odds. When Kale heard that news he was thrilled. He not only made the bet but doubled it, putting down an extra $25,000.

"So, once again, you'll suggest I just stand by – right, Nick?" Kale said with a cocky tone. "I don't really have much of a choice, do I?"

"At this point neither of us does, Kale. By the way, I got a somewhat cryptic voice mail from Sheila Parker yesterday. I think she was trying to say she'd identified the staffer in Congressman Parker's office responsible for contacting your company. Said she'd get back later with details."

"That would be some encouraging news," Kale acknowledged. But Kale was already feeling encouraged. With his two bets confirmed, he was in line to collect $125,000 in a matter of days and be completely out of debt for the first time in his adult life.

"Kale, I've actually got a much more important question for you."

Kale, slurring his words, "Nick, what could be more important than who wins this election in a few days? Please tell me."

"What was your old childhood friend, Manny's last name?"

"What the fuck does that have to do with anything, Nick? And fuck you for bringing him up!"

"Just tell me, Kale. It's important. Trust me."

Kale, mumbled, "My parents adopted him. So, his last name was McDermott. Okay?"

"Kale, what was Manny's parents' last name? Don't pass out on me yet. This is important."

There was a long pause on the line. "Nick, I consider you a good friend, but sometimes, honestly you perplex me to no end. Sometimes I think you're just a plain obnoxious fuck."

"Just tell me his parents' name."

Kale took a big swig of scotch, and then mumbled almost inaudibly, "Little Manny's parents' last name was Sandoval." Kale's phone went silent and then disconnected.

Bozeman, Montana

November <u>2006</u> The Campaign Trail

Confusion, uncertainty and fear is how best to describe the final days of a close political contest. Despite what the polls might indicate or how much momentum one campaign did or didn't have, there was a hard reality over the horizon. Somebody was going to win and somebody was going to lose.

"How are things looking?" Nick asked Waters' State Director, Cody.

"Oh, it's hard to say, but I think things are looking up."

"How so?"

"We just got some internal poll numbers back that put Clarence up by two points statewide."

"That's great!" Nick said.

"And I think a public poll saying the same thing is about to hit the wires acknowledging that Clarence has clawed back and this race is now dead even."

"Cody, that's huge news. That could affect voter turnout! You think the media will report it?" The crumbling line between journalism and political activism was becoming difficult to draw in 2006.

"For sure some would like to bury it. But they may not have a choice. The polling firm will soon be releasing it to all local and national media outlets."

While being ahead or behind in a close campaign is largely an illusion until Election Day, rumors of good poll numbers, or late-erupting scandals involving one's opponent, were always encouraging. Fluctuating levels of self-delusion were a necessity to any committed supporter during the final stretch. Other than that, and forging ahead pursuant to the textbook plan for the closing days, and praying their candidate doesn't say or do something really stupid, there's little else to do during the final hours.

Nick was surprised to be invited to dinner with the Senator and some major donors on the Friday evening before Tuesday's election. They met at a private dining room in an upscale ranch-style restaurant on the outskirts of Bozeman. In attendance were two of the Senator's biggest contributors, one of Clarence's oldest friends, the Senator's state director, the senator's wife and Nick. As they waited for drinks to be served, small talk around the table was fairly upbeat about new poll numbers and confident observations of things turning around at just the right time.

Senator Waters actually looked half rested for the first time in months. They relived some campaign escapades along with a few political jokes.

People were smiling, drinking and feeling generally encouraged right up until someone had to ask: "So, Clarence, what do you really think is going to happen on Tuesday? We really going to pull this thing out?"

The "we" referred to all the money this individual and a few others had contributed to and raised for Waters' campaign and the Montana Republican Party.

"Rooney, I'll tell you what. This is without a doubt the toughest campaign I've ever been in. I've never seen so much personal hatred generated toward myself or my party. And to be honest with you, I don't know what's going to happen on Tuesday. But I'm equally optimistic that we may win as I am worried that we might not. A lot depends on keeping this late momentum of ours and on our get-out-the-vote efforts over the next few days."

"Well that's a frighteningly truthful answer," Rooney replied.

"It's a tough reality. I do think our rally with Senator McMahon this Sunday afternoon will be a big plus," Waters said. "And I think our volunteers are feeling encouraged and energized by the recent poll numbers as we head into this weekend. All very good timing."

Waters was more familiar with the nature, nuance and tactics of campaigns than anyone at the table. His casual way belied how carefully he'd chosen his words. But the Senator's sober assessment did little to unsettle the optimistic energy around the room. They shared some fine wine and ate a delicious meal while Clarence told a few of his favorite tales from his gunny sack of Montana political stories.

Montana

November 2006 Election Day

By Tuesday, November 7th, Election Day, the upbeat mood from the previous Friday night's dinner had faded. For one, Senator McMahon failed to show for the campaign rally on Sunday, which not only didn't help Waters' late momentum, it in fact killed it. Democrats and their allies in the media craftily reported not that McMahon had failed to show, but that he *refused* to show due to Waters' mounting ethical challenges. The Waters campaign had no credible response because McMahon's office would not explain his absence.

Nick drove toward Billings. He turned off the radio, balancing the facts and stats in his head as he gazed beyond vanquished cornfields toward the snow-dusted Crazy Mountains. He also shut off his cell phone. There was little anyone could do at this point and Kale was calling from DC almost every hour. Taking everything into consideration including the unprecedented outside money, Nick believed Waters would win the election. He certainly should win and surely could win – unless he lost. Under a wedge of blue sky, an old freight train with a faded orange locomotive kept a pace running eastward alongside him. It eventually disappeared in his rear view mirror.

Arriving at his hotel near Billings where the victory party would be that evening, he checked into his room. Around six o'clock, a showered Nick Taft, part Florida lawyer, part Washington lobbyist, and of late, part-time Montanan, unassumingly entered the main ballroom. There were big screens mounted on the walls ready to broadcast the news of voting returns. There were also fully stocked bars in every corner. Some volunteers from DC, who'd spent the past week in Great Falls were trading stories of the campaign trail and speculating on the evening's likely outcome.

They decided they all deserved a drink, so headed to one of the corner bars. Some were trying to pace themselves since they knew no meaningful returns would come in until later that evening. Returns from the larger more liberal cities would likely come in first, placing Waters behind in the early part of the evening. Votes from the eastern part of the state and the less-populated counties would be announced later.

By eight-thirty, early returns were in, and the challenger, Evan Sutter, was well ahead. Nick's cell phone rang.

"Hey, I just saw election coverage from Montana. Waters is getting killed!" Nick explained to Lisa the likely order of returns. "So, you think he can win?"

"Yes. In fact he should be behind by more than he is at this point. He's taken a beating by the media like nothing I've ever seen, but I think he'll win."

"How close?"

"I don't know. Maybe a thousand votes."

"Don't tell me that means there'll be a recount."

"There may be if it's within a half a percentage point of the total vote and if either of the candidates requests it. But it may end up being a slightly wider margin."

"By the way, my grandparents' ranch is beginning to come around. I put the furniture from storage back in the living room and dining room. It looks great. I even have a few plants around to liven this old place up a little. Can't wait for you to get here."

"I'll check in with you later."

About nine o'clock, he left the ballroom and wandered into the hotel bar. He'd heard enough nervous talk and wanted a change of scenery. But most of the bar's TVs were also tuned to news channels covering campaign returns. After a few minutes, he couldn't help himself and squinted to see the smaller screen above him. The returns from congressional races around the country were displayed including returns from Florida House races. He thought for a second he saw Congressman Sandy Palmer's race in Florida showing Palmer upside down with his opponent, but knew that wasn't accurate. He downed his drink. His BlackBerry buzzed as an e-mail from an old DC colleague came through:

Nick, very sorry about Sandy – Hally

Nick rushed to the middle of the bar and stood on the railing to see the small TV. He waited impatiently for the scroll at the bottom of the screen to come back around to House returns, then anxiously waited for Florida again. To his disbelief, he saw: U.S. Rep. Sanderson Palmer (R-FL – 21) Defeated. Nick was shocked. The last time he had checked with friends in Florida, Sandy was up by a solid five points in the polls. That was just a week prior. It appeared he had lost by barely one percent. His hometown of Flamingo Beach felt a lifetime away. He thought of his old Florida friends who'd be at Palmer's victory party in Florida.

Then he received a particularly cynical e-mail from Kale in DC: **Has your faith been shaken now???**

He admitted to himself that, as Kale predicted, the Democrats' "Culture of Corruption" strategy was working.[28] Unfortunately, the Florida Member who was caught e-mailing teenagers held the congressional seat geographically adjacent to Palmer's, and the press made little effort to distinguish which Congressman was involved in the scandal – only emphasizing over and over that it was a South Florida Republican. It defeated the man who'd saved Nick from the dispiriting practice of law and given him a chance in Washington.

By eleven o'clock, after another few drinks, the positive returns on Waters' race began to come in. The smaller towns and less populated counties in eastern Montana were beginning to report. Behind by over 10 percentage points most of the evening, Waters had finally pulled ahead. Although Republicans were losing all over the country and at the moment were holding onto the Senate by just one seat, Montanans knew that, as always, Clarence would pull out a victory.

A great feeling of accomplishment imbued those who'd worked so hard. Within an hour, Clarence was up by a full 5 percentage points. The only counties left to report would favor a Republican. The familiar taste of victory hovered in the air.

What Nick had missed while in the bar was that so many college kids had lined up to vote at the University of Montana in Missoula and at Montana State University in Bozeman, that those respective county clerks decided to allow the voting booths on those campuses to remain open for as long as it took for all standing in line to vote. Despite that every other voting booth in the state, pursuant to the state's election laws, had closed on time, polls at these two universities would stay open indefinitely.

Waters' campaign, aware that historically there were relatively few votes on those campuses, had not worked them. In a normal election year, there would be a few thousand students voting from each campus and they would be Democrat and Republican students from all over Montana. But 2006 was not a usual election year and most students waiting to vote that night were not Montanans. Thanks to Senator Mo Kauffman's clever spade work with the State Legislature in Helena, thousands of out-of-state students, regardless of where else they may have been registered, were allowed to register and vote that night in Montana.[29]

By two a.m., the ballroom was more alive than it had been all night. Not only had Waters pulled further ahead, but due to losses across the country, it was clear the outcome of Montana's election could determine if the U.S. Senate stayed in Republican control. It was announced that Democrats had stunned the country with so many victories, they'd recaptured control of the U.S. House for the first time in twelve years. Clarence and his wife made a brief appearance in the ballroom. His voice was hoarse, but he took the microphone and in a scratchy whisper thanked his supporters. He indicated they would not know the outcome of his race until at least the next day.

The magnitude of a Waters' victory had quadrupled. If he won, the President's party might control one chamber of Congress. If he lost, Democrats could control the entire Congress complicating the last years of the President's term. On that night Montana got bigger and smaller at the same time. Bigger in that the sparsely populated state was holding the political future of the country in its hands and smaller because Nick had come to know so many of its good people and felt a part of their fight.

Despite all at stake, Nick was half-asleep at a tabletop. The trickling pace of returns had rendered them all electoral junkies awaiting any ounce of good news. Even with Montana the lone Senate holdout, and only a few thousand ballots yet to be accounted for, Nick had to get some sleep.

He awoke at six a.m. to the sound of people in the hallway outside his room. Although benefitting from only three hours' sleep, a restless energy pushed him out of bed. He turned on the television. The Montana race was still too close to call but reporters were confirming that it was the pivotal race left to be decided. Suddenly the whole country was watching to see if Montana would win or lose the Senate. Sutter had pulled ahead again by just under 200 votes. The total number of votes cast throughout the entire state was just over 400,000.

Everyone knew that Waters had put together a strong effort on absentee ballots during the summer and made sure every Montanan serving in the military around the country and overseas received a ballot. Nick thought that if in the end it came down to only 1,000 votes, Clarence's absentee ballots would put him over the top. He was showered and shaved but looking somewhat rumpled wearing the only clean shirt left from his battered suitcase. He entered the foyer outside the previous evening's ballroom.

Hotel employees were carrying out the big screens and leftover liquor bottles. Waters' campaign team was huddled at a table engaged in what looked like a tense conversation. One television set was left situated by their table with the volume turned low. Reporters were hanging out by the entrance to the room seemingly reluctant to enter. He worked his way toward the table, but as he approached, one of the guys he knew gave him a look that said, "Don't bother us." Nick entered the hotel restaurant where some DC volunteers, just finishing breakfast, were waiting to catch the hotel van to the airport.

"What's the latest?" he asked with some trepidation.

"Sutter is now up by 900 votes."

"900? Ten minutes ago it was barely 200. What happened?"

"Votes from some Indian reservations just came in."

Nicks shoulders slumped, "Oh...wonderful."

"There are delays in vote counting in two Democratic stronghold counties due to technical glitches."

"Technical glitches, my ass," another volunteer snorted. "They're waiting to see how many votes they need."

"There's a rumor Waters is talking about conceding."

"Conceding? Why?!" Nick demanded.

"The margin is getting close to passing the .05% range where a recount would be paid for by the state. And if Waters has to request one, his campaign will have to pay for it."

Another volunteer added somberly, "I doubt his campaign has the money left to pay for all the staff and legal fees required to fund a recount. It's the will of the people, Nick."

"The will of *what* people? Listen, we can raise the money. The national party could help. As little as they've done to help this campaign, they should at least step up now. It's the difference between keeping the Senate or turning the entire Congress over!"

The shuttle driver interrupted. The whole table quickly got up to leave. Lots of handshakes and hugs were exchanged by political comrades. "Good luck, Nick. Keep us posted."

He sat down at the deserted table with cold coffee mugs and half-empty plates of eggs. Then he moved to a clean booth along the wall to order his own breakfast. He drank soothing warm coffee and read the local paper. It detailed how historically close the race was and included a county by county breakdown of returns tallied so far. Waters had been pounded in the reservations and in Gallatin and Missoula counties where the big universities were located. The partisan outcome there was more lopsided than it had been in years.

Nick felt helpless. He wanted to find Clarence and encourage him to buck up and force a recount. He wanted to implore him to forget about the cost, and ignore the media which continued hammering like a never-ending storm. But as his breakfast arrived and he took his first bite of a delicious cheese omelet, Clarence and his wife quietly entered the small restaurant. Nick jumped to his feet.

"Well, you're still standing!" Nick said enthusiastically.

Clarence tried to speak. His voice was completely shot. As they got closer Nick could see he was beyond exhausted. He looked as though he'd aged ten years.

The Senator's stoic wife, with a careworn look spoke up, "Oh, hey Nick. Thanks for your help. You guys have all been such good troopers. Clarence has completely lost his voice and his throat is so swollen the doctor wants him in bed."

Waters reached out and shook his hand. A slight smile bent the harsh lines of his face but could not disguise the assault he had suffered. He whispered, "Thank you my friend. It's been quite a battle. Still some decisions to be made. We're going to get some breakfast." He put a clenched fist up to Nick's chest and walked slowly to his table.

Clarence was wounded by the blitzkrieg of hatred thrown at him. He appeared not only physically drained but spiritually scarred. Nick didn't have the nerve to ask if he was going to challenge any of the lopsided results or request a recount. As he sat back down to eat his breakfast, Nick checked his e-mails. Several friends from DC and Florida had offered heartfelt comments and shock about Sandy Palmer's defeat. Several e-mails from partners and colleagues in his firm wanted the latest scoop from the Waters' camp:

Are they going to seek a recount?

Could Waters win a recount?

Any good gossip?

He ignored them all. As Nick finished his breakfast, Waters' campaign manager and his lawyer passed by to join Clarence and his wife. They unfolded a spreadsheet that looked like precinct maps of the state. Nick assumed they were calculating how many potential votes they might pick up if they forced a recount. Nick recalled it being said that politics is about the science of getting votes, but he thought nothing so haphazard or subject to such personal whims should be considered a science. In the end, politics is really only about math and the math has to add up.

A full recount could take weeks. Lawyers and staff would be retained to counter the firepower of coordinated media and Democrat operatives. For a man of immeasurable contribution to the state he loved, Clarence had been made to appear hated by so many he'd helped. Without a doubt Clarence had made his share of mistakes. He was an old-school politician who did not calibrate his words to avoid attacks. In fact, it seemed at times that he excelled at being politically incorrect. But Nick believed the harsh strategy executed by that unholy alliance of the National Democratic Party and the national media represented a renewed hate- and anger-based sea change noticed by few until the next election, and each one after that.[30]

The reality was the Republican Party was spent. With no money left in its coffers and nothing to show for it, the organization was defeated. Republicans had not beat a single sitting House Democrat or captured a single open House seat, and managed to lose fifteen incumbent House seats.[31] They had also lost almost enough Senate seats to give the Democrats a one seat majority in that body. If Waters could hold on, the split in the Senate could be 50/50; and with Republicans in control of the White House, the Vice President, as President of the Senate, could break the tie and give the President control over one chamber of Congress.

Some would say that Clarence's team had expected more generosity of spirit from their outdated retail politics than the media-driven America of 2006 could give. Though they'd won most absentee ballots, they'd still need to reverse over 1200 votes to win a recount. Waters conceded in a written statement late Wednesday morning. Nick heard that news over his radio as he drove down a cold Montana road. He then heard Senator Kauffman, "Elections have consequences. America can be assured the culture of corruption in DC is over and the power broker industry that fed it is dead. We'll soon pass legislation to reign in the fat-cat lobbyists."

Nick wasn't sure what that meant but was confident it was bad news for just about everyone he knew in DC. His faded airline ticket had expired due to his failure to inform Delta he would be staying in Montana for four months instead of four days. He needed to buy a new ticket back to Washington. When he discovered the cost was prohibitive, he opted to buy a ticket for a flight departing forty-eight hours later. After Waters' loss, he wasn't about to ask his firm to pay. He decided to drive to the friendly town of Three Forks and get a room at the Sacajawea Inn to hibernate and recuperate.

Washington, DC

November 2006 Post Campaign Reality

The shock of the election was slow to wear off of Nick's lobbying colleagues in Washington. The stinging defeat of Members with whom they were close lingered, but more urgent was the frantic scrambling to convince their clients that their representation of them was suddenly more important than ever. They emphasized that the Democrats would have only a one-seat edge in the Senate, the narrowest of narrow majorities, and that they'd hold a very slim margin in the House. But, Republicans of all stripes were generally discouraged by how they had completely lost control of the legislative branch of government.

The Democrats on the other hand were upbeat. A California liberal was poised to become the first female Speaker of the House. The mainstream media was giddy about that unexpected turn of events. Female politicians and business leaders across the country were scheduled back-to-back on cable shows to discuss the impact that a woman Speaker would have.

Nick's firm, which was mostly Republican but employed some Democrats, was frantically looking for new Democratic lobbyists to hire. And they were eyeing which Republicans they could jettison. All the partners were busy drafting a memo to their clients to explain how the unexpected change in power might or might not affect their priorities.

The change in control from Republican to Democrat didn't much affect Nick's clients – the partisanization of non-partisan issues had not yet fully seeped into the Telecom sector. The partners were worried though and asked that he help with a firm-wide memo. The next order of business was to find out who would be the new chairs of key committees, and who their staffers would be.

Did the firm have good relationships with the incoming chairmen or chairwomen? Had they hosted a fundraiser for them lately? Who in the office was closest to the new centers of power and how could they be quickly promoted within the firm? The last critical priority was to keep an eye on any legislation actually being drafted to strengthen lobbying restrictions with Members of Congress. There had to be a way to stop that train wreck.

Western Montana

November <u>2006</u> Post Campaign Reality

Parked in front of the old Sacajawea Inn, Nick stayed in his Jeep for a moment with the windows closed tight as if by doing so he might keep reality at bay. He waited there for a sense of solace, but the consequential loss proved more difficult to accept than to witness. He finally checked in and ordered a drink at the bar, then situated himself in one of the rockers on the vacant front porch. Nick was aware that the political influence of lobbyists ebbed and flowed with the fortunes of Members of Congress with whom they were most closely associated. He had lost his two closest Members in one night, his best ally in the Senate and his best friend in the House.

Putting that analysis off for another day, he thought of what Waters' campaign could have done differently, then realized it was too soon to address that question as well. He reflected back on his ups and downs and adventures across Montana over the past months. He thought of Ava and shots of Jack Daniels, and of Lisa and the twist of fate that brought them back together. He couldn't help but think of the dehumanizing slander so efficiently laced upon Clarence Waters and the razor close finish that would impose such a consequence on his country.[32] It puzzled him that instead of being angry or sad, all he really felt was numb.

Suddenly he thought of Kale. Nick didn't have the energy to deal with his old friend's likely state of mind or ever-growing bundle of issues. He was uncertain of how to tell Kale about *maybe* having come across his old childhood friend, Manny Sandoval, but certain it could change his life forever. The camera with their airport photo on it was safe in his room.

He strolled Main Street, ate at a local diner and lumbered back to the hotel. He awoke the next morning for a big breakfast at the Three Forks Café. The local headline read: *Waters' Loss Turns Senate to Democrats.* The story included the historically close vote and Clarence's concession statement. Nick guessed by the conversations he heard that most in Three Forks had voted Republican.

It was too cold to occupy a rocker on the porch again so he decided to take a drive. He gazed out at the dilapidated wood barns on either side of the road, weathered witnesses to the pending development of the Old West. He passed the Willow Creek Café and recalled being told that it served the best ribs anywhere. He eventually found himself on a lonely road that quietly meandered around the recently lush potato fields of Amsterdam's Dutch farmers and through the little town of Churchill. Then he unexpectedly arrived on the fringes of Bozeman again. He plugged in his BlackBerry to recharge it as he approached the city, and it began to buzz.

Nick pulled over by a ranch where he and some volunteers had spent a half-hour in a strong wind meticulously taping the largest of the *Waters for Senate* signs to a fence facing the highway. He reluctantly checked his voicemails and e-mails. The only call he decided to return was from his firm colleague, Luke Lessman, because he sounded alarmed.

"Hey, Luke. Don't say it. I know we lost. Believe me, we all did everything we could out here. And I know I told everyone that Waters would pull it out. I truly believed he could."

"Nick, are you still in Montana?"

"Yeah. I come back tomorrow."

"Have you talked to anyone back here since yesterday?"

"No. Have all of us Republicans already been let go?"

"Not yet. Nick, have you heard about Kale?"

"No…I haven't." Nick said with a sigh.

"Well, I saw him at the Election Night party at the Capitol Hill Club. He was lit, and not in a good way." Luke paused for several seconds. "Nick, I'm sorry to tell you…"

"What's he done?"

"Nick, I…uh…I know how close you guys…"

"What, Luke?"

"I'm so sorry, Nick. Kale wrapped his car around a telephone pole on Lee Highway early this morning."

"What did you say?"

"I'm sorry my friend. There was only one witness and she said Kale's car seemed to suddenly veer off the road straight into the cement base of a utility pole. He was dead when the EMTs got to the scene."

———————

Nick's body sagged as he hugged the steering wheel of his rental car. An emotional weight he'd never conceived of fell upon him. He turned off the engine, leaned his head against the window and closed his eyes. He wanted to phone someone who knew Kale, but the shock of the news untethered his thinking. Kale had so many acquaintances, but for the life of him, Nick couldn't think of a single close friend. He got out and walked toward the field corralling cold cows. He rested his hands atop a fence post while staring at the fading campaign sign. He absently walked much farther down the fence line than he'd realized until a biting wind forced him back to the car.

Eventually he drove ahead to one of the big gas stations at Four Corners. He washed his face in the men's room and ordered some coffee. There were so many questions – most of which came down to *why*? But all the wrong answers were perilously close. Why hadn't he seen what was happening to his friend? He should have helped more with his illegal loan – and his drinking. Why had he come to doubt his friend's instincts? Kale was right all along about how it would all turn out, predicting the sweeping losses before anybody. Kale was his friend, maybe not the one he deserved, but probably the only real one he had in Washington.

As he got back in his car, the cold rain turned to snow. He knew he had to call Kale's assistant, Jamie, but simply couldn't dial the number. He drove back to the hotel where he put on all his warmest clothes including the wool scarf Lisa had given him, and sat on the front porch bundled up.

He finally thought to get out his cell and call Ava. She was in Logan just down the road. She came right over and talked Nick into getting off the cold porch and into his room. She gave him a long hug and an unexpected kiss on the lips. They sat on his bed and talked about Kale for an hour. She wanted to know if it was a suicide. Nick claimed that it was just a car accident.

They lay down on the bed with her arms around him, both facing a big window. "Sorry about Waters." She said to his back. "And, I'm sorry I never got you any volunteers."

"Oh, Ava, we could have had every able-bodied volunteer in Montana with us and we still would have lost."

She tightened her arms around him. Ava wanted to apologize for every critical word she'd ever spoken to Kale or said about him. She cried in silence for a long time. Nick stared through the window into a blank gray sky until he fell asleep.

Washington, DC

November 2006 Post Campaign Reality

The transition of power began. Staff started boxing up photos and files for Members who had lost their campaigns. They would need to be moved out within weeks. Staffers were also busy sending out resumes to anyone they thought might be interested in hiring. But the job market was flooded. The Republican Senatorial Campaign Committee announced it was laying off ninety percent of its employees; its House-side counterpart had immediately laid off all employees. Those hard realities, coupled with the fact that authority over every legislative committee in the House and Senate would switch to Democratic control, meant that hundreds of Republican committee staffers would soon be let go as well.

Many would move back to the homes from where they had ventured to their nation's capital. Others, in light of their lowered status in DC, might accept some low-paying job on K Street hoping their fortunes would turn around after the next election. Still others would seek political appointments in the President's Administration knowing that many in those posts would begin to leave soon. No current appointee in the Administration would be anxious to await subpoenas from newly-empowered Democratic committee chairs requiring them to testify on any number of things they'd been involved in over the past six years.

Congress would remain in recess until January when new Members would be sworn in. In the interim, leaders of the Democratic Majority would be chosen within their caucus and new committee chairs confirmed. Republicans had little to do but watch from the sidelines. Many were predicting that the colossal defeat marked the beginning of another forty year reign for Democrats in Washington.

Republican Party leaders talked of the need for a weekend retreat to review what had happened, and how to put their beleaguered party back together. There was little agreement on solutions. Hally Stark, having surveyed the changes her organization's efforts reaped, was stunned at how quickly the attention of the media and Washington turned solely to the incoming Democratic leadership and their liberal agenda. Most of the candidates that the *Greater American Foundation* supported had lost.

But Hally was invited along with other willing Republican talking heads to participate on some post-election cable news panels hosted by CNN, MSNBC and FOX. She struggled, as did others, to get a word in edgewise as commentators talked about the epochal thrashing the Republicans had experienced. As Hally tried to offer her best summary of the causes of their defeat, she was interrupted by a woman from a liberal think tank who stated bluntly that the election marked, "the end of the Republican Party as we've known it in our lifetimes." The other pundits and host all nodded. Hally felt what it meant to be out of power in DC.

Western Montana

November 2006 Post Campaign Reality

Nick received the post-election orders from a partner in his firm via his BlackBerry:

First order of business is to secure all clients

Please focus your attention on our firm memo

Report any dubious conversations with clients to Paul

He was not interested in his firm's newfound insecurities or in drafting any pages for their stupid memo. All he could think about was the demise of his friend. He finished packing his suitcase, checked out of the Sacajawea and headed down I-90 toward the airport. He returned the rental car, grateful his firm was picking up that huge tab. He walked to Delta's counter dragging his heavier than remembered baggage. Nick checked in and went up the escalator toward TSA security passing the airport gift shop showcasing the now familiar miniature furry moose, grizzly bears and assorted Montana memorabilia.

As he approached the gate area, his BlackBerry buzzed again reminding him there was a firm-wide conference call scheduled in a few minutes. His plane didn't leave for an hour so he figured he could suffer through some of the painful wordsmithing that call would require. After he dialed into the conference bridge and chimed in just to let his colleagues know he was on the line but at an airport where he couldn't hear very well, Nick put his phone on mute and listened for the first few minutes, then disconnected the call.

He sat in the front row of the mostly empty gate area watching planes take off and land. In the large window he saw his reflected self, a person not wanting to return to DC but not really belonging where he was. He suffered a touch of paranoia upon noticing two staffers to the current four-term incumbent Democratic Senator from Montana waiting to board the same flight. They were looking in his direction and talking.

Clearly, Nick had chosen sides in the bitter political contest there and crossed the transom from being just another telecom lobbyist to one of the defeated along with the rest of his outcast party. His BlackBerry buzzed again. It was a DC area code. As reluctant as he was, he answered it. It was Kale's assistant, Jamie.

In a sad, slow voice, "Hey, Nick."

Nick's voice stalled, "Jamie...I...I can't believe what I've been told. I wish you could tell me it's not true. Somehow it's really not so."

"I'm sorry, Nick." She began to cry. "Nick, he was so depressed lately. He just wasn't himself. I wish you had been here these past few days."

"So do I, Jamie."

"It's the saddest thing, Nick. He was such a nice person. Unfortunately, you need to know, Nick, the DC rumor mill is all about this being a suicide."

"Yeah, I understand." Nick tried to change the tempo. "How's the company handling it?"

"Oh, the executive vice president is coming here tomorrow. They put out a very nice statement regarding how sad they were about Kale's unexpected death. No mention of the circumstances. He's going to begin the hiring process next week."

"Wow. That seems a little soon."

"Doesn't it?" Jamie said, blowing her nose.

"I guess they want to put this all behind them as quickly as possible," Nick offered.

"Yeah...I guess." There was suddenly tension in her voice. "Uhm...Nick, Kale's funeral will be next Thursday at St. Mark's Church by the Capitol. His ex-wife asked if you would speak at it."

The concept of Kale's funeral had not crossed his mind, and his relationship with Kale's ex was not stellar. "Oh, sure. I'll...say a few words. I mean, of course I will. He was my best friend."

"Yeah, yeah, I know that. Okay, I'll let her know."

"Jamie, I'll stop by your office tomorrow when back in town. Maybe we can have lunch."

"Nick. I would so appreciate that. Have a safe trip."

As his flight began to board, he was relieved to see how few passengers were on the big 727. When his plane lifted off, Nick gazed down onto the Bridger Mountains – the first thing he'd seen when he first flew in there years ago. He tried to appreciate their simple beauty as he so often had in the past. While the jet began its gradual turn eastward, Nick strained for a look back at the mountains. Then he stared onto the landscape 20,000 feet below until his view was lost along with the fading light from the west, and they were engulfed by the approaching darkness of the east.

He thought on what he might say at Kale's funeral as he stapled many long memories together. Despite the rumors, Nick was sure his friend had probably been lighting a cigarette, dropped it in his lap and lost control of his car. He half-smiled and shook his head. Nick was convinced Kale would never have taken his own life.

He gazed out the window then felt a slow trickle down the side of his face for the first time in years. He swallowed hard, wiped his cheek and composed himself as a flight attendant passed by. He thought about cleaning up his files at his firm and visiting Lisa's ranch in Texas – maybe it would be a new start to an unpainted future. Nick leaned his head against the window and slept the rest of the flight. He would never again return to Montana.

Epilogue

Since the outcome of political campaigns and the many decisions that bring them to their ultimate conclusions cannot be appreciated until the last vote is counted, their inevitability prepares one badly for the miscalculations that were never taken into account when first planned. In the end, Waters' team was ill-prepared for the onslaught an around-the-clock, hate-filled internet and media campaign could bring. It was an early crossing of a journalistic fault line that would come to characterize electoral politics in America for years. So, after two decades of a long and frenzied political career full of passion and accomplishment on behalf of the people of Montana, Clarence Waters exited the U.S. Senate gently, quietly and almost unnoticed.

It is true that unlimited money, regardless of its source, to fund negative ads can win political contests. It is also accurate that a kernel of truth can sustain a full-scale negative campaign for a predisposed media. But it was false that Clarence Waters was a dishonest man, was ever asked to testify, or even interviewed by a prosecutor much less charged with a crime in any investigation. For months the media had painted an intriguing and sinister picture for their readers, but it was inaccurate. A Washington, DC Justice Department bureaucrat confirmed that months after the election.

FBI Agent Braggs came through on his promise to track down the owners of the prison. Zach Gerkin and his once future father-in-law were indicted for tax evasion and money laundering. Both pled guilty but avoided jail time. None of the Senator's other staff, whose involvement with Dick Hanov bolstered the media's leverage to diminish Waters, were ever charged with a crime. Waters' former long-serving staffer, Thurlow Carmine, despite his reputation as an unbridled cowboy, proved to be a true friend to Clarence and helped him in many ways during his later years.

Hally Peters-Stark left Washington to carry on a fairly normal life as a wife, mother and transactional lawyer in Boston. She had been involved in only quasi-borderline fundraising activities, but skirted any consequences. Her, Tad's and others' early flirtations on the edge of campaign finance laws ultimately paved the way for future creative dynamics that led to what became known as dark money – absolutely legal and absolutely untraceable. As it turned out, she never had an affair with Senator Raines; they'd simply become friends because her estranged brother and Raines served in the same platoon together in Vietnam. The two would meet for lunch in DC a few times a year and occasionally Hally would be invited.

Tom Whitaker served in the next Democratic Administration as Counsel to the President for Political Affairs. He worked in that capacity from 2009 until 2014 and then moved on to have a successful business career in Washington DC. He started a head-hunting firm that became one of the most powerful in Washington at helping former political staff find lucrative jobs in the private sector.

Democratic Congressman Judd Parker would serve only two terms in the majority in Congress, 2007-2008 and 2009-2010. He would be defeated in the sweeping Congressional elections of 2010 when Republicans took control of the House again. He and his wife, Sheila, were divorced, then remarried and then divorced again. Some say he remarried her just to get the better of her in the second proceeding only to find out she'd already spent all the money she'd won in their first divorce. As the years went by, Sheila would fade into relative obscurity. Judd, on the other hand, was appointed to a state circuit court judgeship by the next Utah Governor.

Democrats in Congress made good on their promise to pass a law reining in many of the activities of DC lobbyists. With regard to the lavish spending on elected officials, they banned the buying of drinks, meals, airfare, hotels, golf fees and just about anything else of value by any registered lobbyist. As opposed to past attempts via House or Senate rules to restrict lobbyists, the new Democratic-controlled Congress passed a federal statute enforceable by the DC U.S. Attorney thus sealing all the alligators into their swamp.[33]

But political interaction in a free society is hard to abate. Ironically, the effect of the new federal ethics law was to make interactions between elected politicians and lobbyists even more transactional than they previously were. Most of the previous activities continue today, not as randomly at bars, restaurants or sports events, but at fully scripted PAC-sponsored dinners and sporting events, and at ski or golf resorts paid for not with corporate credit cards but with corporate PAC checks. In lieu of paying $300 to a restaurant in order to sit down for lunch with a Congressman, today lobbyists pay up to $5,000 in political contributions for the same honor.

At some point, all politics – lobbying in DC, campaigning in the countryside or fundraising anywhere in between – becomes one streaming conflict of priorities. And a river of money runs right through the middle of it.

The gold mine-backed campaign operation and its money evaporated into the wind overnight. As soon as the tribal election was over, the dealers scrubbed the prison and returned to Mexico. Among the FBI's findings, the fingerprints lifted turned out to have no match, the license plate numbers Burch emailed to Texas did not exist and they identified the chilled body in the fridge as Mr. Sidney Lucas. The owners of the Canadian company and the H.H.S. ALES were convicted of laundering millions of dollars through night clubs like The SeLaSsh. The money was from cocaine, heroin and meth sold throughout the country. Despite the unprecedented success of the Mexican cartels, the State of Montana made a substantial effort to tackle the meth issue head-on with some early success.[34]

Tad Larson eventually went on to be head of congressional affairs at the ACC, but it closed its doors in 2001. He then formed his own law firm. If he'd had any idea of the depth of the creativity of Hally's fundraising schemes, he probably would have sought to remove her from the ACC within months. But his own involvement in a presidential exploratory committee spooked him. Tad also avoided any consequences for his somewhat questionable campaign activities. In 2007 he married a supermodel and retired altogether.

Cotter Anderson remained in the PR business in Salt Lake City, but managed to get pulled over one night and – recalling Kale's strong advice – refused a breathalyzer test. He had to defend that decision to the judge assigned to his case. New Judge Parker, frustrated by a lack of evidence, could not convict him of a DUI; so instead issued an order requiring Cotter install the latest of breathalyzer-car-disability technologies in his Mercedes. One of the first orders of its kind in the state, it required he randomly pull over and breathe into a device on his dashboard. The ever-cagey Cotter simply quit driving his car, and got a license from another state. He also started very publicly dating Sheila Parker again.

The dealers who provided the powerful meth that killed young Jacey were never caught. Her sister lived on to see her native tribe decimated by use of the drug. Neither she nor anyone else knew how to stop it. The only thing they did know was where it came from. It arrived via Mexican cartels, and came into Montana straight up from the U.S.-Mexico border. It has become just another of many sad chapters in the reality of America's ever more destructive open border.[35]

Lobbyists have long endured an image as unscrupulous and greedy. Dick Hanov personified that for all to see, and was sentenced to several years in jail and fined millions of dollars for his illegalities. His reckless representation of clients not only damaged the already beleaguered reputation of the lobbying industry, it inflicted incalculable harm on the Republican Party. Nick believed the majority of lobbyists were conscientious, hard working men and women who served an important educational function for elected officials and staff. Hanov was not one of them.

Senator Mo Kauffman, though congratulated for his electoral victories, did not seek reelection to the Senate. As it turned out, he had nothing to do with the Mexican drug cartel or knowledge of his fundraiser's involvement on the Crow Reservation. When facts surrounding those actions came to light, including Sid Lucas' murder, Kauffman confronted Hugh Haddad. But Hugh reminded Mo that with Sid Lucas dead, the only other person the Jersey City police had on their radar for the unsolved Alexandra Martin case was Mo Kauffman. Mo retired from politics altogether and joined a law firm in New Jersey where he lived out a successful, but very non-public life.

Burch Maloney returned to Texas and began a run for Congress in the next election to help his party's political comeback. He fought a tough campaign and defeated an incumbent Democrat from his hometown. He was married just after that election to his campaign manager, a woman he'd dated in college and stayed close with for years. Burch became involved as a young leader in the U.S. House and helped the Republican Party rebuild their majority in that chamber. While in Congress he would join the ever-losing battle to secure the U.S.- Mexico border.

Manny Sandoval never heard the story of his childhood friend's quest to find him. As curious as Nick was to close that loop, whatever good might have come from it, would not. Nick decided to let Kale's death bury the grief of his past. Manuel served as a staffer in Burch Maloney's congressional office and worked hard to document evidence of the brutal activities of Mexican cartels. His findings were wasted on another one of Congress' failed attempts at immigration reform. He eventually tired of the politics and the media's indifference to the realities on the border. He gave up after two years to return to work as a private investigator.

Ava Mueller got her degree in journalism and became a free-lance writer in the Rocky Mountain West. She was married a year after the campaign to a third generation Montana rancher. The first article she wrote was about how unfair the coverage of the 2006 Montana Senate race had been. But no publication would print it. Her career took off though when she covered the next political campaign in Montana and gave specific examples of verifiable media bias and misstatements of fact that had been written or spoken. She was rewarded for her work.

Lisa Castile was a part-time lawyer living on her grandparents' ranch in Texas. She continued to work for a legal aid society, but only as of counsel so was able to work mostly from home. She and Nick lived in the ranch style log cabin there for years to come, and Nick discovered a healing peace in Texas' open spaces he'd not found before. He worked for a family-owned manufacturing company where he learned that small businesses and the local communities they support was where the rational soul of America would survive. He occasionally fly-fished the rolling rivers of the Lone Star State or its quiet saltwater flats, but they were a far cry from Montana's cold and swift streams.

News of Waters' passing came via a late night e-mail from Thurlow Carmine: "Clarence Waters passed away peacefully at his home in Wisdom, Montana yesterday afternoon." The words struck Nick hard. He felt it was the passing of a political era as much as that of a person he had liked and admired.

Soon thereafter was a fitting sendoff for a man whose optimism for the West and sense of humor would endure like a character from an old movie. Hundreds attended Clarence's funeral offering one last-thank you for giving so much back to Montana. Friends of all stripes were at the service, many wearing dark suits and muted ties, others in jeans and bolo ties and a few sporting *Waters For Senate* T-shirts. Also in attendance were former staffers along with the dishwasher and waiter from his favorite coffee shop as well as current and former governors, senators and congressmen. Despite the large crowd, it seemed as if everyone sort-of knew each other.

The pastor, though personifying the somberness of the occasion, did an admirable job of recalling Clarence as the full of humor, down-to-earth man he was despite the lofty positions reached in his life. He did not struggle to make sense of Waters' death. Instead, he respectfully acknowledged how Clarence had been servile to nobody's politically established tastes, and had lived life by his own standards. That inspiration to the attendees is how they would remember him.

Recollections of his friendships with Kale McDermott and Clarence Waters would stay with Nick Taft for years to come. They would occasionally lead him to look back with a profound sense of sadness and loss, but mostly to just laugh out loud from time to time.

Acknowledgements

I would like to give special thanks to the following for their inspiration, help, political insights, encouragement, fact-checks, memories, editing, reality checks and research on this book: Louise Rockwell, Linda Willard, Joseph Gibson, Patrice Taylor, Geoff Feiss, Linda Anderson, Jeff Bragg, Helen Wayne, Patrick Thompson, Steven Voljavec, Joanne Fleming, Bob Pipkin, Vicky Irvine, Chris Gallagher, Jonas Neihardt, Jaime Horn, Bill Barloon, Patricia Voljavec, Andrew Talley, Jana McKeag, Susanna Soper, Russell Rockwell, Joelle Ziemian, Agent Garrett Hays, Kirk Lundby, and Alice Thomas. I would also like to thank the Sacajawea Hotel in Three Forks, Montana for the peacefulness of its front porch and the Coral Sands Hotel in Harbour Island, Bahamas for the quiet of its beach and balconies.

Notes

1. A number of government relations people in Washington have no legislative experience but come from some corporation's headquarters because the executives there didn't know what to do with them next. They may also come from the most recent presidential campaign landing in government relations due to the efforts of a politically connected headhunting firm.

2. Political Action Committees (PACs) are required by federal law to be formed by any corporation which intends to contribute more than $1,000 to any federal candidate. Before that requirement, corporations were allowed to give unlimited amounts of money directly from their treasuries to candidates for federal office and to political parties. Under current law, contributions by corporate PACs are highly regulated and must be reported to the Federal Elections Commission. Corporations are no longer allowed to give any funds directly to a federal candidate, but instead must create and register a PAC to which employees of a company may contribute, which may then be disbursed from the PAC to a campaign under certain restrictions. Pursuant to the law, a PAC must report to the federal government the name of all campaigns to which it has contributed, the date on which any check was delivered, and how much money was given. PACs are also restricted as to how much money they may contribute to any federal candidate per election cycle.

3. In 1974 when Congress effectively forced states to adopt a national speed limit of 55 MPH, Montana did not have a daytime speed limit, operating instead under a "basic rule" which mandated a rate of speed no greater than is reasonable and proper under the conditions existing at the point of operation. See, Section 61-8-303 Montana Code Annotated (1997). After Congress threatened to withhold highway funding if Montana failed to enforce the 55 MPH limit, a fine of $5.00 for "wasting a natural resource" was created to incentivize drivers. This fine never became part of any driving record, could be paid on the spot, and actually cost the state more than four times that amount to process. After Congress removed the 55 MPH speed limit requirement in 1995, the only existing limit Montana had left was the "basic rule" which meant that drivers could drive as fast as they wanted as long as it was not reckless. In response to the Montana Supreme Court striking down the "basic rule" in 1998 as overly vague, the state finally created a daytime

speed limit of 75MPH which was later increased to 80MPH. See, "Recent history of highway speed limits in Montana," Independent Record, November 30, 2014, http://helenair.com/news/local/recent-history-of-highway-speed-limitsin-montana/article_a27bf2e5-ca02-5353-8499-57ac7068a777.html; Jim Robbins, "Montana's Speed Limit of ?? M.P.H. is Overturned as Too Vague," The New York Times, December 25, 1998, https://www.nytimes.com/1998/12/25/us/montana-s-speed-limit-of-mph-is-overturned-as-too-vague.html

4. Most Political Action Committees (PACs) are built by payroll deductions contributed to a corporation's PAC by employees of the company. Companies may, pursuant to specific guidelines, encourage their employees to contribute portions of their pay to a company PAC in order to allow the company to contribute to candidates for office. In most circumstances, those PAC dollars are contributed so that either an in-house lobbyist for the company or political consultants to the company may attend some of the thousands of political fundraising events held every year. While the majority of those events for federal candidates take place in Washington, DC, many of them are hosted at ski and golf resorts or spas at popular vacation destinations throughout the country. Skiing, golfing, fishing, hunting and spa visits are in many cases an adjunct to the fundraising event and may, in some instances, be covered by PAC funds.

5. The Digital Divide is a term that has been used in the telecommunications space for decades. The concept is manipulated by some companies to get funds from the federal government or to affect a government policy which may or may not, in fact, have anything to do with an actual divide. Generally speaking, the digital divide refers to an inequity regarding access to or use of the communications technology of the internet. But recent factors, including the exponential growth of mobile phone penetration, indicate the divide is changing to more of a relative inequity between those who have more or less bandwidth with which to utilize communications technology. While that shifting divide appears to be closing for some demographic communities, the gap between rural and urban populations remains fairly consistent. According to a U.S. Commerce Department National Telecommunications and Information Administration (NTIA) report, even as internet use in the United States overall has increased dramatically, a substantial rural/urban divide remains. See, Carlson, Edward and Gross, Justin,

"The State of the Urban/Rural Digital Divide," NTIA (blog), U.S. Department of Commerce, August 10, 2016. https://www.ntia.doc.gov/blog/2016/state-urbanrural-digital-divide; See also, Steve Lohr, "Digital Divide is Wider Than We Think, Study Says," The New York Times, December 4, 2018, https://www.nytimes.com/2018/12/04/technology/digital-divide-us-fcc-microsoft.html; Kim Hart and Sara Fischer, "Faster internet is coming, but only for a few," Axios, August 6, 2019, https://www.axios.com/fasterinternet-5g-rural-gaps-a4658995-3629-4f23-a391-d94941481dda.html

6. In 2007, Congress passed H.R.1136 - The Ethics Reform Act of 2007. That substantial reform bill received widespread bipartisan support and passed the House and Senate 411-8 and 83-14, respectively. The law prohibits Members and staff from accepting gifts in any form (including dinner, drinks or sports tickets) from a registered lobbyist and requires members to pay charter rates when flying on private jets. The law also requires lawmakers to disclose the amount of campaign money federal lobbyists have raised for, or contributed to them; and it instituted new minimum time restrictions before which a former Member of Congress can become a federal lobbyist. See, e.g., H.R. 1136 – Ethics Reform Act of 2007, https://www.congress.gov/bill/110th-congress/house-bill/1136/all-info; Gail Russell Chaddock, "First steps towards ethics reform in Congress," The Christian Science Monitor, December 15, 2006, https://www.csmonitor.com/2006/1215/p03s02-uspo.html; Gilbert Cruz/Washington, "Is Congress's Ethics Reform Serious?" Time, July 31, 2007, http://content.time.com/time/politics/article/0,8599,1648556,00.html; Jeff Zeleny and Carl Hulse, "Congress passes ethics overhaul bill," The New York Times. August 3, 2007, http://www.nytimes.com/2007/08/03/world/americas/03iht-ethics.1.6970027.html

7. The U.S. Senate election between the Republican incumbent and Democratic challenger set a record for spending in Montana in 2006 with over $14 million spent by both sides, and 3.5 million or approximately 25% from outside PACs. That outside spending spiked in the following years. In the Senate election for that same seat in 2012 a total of $47 million was spent with $25 million or approximately 50% coming from outside of Montana. In the campaign for that same Montana Senate seat for the 2018 election, a final tally of almost $73 million was spent in total with even more coming from outside the state. At least 70% of the candidates' campaign contributions came from outside of Montana.

See, "Montana - Senate 2006 Election - Candidate financial totals," U.S. Federal Election Commission, https://www.fec.gov/data/elections/senate/MT/2006/?tab=comparison; Matthew Brown, "Spending in Senate Montana race reached record $47 million," Missoulian, December 10, 2012, https://missoulian.com/news/local/spending-inmontana-senate-race-reached-record-million/%20article_707af262-42e4-11e2-8a31-001a4bcf887a.html and Associated Press, "More than $70 million spent in Montana US Senate race," *Independent Record*, December 10, 2018. https://helenair.com/news/government-and-politics/more-than-million-spent-in-montana-us-senate-race/article_caa0a37a-a7c7-517a-84a1-9a1c861077b6.html

8. Legislation providing for same-day voter registration in Montana was in fact passed during the 2005 session. Supported at the time by both parties, SB 302 passed the Senate 50-0 and the House 96-2 with the Democratic Governor signing it on April 19, 2005. The law went into effect on July 1, 2006, three months before Election Day. See, MCA Title 13: Elections. According to the Secretary of State's office, approximately 50,000 people have utilized same-day voting since the law was enacted. However, since the law was passed, there have been multiple efforts to repeal it. In 2011 a bill repealing the law passed both the Montana State House and Senate but was vetoed by the Governor. In 2014, Legislative Referendum 126 was created to accomplish the same goal but was ultimately unsuccessful. See, e.g., Martin Kidston, "Election Day voter registration? Referendum could end it," The Billings Gazette, October 14, 2014, https://billingsgazette.com/news/%20state-and-regional/montana/election-day-voter-registration-referendumcould-end-it/article_f44e75ba-b700-5e0b-9fe0-53293e9b0716.html

9. Montanans have never shied away from serving their country, and many families can trace back generations of military service. More than 10% of the state's population served in World War I and others later by the same percentage in World War II, one of the highest per capita ratios in the country. That pattern continues today with Montana maintaining the second highest number of veterans per capita, and where more than 15% of civilians have served at some point in the U.S. military. That figure does not include individuals on Indian Reservations located within the state. Native Americans have served with the highest per-capita ratio of any distinct group since the Revolutionary War. Montana also holds prestige in the Special Forces. See, e.g., Niraj Chokshi, "What each

state's veteran population looks like, in 10 maps," The Washington Post, November 11, 2014, https://www.washingtonpost.com/blogs/govbeat/wp/2014/11/11/what-each-states-veteran-population-looks-like-in-10-maps/?utm_term=.5dcc25cfb8e1; Kevin Gover (Pawnee), "American Indians Serve in the U.S. Military in Greater Numbers Than Any Ethnic Group and Have Since the Revolution," The Huffington Post, December 6, 2017, http://www.huffingtonpost.com/national-museum-of-the-americanindian/american-indians-serve-in-the-us-military_b_7417854.html

10. The U.S. House and Senate Clerks' offices require a myriad of reports to be filed by registered lobbyists including reports regarding any personal contribution made of $200 or more to any candidate for federal office. Those reports must include the name of the candidate or campaign, the amount contributed, and the date of the contribution. Most reported data for candidates can be found on the FEC website. See, https://www.fec.gov/data/; and Tom Murse, "How Much You Can Give to Political Candidates and Campaigns," ThoughtCo., July 3, 2019, https://www.thoughtco.com/how-much-you-can-donate-3367617

11. See, endnote 5.

12. See, e.g., Kim Hart, "The large parts of America left behind by today's economy," Axios, September 25, 2017, https://www.axios.com/the-large-parts-of-america-left-behind-by-todays-economy-1513305693-70d3114b-c79c-403d-902c-ec5b128f793f.html; and Economic Innovation Group - 2018 Distressed Communities Index, https://eig.org/%20dci. See also, Emily Badger, "How the Rural-Urban Divide Became America's Political Fault Line," The New York Times, May 21, 2019, https://www.nytimes.com/2019/05/21/upshot/america-political-divide-urban-rural.html

13. Montana is one state that tried to limit corporate contributions to political candidates, but was thwarted by the U.S. Supreme Court's ruling in Citizens United v. FEC. See, American Tradition Partnership, Inc. v. Bullock, 2011 MT 328; and American Tradition Partnership v. Bullock, 567, U.S. 516 (2012).

14. See, e.g., Kyle T. Bernstien, et al., "Cocaine- and Opiate-related fatal overdoses in New York City, 1990-2000," BMC Public Health, March 2009. https://bmcpublichealth.biomedcentral.com/articles/10.1186/1471-2458-7-31. See also, Juan Carlos Puyana, et al., "Drugs, Violence and Trauma in Mexico and the USA," Medical

Principles and Practice, Karger Publishers, August 2017. https://www.ncbi.nlm.nih.gov/pmc/articles/PMC5768117/; and Gustavo Solis, "Drug smuggling and the endless battle to stop it," The Dessert Sun, USA Today Network, 2017. https://www.usatoday.com/border-wall/story/drug-trafficking-smuggling-cartels-tunnels/559814001/

15. See, Simone Pathe, "Montana Candidates Court Native American Voters – With Good Reason," Roll Call, September 5, 2018, https://www.rollcall.com/news/politics/montana-candidates-court-native-american-voters-good-reason

16. See, Chris La Tray, "Rethinking the System," Montana Quarterly, Vol. 14, No. 2 (Summer 2018); and Howard G. Buffett, "Our 50-State Border Crises How the Mexican Border Fuels the Drug Epidemic Across America," New York: Hachette Books, 2018.

17. See, John Ladarola, "How the media can save itself, before Donald Trump destroys it," The Hill, September 2, 2019, https://thehill.com/opinion/technology/459590-how-the-media-can-save-itself-before-donald-trump-destroys-it; and Evan Siegfried, "Media bias against conservatives is real, and part of the reason no one trusts the news now," Think, NBC News (blog), July 29, 2018, https://www.nbcnews.com/think/opinion/media-biasagainst-conservatives-real-part-reason-no-one-trusts-ncna895471

18. See, Ina Fried, "YouTube tightens hate speech policies," Axios, June 5, 2019, https://www.axios.com/youtube-tightens-hate-speech-policies-c840d9e6-fbc7-49bc-aaf5-76f818b76190.html   See also, Jeff Kosseff, "The Twenty-Six Words That Created The Internet," New York, Cornell University Press, 2019.

19. State legislation, SB 302, to change the voting laws in Montana was actually debated in 2005 and took two months from the first committee hearing convened until it was signed into law by the Governor. See endnote 8.

20. See, Sylvia Longmire, "How Mexican Cartels Are Changing the Face of Immigration," The Fletcher Forum of World Affairs, Volume 38, No. 2 (Summer 2014). https://static1.squarespace.com/static/579fc2ad725e253a86230610/t/57ec73bbd2b85737540592 3c/1475113923588/Longmire_Vol38No2.pdf; See also, endnotes 14 and 16.

21. From the 1980s to the early 2000s, U.S. law regarding campaign fundraising was all over the map, constantly in flux and sporadically

enforced. From the Supreme Court ruling in Buckley v. Valeo in 1976 to the McCain-Feingold Act that passed Congress in 2002, and then later the Citizens United Supreme Court decision, it is fair to say that what was legal or specifically illegal was subject to wide interpretation and a moving target. See, Buckley v. Valeo, 424 U.S. 1 (1976); The Bipartisan Campaign Act of 2002, Pub. L. 107-155 enacted March 27, 2002; and Citizens United v. Federal Election Commission, 588 U.S. 310 (2010).

22. See, Congressional Record, September 14, 2006, House Proceedings, Roll Call 446.

23. See, Congressional Record, September 14, 2006, House Proceedings.

24. See, James Madison, Clinton Rossiter, The Federalist Papers, New York, New York: Mentor, 1966; and Ralph Ketcham, The Anti-Federalist Papers and the Constitutional Debates, New York: Signet, 2003.

25. A Montana citizens' initiative passed by referendum banned open pit heap leach mining using cyanide in the state in 1998. See, Section 82-4-390 Montana Code Annotated. Tribal lands, however, are governed by their own laws.

26. Interview with OJS Crow Agency, Chief of Police, Jose Figueroa by author (October 22, 2018). See also, Methamphetamine in Indian Country: An American Problem Uniquely Affecting Indian Country, The National Congress of American Indians, Nov. 2006, https://www.justice.gov/archive/tribal/docs/fv_tjs/session_1/session1_presentations/Meth_Overview.pdf

27. Approximately 100% of the meth entering the Crow Reservation comes in across the US-Mexico border, and it is no longer referred to simply as cartel meth but (due to the availability of chemical testing identifying which specific cartel meth comes from) is referred to as Sinaloa meth. See note 26, interview of Jose Figueroa. See also, Kathleen J. Bryan, "Cartels replace local labs as cheap methamphetamine floods Montana," The Montana Standard, Dec 15, 2016, https://missoulian.com/cartels-replace-local-labs-as-cheap-methamphetamine-floods-montana/article_b9e0350a-9af1-5371-8004-93bceef80ba8.html

28. Several Republican Members had either been indicted or resigned from the U.S. House during that congressional cycle. This provided much fodder for the Democrats' "Culture of Corruption" campaign theme. Congressman Duke Cunningham (R-CA) resigned from the

House in November 2005 after pleading guilty to federal charges of conspiracy to commit bribery, mail fraud and tax evasion. He was sentenced to eight years in prison. Congressman Tom Delay (R-TX) resigned from the House in September 2005 after being charged with violating campaign finance laws. Delay was initially found guilty in 2010, but that conviction was overturned in 2013. Congressman Mark Foley (R-FL) resigned from the House in September 2006 due to allegations that he sent sexually explicit e-mails to teenage boys. In 2008 those charges were thrown out and the case dismissed for lack of evidence. Congressman Bob Ney (R-OH) resigned in November 2006 after pleading guilty to charges of conspiracy and making false statements in relation to the Jack Abramoff lobbying scandal. He served thirty months in prison.

29. See, endnote 8.

30. See, Joanne Freeman, "America Descends Into the Politics of Rage," *The Atlantic,* October 22, 2018, https://www.theatlantic.com/ideas/archive/2018/10/trump-and-politics-anger/573556/

31. The 2006 mid-term elections were a disaster for Republicans. The Democrats gained control of the entire Congress for the first time since 1994. It was the only election since the Republican Party's creation in 1860 in which no Republican won a Senate, House, or Governor's seat held by a Democrat. Democrats won 6 Senate seats, 31 House seats, and 6 Governor's mansions. Additionally, the Democrats picked up over 300 state legislative seats, gaining control of 23 State Legislatures. See endnote 4. See also, CNN Special Report: America Votes 2006, Democrats Retake Congress, https://www.cnn.com/ELECTION/2006/.

32. One, an unknown freshman Senator from Illinois was allowed the privileges of being in the majority, including the chairmanship of the plum European Affairs Subcommittee. See, Legislative Activities Report (111th Congress) U.S. Senate Committee on Foreign Relations, Senate Report 111-12. Two, the new majority advocated against, delayed and almost defeated Congressional approval of a troop surge in Iraq, which in historical context, proved to be the turning point in that war in 2007 and gave the U.S. operational control of the country; three, helped elect a new President in 2008 who forfeited operational control of Iraq by pulling all U.S. combat troops out of that country in 2011; and four, gave the new Democratic majority just enough votes to pass the Senate by a one

vote margin on Christmas Eve of 2009, The Affordable Care Act, uprooting the system of health care insurance that had existed in the U.S. for over a half century.

33. See, Title 2 U.S. Code sec. 1601 et seq.

34. See, e.g., Montana Meth Project (MMP) Website: http:// montanameth.org/; Kate Zerike, "With Scenes of Blood and Pain, Ads Battle Methamphetamine in Montana," The New York Times, February 26, 2006, https://www.nytimes.com/2006/02/26/us/with-scenes-of-blood-and-pain-ads-battle-methamphetamine-in-montana. html?mtrref=www.google.com&gwh=C1717DF2A8CED9BC69185 EED13ED1ED9&gwt=pay&assetType=REGIWALL. In 2005, the Montana State Legislature passed SB 287 which severely restricted the sale of ephedrine and pseudoephedrine – over-the-counter ingredients that are key components of meth production. At the time, household and small lab producers were the primary source of retail meth in Montana. As a result of the new law, local producers were severely hampered in acquiring critical components to make the drug. See, http://leg.mt.gov/bills/2005/billpdf/SB0287.pdf. Despite those efforts, meth use has increased exponentially in the state due to the importation of "cartel meth" from out of state sources. According to a Montana Board of Crime Control report, the number of meth-related drug violations has nearly tripled since 2005. Approximately 90 percent of the meth that enters the entire United States today comes in across the U.S. – Mexico border. See, e.g., Mike Gallagher, "The Cartels Next Door: Mexican drug lords corner meth market, Albuquerque Journal, Feb. 15, 2017, https://www.google.com/ amp/s/www.abqjournal.com/950174/nextdoor.html/amp; and Stewart Ramsay, "Inside Mexico's Infamous Meth 'Super Labs'", Sky News, July 8, 2015, https://news.sky.com/story/inside-mexicos-infamous-meth-super-labs-10353255.

35. See, endnotes 14, 16, 20, 26, and 27.

ABOUT THE AUTHOR

———————

Roger Fleming, who is also the author of Majority Rules, was born and raised in Florida. He served as Legislative Director to U.S. Congressman E. Clay Shaw, Jr., as Majority and Minority Counsel on the Judiciary Committee of the U.S. House of Representatives, and as a political appointee in the Administration of President George H.W. Bush.

Roger is a graduate of Emory University and lives in Alexandria, Virginia and Bozeman, Montana.